About the author

Harriet Roth trained as a nutritionist, going on to teach French and Italian cooking for 18 years. She began adapting *haute cuisine* to strict dietary standards when her husband's coronary problems demanded a new culinary approach. Formerly Director of the Pritikin Longevity Center Cooking School, she now runs a private dietary consulting service in Los Angeles, California, where she lives with her husband and two children.

NOTE TO THE READER

The information contained in this book is not intended as a substitute for consulting with your doctor. All matters regarding your health require medical supervision.

The majority of the less usual ingredients mentioned are relatively easy to find, mainly in health food shops. However, use the nearest equivalent if necessary, for example use low-fat milk and yogurt if non-fat is unavailable; use skimmed evaporated milk when non-fat is unobtainable; use Parmesan cheese when Sap Sago cheese is hard to find.

Also available from Century

The Bristol Diet Dr Alec Forbes
Dieting Makes You Fat Geoffrey Cannon & Hetty Einzig
The Food Scandal Caroline Walker & Geoffrey Cannon
Raw Energy Leslie & Susannah Kenton
The Right Food for your Kids Louise Templeton
Sprouting Beans and Seeds Judy Ridgway

✥ DELICIOUSLY LOW ✥

A Gourmet Guide to Low-salt, Low-fat,
Low-cholesterol, Low-sugar Cooking

———————

HARRIET ROTH
Foreword by John W. Farquhar, M.D.

CENTURY PUBLISHING
LONDON

First published in Great Britain in 1984 by
Century Publishing Co. Ltd,
Portland House,
12–13 Greek Street, London W1V 5LE

ISBN 0 7126 0960 1

Filmset by Deltatype, Ellesmere Port
Printed in Great Britain in 1984 by
The Guernsey Press Limited, Guernsey, Channel Islands

This book is dedicated to the health of my family

my daughter, Sally

my son, Larry

and my husband, Harold,
whose love and encouragement
provided the energy for
writing this book

❧ Contents ❧

❧ Acknowledgments ❧

No book just happens, and this one is no exception. There are years of learning, teaching, anticipation, and, finally, realization. I would like to say thank you to *everyone* who contributed to this process for their sound advice, ideas, recipe-testing, editing and proofreading, typing, and always enthusiastic encouragement.

I will not enumerate what each individual has contributed, merely list them alphabetically. They are: Sandy Ackerman, Molly Allen, Irene Baron, Sharon Berryhill, Barbara Curry, John Dodds, Annette Drandell, Helen Eisenbach, John W. Farquhar, M.D., Barbara Frances, Harriet Friedman, Kenny Gonzales, Susan Herner, Lee Hochman, Esther Holsenberg, Ronny Johnson, Barrett S. Litt, Jill Neimark, Maryann Palumbo, Marge Perlow, Irene Pink, Nathan Pritikin, Harriet Root, Richard Rossiter, Penny Saltsburg, Eva Silver, David S. Sobel, M.D., Edith Wahl, Barbara Wolf, and my many friends and participants from the Pritikin Longevity Center, and Computrition, Inc.

A special note of thanks to my editor, Carole Hall, Joe Kirschbaum, and George Epstein for their guidance.

Again, my heartfelt thanks to you all.

—H.R.

❧ Foreword ❧

This excellent book provides both the neophyte and the seasoned veteran of culinary battles with a fresh, new approach to nutrition. Harriet Roth leaps into the future instead of timidly creeping toward a prudent lifestyle.

Too many "health" cookbooks heretofore have not addressed the central issue of our nation's need to *dramatically* alter its eating habits in order to eat lower on the food chain. The economic reasons have been most cogently described by Frances Moore Lappe. The health reasons for changing our eating habits in this manner have been put forth by the Stanford Heart Disease Prevention Program and by many other national and international health groups. Most recently the World Health Organization added its vote to the urgency of adopting a lowered sodium, low fat, and high complex carbohydrate diet as a means of preventing coronary heart disease. Similarly, a recent committee of the National Academy of Sciences advocated this nutritional change as a means of preventing various cancers.

Given this consensus, many people rightfully want to know how to change their eating habits. Harriet Roth gives us recipes with nutrient contents that will allow us to practice the art of changing our diets in a palate-pleasing manner. How better to avoid the familiar trap and common fear that the path toward health will be painful? This book will be a most welcome resource for millions of families.

—JOHN W. FARQUHAR, M.D.
Director, Stanford Heart Disease
Prevention Program

❧ Introduction ❧

In 1978, my husband, Dr. Harold V. Roth, developed a coronary problem. At the time, I was steeped in a background of *haute cuisine*, having studied with some of the finest cooks in the world—Simone Beck, Roger Verget, Camille Cadier. In fact, for thirteen years I had been conducting cooking classes in the preparation of French and Italian foods. Suddenly I had to face the fact that the traditional style of cooking I loved might be dangerous to my husband's health.

Fortunately, I discovered Nathan Pritikin's concepts of lifestyle and nutrition and began to prepare food at home in accord with his ideas; that is, making sure that my husband's diet was high in complex carbohydrates, low in sodium and fat, and low in protein (also making it low in cholesterol)—with no added sugar. I found it fairly easy to follow these recommendations by eliminating added salt and sugar, and using fresh fruits and vegetables, whole grains, legumes, and only minimal amounts of animal protein.

I had always delighted in preparing elegant meals for my family and friends, and while it was not difficult to minimize the sodium, fat, cholesterol, or sugar in my favourite recipes, it was an enormous challenge to limit all four of those menaces at the same time. Determined to continue to prepare a wide variety of delicious and attractive meals but keep them very low in potentially harmful elements, I developed and tested countless new recipes. My husband was responding beautifully to the Pritikin diet, and seeing his health improve was all the incentive I needed to persevere.

I also got tremendous encouragement from an unexpected source—my cooking students. I had begun to experiment with Pritikin principles in my cooking classes because I could no longer reconcile myself to teaching people how to prepare food that did not contribute to their optimum health.

To my constant delight, every new class presentation was a success. I found that most of my favourite recipes could be modified to conform to low-sodium, low-fat, low-cholesterol, low-sugar standards. The new ingredients and cooking techniques produced very attractive, delectable, uniquely healthful dishes which I proudly served in my home—to both family and guests.

In 1981 my teaching and experimentation led to my appointment as Director of the Pritikin Longevity Center Cooking School. Fuelled by the enthusiasm and needs of the participants at the Longevity Center—as well as by my husband's return to vigorous, tennis-playing good health—my personal culinary exploration became even more intense as I instructed others to prepare and create along with me so that when they left the Longevity Center they could take the Pritikin diet into their own kitchens, stick with it, and still enjoy eating.

A Pritikin-Style Diet to Live With

Many of my students had a misconceived image of wholesome cooking. Some thought that if you eliminated sugar, salt, refined flour, and the like from your diet, all you'd have left to cook with would be seaweed and lecithin. To the contrary, eliminating dangerous foods from your cooking can open the door to discovering scores of familiar foods and food products that you may have just never taken the time or effort to imaginatively prepare or even try. You don't have to be nutritionally deprived in order to feel gastronomic satisfaction. You *can* have healthful food and eat well at the same time.

Let me give you an example. Recently, I had an occasion to prepare lunch for some dear friends I hadn't seen for years. My friends went wild for the pasta salad with Chinese dried mushrooms and couldn't believe that the salmon mousse was neither fattening nor illegal. We had wonderful whole wheat muffins with a delightful sugar-free apple and blackcurrant spread I'd found at the supermarket. And I filled an enormous basket with vegetables fresh from the grocer—not only the usual carrots, broccoli and cauliflower, but lovely, crisp, mange tout peas, swedes, turnips, Japanese radishes, and fennel as well—to serve with a piquant spinach dip. For dessert, I served my Perfect Pears in a gorgeous crystal bowl, its beauty only surpassed by the wonderful, natural flavour of the fruit.

It is my hope that nutritious foods, exotically flavoured and handsomely displayed, will inspire you to take positive steps toward a healthier life through better cooking. This book is not intended as a cure-all, but every recipe has been carefully, creatively designed to show that beautiful, richly satisfying meals can be prepared in accordance with modern theories of healthful eating. For years we have been hearing that health problems related to diet begin very early in life, and that how we eat can make all the difference between being sick and being well. If you are still regularly eating foods that are high in salt, fat, cholesterol and sugar, though, you may be wondering just what those modern theories are. The United States Department of Health and Human Services sums them up in the following recommendations.

1. Avoid Too Much Sodium and Salt

The average person consumes 10 to 20 times more sodium than he needs. Limited amounts of sodium are necessary so the body can maintain a proper water balance, but in excessive amounts sodium causes the body to adjust to holding excessive fluids and contributes to high blood pressure, edema and kidney disease.

There is enough sodium in the natural food and water we consume to answer our basic metabolic needs. Additional sodium is hidden in various products such as medications and dentifrices. The recipes in this book add no salt in food preparation, and will help you decrease your use of sodium-packed convenience and fast foods. Whenever my recipes call for prepared ingredients, I'll be recommending either low-sodium or no-sodium products or ways to dilute the sodium content of commercial products that are not low-sodium already.

2. Avoid Too Much Fat and Cholesterol

About 40 percent of the total calories the average person consumes are derived from fat. 25g/1 oz of fat contains over twice as many calories as either protein or complex carbohydrates, and high fat diets have been shown to contribute to heart disease, hypertension, coronary artery disease, cancer and diabetes. My recipes are designed to help you lower your fat intake to a safer 15 to 20 percent of your total calories by avoiding vegetable oils, mayonnaise, prepared salad dressings, margarine, butter, lard, bacon, pork, lamb, chicken fat, ice cream, whole milk products and cheeses, and too much beef.

Cholesterol is a sterol, not a fat. It is naturally manufactured by the body and found in all foods derived from animal sources but not in foods from plant sources. For example, egg yolks, not whites, are high in cholesterol but relatively low in fat and calories, while chocolate is *high in fat* and *calories* but contains *no cholesterol*. Cholesterol is another part of our diet that bears watching. Because we all manufacture different amounts of cholesterol in our bodies, the American Heart Association recommends that we control the amount of cholesterol we include in our diets and hold the amount down to 100 to 300 milligrams per day, depending upon the state of your health. One egg yolk contains 285 milligrams. Other high-cholesterol foods to avoid are beef, veal, lamb, pork, some shellfish, organ meats, butter, ice cream, and whole milk dairy products, such as sour cream, cheeses, and yogurt—all examples of animal protein.

Nathan Pritikin recommends we reduce our fat intake to less than 10 percent of total calories and limit our cholesterol intake to 100 milligrams per day. Even with this cholesterol limitation you can still eat as much as a total of 675g/1½ lb of fish, fowl, and/or meat in a week. On a daily basis, this is about 75–100 g/3–4 oz; practically all my recipes, with the exception of those using ricotta and mozzarella cheeses, meet these limitations.

The recipes in this book use nonfat dairy products and will help you limit the amount of animal protein you consume. Judging by the diets of most people, the role of and need for protein are grossly misunderstood. For decades, we have been taught that a healthy diet should contain generous amounts of protein, the more the better. On the contrary, nutritionally, this is no advantage, but rather a disadvantage. Recent studies have found that excess protein prevents absorption of calcium in the body and may contribute to osteoporosis. Animal protein, in particular, poses the danger of excess fat and cholesterol. Not only do we need less protein—no more than 12 to 15 percent of our caloric intake, but less should come from animal sources and more from other sources such as vegetables, legumes and whole grains.

3. Avoid Too Much Sugar and Eat A Diet High in Complex Carbohydrates and Fibre

We know that excessive sugar in our diet contributes to tooth decay and obesity but current research points to the fact that a high sugar intake also contributes to the development of heart disease. (Refined, simple sugars tend to increase triglyceride levels in the blood.) To maximize the nutritional benefits of the calories you consume it makes sense to limit your sugar intake. It's up to you to avoid sugar-laden soft drinks, cakes, cookies, and candy, but I've included recipes in this book to satisfy your desire for sweets while limiting all sugars, including molasses, honey, and syrups.

There is more to the low-sugar story. According to Dr. John W. Farquhar of Stanford University, "Complex carbohydrates found in grains and vegetables are a common casualty of a sugar-rich diet. Complex carbohydrates once constituted a major and valuable part of the American diet. Unfortunately, starch and carbohydrates have fallen into disrepute in recent years because of popular fads, including 'low-carbohydrate high-protein' diets. In fact, complex carbohydrates are potentially the slimmer's greatest ally. As a group they not only provide more complex nutrition than do refined carbohydrates, but are also lower in caloric density than are fatty or sugary foods; they tend to slow down the rapid intake of calories that often leads to weight gain." An additional benefit of a diet high in complex carbohydrates is that it will also be naturally high in fibre, a known protection against certain forms of cancer.

My recipes will help you restore complex carbohydrates to their proper place in your diet. You will be using more dried peas, beans, lentils, whole grain cereals, whole grain breads, whole grain pastas, whole raw vegetables, and whole raw fruits and enjoying them more. Why waste your calories?

4. Maintain Your Ideal Weight

If you've seen a table of desirable heights and weights, it was probably based on the one developed by the Metropolitan Life Insurance Company. The latest table developed by Metropolitan allows you 1.5 to 7 kg/1 to 16 lb more (depending on your height) than the older one did. But it is important to remember that these tables were never meant to be taken literally, and the new standard should not be used as an excuse to fatten up. The figures are simply a useful guide that points in the direction of a longer, healthier life. Cardiovascular disease, diabetes, gout, osteoarthritis, gallbladder disease, and high blood pressure have all been associated with obesity.

My recipes will help you keep your weight down because they will help you minimize the amount of fat, sugar, fluid-retaining salt, and high-calorie animal protein in your daily diet.

Compare the Difference

Every recipe in this book has been computer-analyzed for its per-serving calorie count and its content of eighteen essential nutrients plus fibre. The analysis is printed at the foot of each recipe based on data compiled by Computrition, Inc., Chatsworth, California. You can use this information if you are closely monitoring and controlling your diet.

If you're wondering how well my recipes stack up against conventional recipes, the computer analyses will convince you that there's a major improvement. I asked Computrition to analyze a few of my old recipes so I could compare them to the ones I've recently created, and even I was astonished by the degree of difference that my approach to cooking made in lowering the sodium, fat, cholesterol and caloric content of conventional dishes.

Rumaki, for instance, is an appetizer high in popularity, but even higher in sodium, fat, cholesterol and calories. Here are the ingredients for 12 servings from my old favourite rumaki recipe:

12 chicken livers, cut in half
12 slices bacon, cut in half
120 ml/4 fl oz soy sauce
2 tablespoons sugar
2 tablespoons sherry or sake

2 tablespoons water
1 teaspoon garlic powder
1 teaspoon ground ginger
4 tablespoons tomato ketchup
2 tablespoons Dijon mustard

Computrition analyzed the key nutrients in that recipe as follows: 245 calories, 991 milligrams of sodium, 20.8 grams of fat and 177 milligrams of cholesterol per serving.

The ingredients in my new recipe, which follows, produce a comparable taste sensation, but without the health risk.

Chicken Rumaki

Serves: 12

275 g/10 oz slightly frozen skinned and boned chicken breasts

12 fresh or canned unsweetened pineapple chunks

12 whole canned water chestnuts, drained

2½ tablespoons mild soy sauce

4 tablespoons water

2 tablespoons frozen unsweetened pineapple juice concentrate

2 tablespoons dry sherry or sake

1 teaspoon garlic powder

1 teaspoon ground ginger

Chicken Rumaki has only 48 calories, 163 milligrams of sodium, 0.33 gram of fat and 14 milligrams of cholesterol per serving.

In case you think rumaki is just an especially dramatic example, I'd like to compare three more sets of recipes to demonstrate how contrary to good health traditional recipes can be and how my recipes can help you make a change for the better. The ingredients in Veal Tonnato, an Italian main dish, are a high-cholesterol case in point.

According to Computrition, they add up to 572 calories, 523 milligrams of sodium, 41.9 grams of fat and 131 milligrams of cholesterol per serving.

In my recipe on page 129 I changed the veal to turkey, tuna in oil to tuna in salt-free water pack, and omitted the anchovies and mayonnaise. This vastly improves the nutritional quality without sacrificing flavour.

Each serving has only 200 calories, 96 milligrams of sodium, 3.7 grams of fat and 85 milligrams of cholesterol. The nutritional advantage is impressive, and—served as I suggest, with a colourful garnish of tiny tomatoes and radish roses accompanied by a cold rice salad—so is the dish.

You will find my recipes provide new rewards for your palate that more than compensate for an inevitable loss of certain familiar flavours that come from the liberal use of salt, butter, egg yolks, cream, and the like.

Sometimes even recipes with healthy-sounding names can be loaded with potentially harmful ingredients. A muffin recipe I used to enjoy is a perfect example. The difference in the calorie count between these muffins and my adaptation is only about 50 calories per muffin, but there is an enormous difference in the nutritional quality. One recipe I used to use contained 181 calories, 179 milligrams of sodium, 5.6 grams of fat, and 27.8 milligrams of cholesterol per serving.

My recipe for Geneva's Extra-Special Muffins on page 201 is high in fibre and has only 126 calories, 56 milligrams of sodium, 0.8 grams of fat, and no cholesterol per serving. To get these results I use unsweetened cereal, fruit instead of sugar, whole grain flour instead of bleached white flour, and eliminate oil and egg yolks.

Sometimes you can feel your arteries hardening as you read traditional ingredient lists. Eggs Benedict is a good example: there are an incredible 1142 calories, 3912 milligrams of sodium, 81 grams of fat, and 1132 milligrams of cholesterol per serving.

My Tuna Benedictine on page 209 is an attractive, considerably lighter substitute with only 148 calories, 185 milligrams of sodium, 1.47 grams of fat, and 16 milligrams of cholesterol per serving.

Where There's a Will, There's a Way

In changing from *haute cuisine* to healthful cooking, I learned many new things. They include cooking methods, that now have become second nature to me. Once you learn them yourself, you can begin to improvise your own low-sodium, low-fat, low-cholesterol, low-sugar recipes. Here are some of the methods I've adopted.

Substitutions

Instead of	Use
canned fruit	fresh fruit
fruit juice	whole fruit
fat or oil	nonstick spray, nonstick pan, or stock for sautéeing
canned soup	homemade or acceptable commercial product
sugar, molasses, or syrup	unsweetened fruit juice or fruit concentrate or ripe banana
sour cream, cream cheese, or mayonnaise	nonfat yogurt
oil-packed tuna	water-packed tuna
whole milk	nonfat milk and milk products, dry skim milk plus water, or canned skim milk
whipped cream	whipped nonfat milk, whipped nonfat evaporated milk, or whipped dry skim milk
white breads or flours	use whole grain breads or flours
whole eggs	egg whites only
salt	low-sodium vegetable seasoning, herbs and other piquant seasonings such as pepper

Better Recipes for the Basics

Instead of	Use
chicken stock	Basic Chicken Stock (see page 22)
stock cubes	Stock Cubes (see page 21) This low-sodium alternative is handy for stir-frying, sautéeing, or seasoning.
cream cheese or sour cream	Our Cream Cheese and Sour Cream (see page 23) The key to making these nonfat

	alternatives is to use only the freshest ingredients.
salt	Harriet's No-Salt Vegetable Seasoning (see page 24) or an acceptable low-Sodium Seasoning
packaged breadcrumbs	Seasoned Breadcrumbs (see page 25)

How to Start Eating Better

It is my sincere hope that after you try some of my recipes, you will be motivated to change your cooking and eating habits. But the degree to which you follow my suggestions is up to you. Any positive changes that you make will be in your best interests, so don't be discouraged and feel that if you don't radically change all your food habits at once, you can't change at all.

You may start by omitting salt—omitting added salt in your cooking and removing the salt shaker from your table.

Using nonfat dairy products is most desirable, but you can *start* by changing to low-fat dairy products—that's a 50 percent reduction in your fat intake. Using oil-free salad dressing, light salad dressings, or yogurt instead of mayonnaise or sour cream and baking and grilling foods instead of frying will all help reduce your total fat intake.

You may have been having eggs or even bacon for breakfast every morning, and red meat four to five times a week. Limit your red meat to no more than a weekly serving of very lean beef such as top rump steak, topside or rump, and increase the use of fish and poultry. Have an egg just once a week, if you must. This will enormously lower your intake of cholesterol.

Try satisfying your "sweet tooth" by choosing some of the wonderful seasonally fresh or dried fruits available in the market today or preparing a sorbet or treat as listed in Sweets and Treats (pages 180–198). Fruit concentrates can take the place of refined sugars usually found in "traditional" recipes. Be creative and try adjusting some of your favourite recipes with the ingredients listed in the next section.

❧ Helpful Hints ❧

Preferred Products

Caveat emptor means "let the buyer beware". Indeed, as prudent consumers we must use judgment and take the *time to read labels*. Be aware of the sodium, fat, sugar and preservatives that are being added to the foods you buy. Keep these general shopping guidelines in mind:

1.   Avoid buying food with any of the following ingredients listed on the label, as they raise the *sodium content* of the product: salt (should be listed at least after the third ingredient), sodium chloride, sea salt, MSG (monosodium glutamate), sodium saccharin, sodium nitrite, sodium nitrate, sodium propionate, sodium benzoate, sodium bisulfite, or any ingredient with sodium in its name should be shunned.

2.   Do not buy seasoning such as onion salt, garlic salt, celery salt, ketchup, chilli sauce, barbecue sauce, cooking wines (salt is added), miso, soy sauce or tamari (unless low-sodium), and prepared mustard (unless salt-free). Capers must be rinsed before using to remove some salt and then used only as a seasoning. Worcestershire sauce contains 150 milligrams of sodium per tablespoon; use it judiciously as a seasoning.

3.   If you use salt-free tomato products instead of the usual canned tomato products you will subtantially further lower the sodium content of our recipes. 225 g/8 oz canned tomatoes contains 250 to 300 milligrams of sodium, whereas 225 g/8 oz salt-free or no-salt-added tomatoes contains 30 milligrams of sodium.

4.   Sugar on labels appears under listings such as sucrose, glucose, dextrose, lactose, fructose, corn sugar, golden syrup or corn sweetener, cane sugar, raw sugar, sorghum, molasses and

honey. Avoid buying products with any of these ingredients.

5. Fat content in processed foods is listed as shortening, oil, mayonnaise, butter, margarine, monoglycerides, diglycerides or triglycerides, lard, tallow, suet, chicken fat, egg yolks, lipids or lecithin. Avoid these if you can.

6. When buying cereals, choose whole grain cereals that have no salt or sugar added.

7. Whole grain flours are preferred. If you buy white flour, at least buy the unbleached variety.

8. If you use canned fruits purchase only those canned in natural, unsweetened fruit juices. Frozen fruits should be unsweetened.

9. Canned soups should have no fat, MSG or sweetener added. If any salt is added, it should appear after the third ingredient listed. Try making your own soup. It will taste better and be cheaper and more nourishing.

10. Above all, be an alert and concerned consumer. Become a detective. The quality of the products that appear in our markets is improving daily. This is only because consumers like you and I have requested, in some cases demanded, nourishing food products not disturbed by unnecessary processing, additives and preservatives.

A Note on Herbs and Spices

My recipes always use dried herbs unless fresh herbs are specified. Of course, if you have access to fresh herbs, use them. They will add a gentle seasoning you will enjoy. To convert from dried to fresh herbs, triple the amounts specified for dried.

Herbs and spices should be stored in a cool, dry, dark place (not over the cooker). They have a shelf life of about six months, so the ones you do not use a great deal should be divided at the time of purchase and placed in plastic bags in the freezer. I write the date on my herb jars when I fill them and empty those not used within six months. Stale herbs taste like sawdust, not a very delicate flavour to add to your foods, so do not buy in bulk and only buy herbs and spices in sealed containers.

Our Vinaigrette or Italian Dressings

Whenever the recipes call for our Italian or our Vinaigrette Dressing, you may use any commercial Italian or vinaigrette dressing that is low-sodium and sugar-free. Any commercial product is acceptable if it meets those standards. If you buy a commercial dressing that is low-fat and sugar-free but not low-sodium, you can make it acceptable by making two bottles out of one. Here's how: mix your bottled dressing with an equal amount of a solution that is half water and half of a quality vinegar.

Useful Ingredients

Baking Powder
In an emergency 1 teaspoon of a tartrate baking powder may be substituted for ¼ teaspoon of bicarbonate soda and ½ teaspoon of cream of tartar.

If not using a low-sodium baking powder, I recommend baking powder without aluminium or alum.

Bananas
A very ripe banana is a good sweetener. Bananas may be flash-frozen on a baking sheet and stored in tightly closed plastic bags. Defrost slightly before using, except in preparing sorbet.

Bouquet Garni
A bouquet garni is a combination of parsley, thyme, bay leaf and crushed red pepper used in flavouring soups, stews, vegetables and sauces. Combine the ingredients in muslin tied with string or unwaxed dental floss.

Buttermilk
When using buttermilk always strain fat globules, which have been added at the dairy, before using. If a recipe calls for buttermilk, you may substitute milk which has been soured in this fashion: Add 1 tablespoon of brown rice vinegar to 250 ml/8 fl oz of nonfat milk. Let stand a few moments until it curdles.

Carob Powder
Carob powder is made from the dried pods of the carob tree. It is

used as a substitute for chocolate or cocoa (which contains caffeine). There is a difference in flavour, but it is quite acceptable. A rule of thumb for substitution is 3 tablespoons of carob plus 2 tablespoons of liquid equals one square unsweetened chocolate. Sugar substitutions are made with fruit juice concentrate or ripe banana to suit your taste.

Chicken Stock (see recipe page 22)
Save skin, bones, giblets and wing tips from poultry and freeze in plastic bags. Use as part of base when making chicken stock. (Chicken necks and backs are good and cheap to use in making stock.)

TO CLARIFY CHICKEN OR FISH STOCK
Add 1 egg white plus 2 teaspoons of water, and the eggshell to 1 litre/1¾ pints boiling stock. Boil 2 minutes and strain.

TO ADD A RICH BROWN COLOUR TO CHICKEN STOCK
Add 1 tablespoon tomato paste to 1 litre/1¾ pints stock.

Duxelles
Minced mushrooms and shallots sautéed in our Stock Cubes (see page 21) as follows: Take 225 g/8 oz mushrooms and mince in food processor. Squeeze dry in corner of kitchen paper towel. (Save juice for soup or sauce.) Add to finely chopped spring onions or shallots and sauté in 2 Stock Cubes and 2 tablespoons of dry vermouth. Stir frequently until mushrooms are dry and begin to separate. Add 1 teaspoon of vegetable seasoning (see page 24) and sauté a few more minutes. Store in refrigerator for several weeks in airtight container or freeze. Used in sauces, stuffings, and vegetable purées, this will be a cherished ingredient.

Flours, Cereals
Flours and cereals should be stored in airtight jars. Because the germ is not removed in whole grain products, they are a little more perishable. (The fat content of germ causes this.) I keep my whole wheat flour in the freezer. Odds and ends of dry cereal may be pulverized, appropriately seasoned, and used to bread fish or chicken or as a topping for vegetables.

Garlic
If you are a garlic lover as I am, try adding a little additional very finely chopped garlic to a dish ten minutes before the cooking time is over. It gives a fresh, delicious taste to the food.

To make garlic toast croûtons, toast whole wheat bread and rub whole cloves of garlic on hot toast. It will melt into toast and make a flavourful garlic toast—without fat. If croûtons are desired, cut into cubes and toast on baking sheet in 200°C, 400°F, Gas Mark 6 oven until crisp. (If your hands smell garlicky, rinse in cold water and rub in salt; we finally found something it is good for.)

Ginger Root
May be stored in a plastic bag or the freezer or in a bottle of dry sherry if you promise not to nip.

Spring Onions or Scallions
The white portion may be used to substitute for shallots in cooking, and the green part for chives.

Leftovers
YESTERDAY'S VEGETABLES BECOME TODAY'S SALAD
Mix our Vinaigrette Dressing (see page 13) in a generous-sized jar. Each day, add any leftover bits of raw or cooked vegetables. (Exception is salad greens.) In a few days, lift marinated vegetable mixture with slotted spoon onto lettuce leaves and serve as a delicious salad. You will discover unusual and flavourful mixtures this way.

LEFTOVER COOKED MEATS
Use leftover cooked meats (chicken, turkey or top rump steak) in salads; purée and use as a seasoned sandwich spread or as a pâté appetizer.

LEFTOVER COOKED RICE OR SPAGHETTI
May be used in salads, soups or as a crust. Season and blend with lightly beaten egg white and Weight Watcher's cottage cheese. Press over bottom and sides of pie plate, and fill with vegetable mixture and bake.

Lemons

Lemon juice is a marvellous flavour enhancer to be used on fish, chicken, game and turkey. It develops a flavour without a lemony taste, if used judiciously. Add grated lemon rind to salads or vinaigrette dressings. Float lemon slices on some soups or serve with jellied consommés. Lemon wedges served with fresh melon add extra zip. Lemons may be stored at room temperature for about ten days and in the refrigerator in crisper or plastic bag for about six weeks. Lemons yield more juice when at room temperature. If chilled, place under hot water or in a microwave oven for about fifteen seconds. Roll on worktop before squeezing to release more juice.

Mirepoix

A mirepoix is a mixture of 1 carrot, 1 small onion and 1 stalk of celery (sometimes a shallot) that have been chopped and sautéed in chicken stock until transparent. It is used as a base in roasting or braising meat or chicken and sometimes with added liquid as a base for poaching fish.

Popcorn

May be seasoned with vegetable seasoning, curry powder, garlic powder or onion powder as a snack substitute for "junk foods".

Sap Sago Cheese (nonfat herb cheese from Switzerland)

When using Sap Sago cheese as a seasoning or topping, grate it fine, then place it on a baking sheet in a 190°C, 375°F, Gas Mark 5 oven until golden brown. Stir from time to time while toasting. If it lumps, do not become alarmed, simply crush it between your fingers until it resembles the texture of Parmesan, for which it is frequently substituted. Sap Sago cheese may be frozen.

Soy Sauce

Use only mild soy sauce. If you cannot find mild salt-reduced soy sauce, you can dilute regular soy sauce (1 part water to 1 part soy sauce) before measuring and using.

Thickeners

For thickening a sauce, 1 tablespoon of cornflour, arrowroot or potato starch equals 2 tablespoons of flour. Use cornflour, arrowroot or potato starch when you want a translucent look. Mix thickener with cold water before adding to hot liquid.

Tofu (soy bean curd)
Tofu is a vegetable cheese made from soy milk. It has been used as a meat exchange in China and Japan for centuries as a major source of protein. Since it is not of animal origin, it contains no cholesterol. Because of its fat content, it must be used as an exchange for fish or poultry; however, it has fewer calories— about 72 calories in a 100 g/3½ oz serving, whereas a skinned chicken breast has about 110 calories.

Tofu has a bland taste, but it absorbs the flavour of the food with which it is combined. Hence, it lends itself to marinades or stir-frying. When cubed, it is a good protein addition to soups. It may be blended in your food processor and used as a cheese in lasagna, as a substitute for mayonnaise, or seasoned and used instead of yogurt in a dip.

Tomato Products
Blend 1 can of salt-free tomato paste with 1 can of cold water to make a salt-free tomato purée, 2 cans of water with paste to make a sauce, and 3 cans of water plus 1 teaspoon of apple juice concentrate, lemon juice and Tabasco to make a pleasant-tasting (and less expensive) tomato juice. It is important to blend juice well and chill before serving.

For ketchup, combine a 175 g/6 oz can of salt-free tomato paste, 2 cans of water, 2 tablespoons of apple cider, brown rice vinegar or raspberry wine vinegar, and 1½ tablespoons of frozen unsweetened pineapple juice concentrate. Blend well and refrigerate. (If you like a spicier ketchup, a few drops of Tabasco may be added.)

Truffles
Truffles are round, wrinkled, black or white aromatic fungi, which are dug up by pigs in certain regions of France and Italy. They are expensive, especially the fresh, which are seldom found in the United States. The flavour of canned truffles can be enhanced by sprinkling 1 tablespoon of Madeira over them a short time before serving. They lend exquisite flavour to sauces and salads; leftovers, if you can use such a plebian term in connection with truffles, may be frozen and are wonderful shredded and added to pasta.

Vinegar
There is a soggy mass that may develop in vinegar when it ages. This is called mother-of-vinegar. If it is present, you may make your own vinegar by adding leftover wine (white or red depending on the vinegar) to it and letting the bottle stand in a cool, dark place for several weeks before using.

Herb vinegars are more expensive. You may make your own by adding a bunch of fresh basil, tarragon, dill or 3 crushed garlic cloves to the plain vinegar of your choice. (It makes a lovely gift, also.)

Wine
Don't be concerned about adding wine to your cooking; 85 percent of the calories and all of the alcohol cook off at about 80°C, 175°F.

Yogurt
Contains the same nutrients as the milk from which it is made. Therefore, 250 ml/8 fl oz of nonfat yogurt contain about 90 calories. Compare this to 250 ml/8 fl oz of sour cream with 485 calories, or worse yet, 250 ml/8 fl oz of mayonnaise with 1400 calories. Yogurt is also a good source of protein, calcium, potassium and other minerals. It is a perishable dairy product and must be refrigerated. The longer it is stored, the more tart it becomes. Yogurt made from a Bulgarian starter is innately more tart. Liquid naturally separates from the solid as it stands, so for a thicker yogurt, drain off the liquid before stirring it. Commercial yogurt has a date stamped on the bottom to indicate the last day it can be sold. Yogurt may be used in dips, as a base in desserts or fruited toppings, in baking, in soups, and in marinating or cooking poultry, fish or meats. Naturally, it can be adapted and substituted whenever sour cream or mayonnaise is used.

Cooking Tips

To Beat Egg Whites
The bowl, beaters and egg whites should be at room temperature to increase the volume of the beaten egg whites. Do not use a plastic bowl because it retains grease from previous cooking and inhibits egg whites from becoming stiff. If you add half of a very

ripe banana, puréed, to softly beaten egg whites, you will further increase their volume.

To Whip Skimmed Evaporated Milk
Canned milk should be thoroughly chilled for about one hour or two in the freezer. The bowl and beater to be used should also be chilled in the freezer first. If all ingredients and utensils are thoroughly chilled, milk will triple in bulk when beaten.

Steam, Grill, Use Pressure Cooker or Microwave Raw Vegetables to Preserve Vitamins
When possible, eat raw. Don't thaw frozen vegetables before cooking, and use as little water as possible to cook them. (It saves the nutrients.) Any leftover vegetable liquid should be saved for soups, sauces or gravy.

To Remove Fat from Liquids
Let liquids chill so that the fat rises and hardens. Remove the fat several hours later or the next day. If you want to remove fat immediately, there is a wonderful piece of equipment called a gravy strain that removes all fat from liquids by just pouring. The spout is on the bottom so that de-fatted liquid can be removed quite simply.

To Prepare Dried Orange Peel
To prepare dried orange peel, remove rind of orange (not white part) with vegetable peeler and let it hang in your kitchen for several days to dry. When dried, store in airtight spice jar or in freezer for future use.

Taste Your Marinara Sauce
Dip a small piece of whole wheat or Italian bread into your marinara or tomato sauce while cooking to check the seasoning. It will give you a good idea of what the sauce tastes like served over pasta. (Besides, it also gives you an excuse to dunk while cooking.) If you are concerned about calories, try the following: blanch fresh bean sprouts in boiling water about one minute. Drain *quickly* and serve with marinara sauce. *Voilà*—almost-pasta with few calories.

Control Yogurt Curdling

Yogurt is very sensitive to heat. It curdles under high temperatures. When a recipe calls for you to heat yogurt, start with it at room temperature and add it to the other ingredients at the end of the cooking time. Continue cooking at a low temperature for a brief period of time. Cornflour blended with yogurt—1 teaspoon of cornflour to 120 ml/4 fl oz of yogurt—also helps stabilize it.

To Process Garlic

Add garlic while the machine is in motion; otherwise, it may lodge under the blade of the processor and not be chopped.

To Clean Mushrooms

Wipe with damp kitchen paper towels or a mushroom brush. As a last resort, you may wash quickly under cold running water. *Never* soak mushrooms in water to clean. They absorb too much water and dilute flavour in cooking. If mushroom caps are not tightly closed and you can see the gills, the mushrooms are too old and you should not buy them. If, however, you have them at home, they can be used. Mushrooms can be sliced and placed in freezer bags for future use in cooking.

To Cook Whole Onions

Cut an × in the root end of an onion to prevent it from slipping apart in cooking.

To Plump Raisins

In order to enhance the flavour and texture of raisins, they need to be plumped in a hot liquid of your choice such as fresh orange juice, water, sherry or brandy. Simply cover raisins with hot liquid for fifteen minutes and drain well before using. They may also be heated in the microwave oven on high for three minutes.

To Peel Tomatoes

Immerse in boiling water for two minutes. Rinse in cold water, core and peel. They may also be placed on a fork over an open flame and turned until skin bursts, then peeled. To seed tomatoes, cut in half crosswise and gently squeeze to remove seeds.

❧ Six Easy Basics ❧

Stock Cubes
Basic Chicken Stock
Our Cream Cheese and
  Sour Cream

Harriet's No-Salt Vegetable
  Seasoning
Seasoned Bread Crumbs
Basic White Sauce

Stock Cubes

450 ml/¾ pint our Basic
Chicken Stock (see page 22)
120 ml/4 fl oz dry white wine
  or vermouth

1 bay leaf
2 shallots, chopped

1. Combine above ingredients.

2. Simmer until reduced to 250 ml/8 fl oz. (If by chance you have stored your chicken stock in the refrigerator for more than 3 days, bring the stock to the boil before using in order to destroy any harmful bacteria.)

3. Pour into ice cube tray and freeze.

4. Remove from tray and seal tightly in plastic bags. (Don't get cubes wet when removing from ice cube tray or they will stick together.) These are handy to use in stir-frying or sautéeing ingredients, instead of fat or oil. Also nice for seasoning steamed vegetables.

Per serving: 5 calories; 0.4 gm protein; 0 gm fat; 0.8 gm carbohydrate; 0 gm fibre; 0 mg cholesterol; 0 mg iron; 0.7 mg sodium; 0 IU Vitamin A; 0 mg thiamine; 0 mg riboflavin; 0 mg Vitamin C; 0 mg potassium; 0 mg zinc; 0 mg niacin; 0 mcg Vitamin B_6; 0 mcg Vitamin B_{12}; 0 mcg folic acid

Basic Chicken Stock

Yield: about 2 litres/3½ pints (250 ml/8 fl oz = 1 serving)

The preparation of a delicious low-fat, low-sodium chicken stock is essential in our type of food preparation. It serves as the base of many other soups, is an essential cooking liquid in a large variety of dishes and sauces, and is required in making your own frozen stock cubes to use in stir-frying, sautéing and seasoning. As of this writing there is no chicken stock available commercially that has no salt, MSG, sugar or fat added. Besides, yours will taste much better. You can make it in bulk once a month to freeze for future use. If by chance you have stored your chicken stock in the refrigerator for more than 3 days, bring the stock to the boil before using in order to destroy harmful bacteria—Salmonella—that increase with lengthy storage.

3.75 ml/¾ pints cold water
1.8 kg/4 lb chicken necks and backs (all visible fat removed)
2 whole chicken breasts, halved
3 carrots
3 stalks celery with leaves
1 parsnip
2 leeks, well washed

1 turnip
1 bouquet garni (4 sprigs parsley, ½ teaspoon crushed red pepper, 2 bay leaves, 1 teaspoon thyme, 1 table-spoon dried soup greens or similar)
1 onion stuck with 4 whole cloves

1. Place chicken necks and backs in a large stainless steel stock pot.
2. Cover with *cold* water.
3. Bring to the boil; remove scum.
4. Add remaining ingredients, lower heat and simmer for 2½ hours, partially covered. (Remove chicken breasts after 1 hour of cooking.*)
5. Strain through a stainless steel triple-mesh strainer, cool, and place in refrigerator overnight. Remove congealed fat before

---

* Reserve chicken breasts for use in salads or sandwiches, or serve as chicken in the pot with stock for dinner!

using or freezing. Keeps in refrigerator 3 days. For longer storage, freeze according to instructions on page 46.

To Use: Reheat and serve as stock or use as the base for a soup. (If you like, add fresh dill to the stock when reheating—it adds a surprisingly fresh flavour. Remember to remove the sprigs of dill before serving.) Use some to prepare our valuable Stock Cubes (see page 21).

Helpful Hints: Always use cold water in starting a stock. It allows the flavour to flow into the stock instead of being sealed in the bones or meat.

There is a cup called a gravy strain that may be used to defat stock *before* chilling or freezing.

Per serving: 34 calories; 2.6 gm protein; 0 gm fat; 5.5 gm carbohydrate; 0 gm fibre, 0 mg cholesterol; 0 mg iron; 5 mg sodium; 0 mg calcium; 0 mg phosphorus; 0 IU Vitamin A; 0 mg thiamine; 0 mg riboflavin; 0 mg Vitamin C; 0 mg potassium; 0 mg zinc; 0 mg niacin; 0 mcg Vitamin B_6; 0 mcg Vitamin B_{12}; 0 mcg folic acid

Our Cream Cheese and Sour Cream

Yield: about 450 g/1 lb (1 tablespoon = 1 serving)

This is a nonfat substitute for cream cheese and sour cream that is not only easy to prepare but may be frozen for future use.

225 g/8 oz *fresh* hoop cheese or skim milk ricotta
120 ml/4 fl oz fresh nonfat yogurt, or more to reach desired consistency

120 ml/4 fl oz buttermilk, strained to remove fat globules (for sour cream only)

1. Crumble *fresh* hoop cheese into a food processor or blender.
2. Process cheese until it forms a ball.
3. Add yogurt gradually while creaming. *This produces a cream cheese.*
4. *When a smooth, sour cream consistency is desired*, add 120 ml/4 fl oz buttermilk and process until smooth.
5. Keep in refrigerator for 1 week; for longer storage, put in freezer.

To Use: May be served or used as a cooking ingredient

whenever cream cheese or sour cream is indicated. Try the cream cheese on bagels for Sunday brunch, the sour cream as a topping for baked potatoes. If frozen, defrost and blend well before using.

Variation: If hoop cheese is not available, sour cream can be made by pureeing 1%– or 2%–fat cottage cheese in the food processor until smooth. Use as a sour cream topping.

Per serving: 9 calories; 1.8 gm protein; 0.09 gm fat; 0.63 gm carbohydrate; 0 gm fibre; 0.08 mg cholesterol; 0 mg iron; 22 mg sodium; 12 mg calcium; 8 mg phosphorus; 33 IU Vitamin A; 0 mg thiamine; 0.01 riboflavin; 0.04 mg Vitamin C; 13 mg potassium; 0.05 mg zinc; 0 mg niacin; 2.67 mcg Vitamin B_6; 0.03 mcg Vitamin B_{12}; 0.58 folic acid

Harriet's No-Salt Vegetable Seasoning

Yield: 6 tablespoons (½ teaspoon = 1 serving)

If a low-sodium vegetable seasoning is not available in your area, try making your own. It is quite simple, and you may even find that you prefer it to those commercially available.

15 g/½ oz dried soup greens or similar
1 tablespoon dried shallots or dried mushrooms
¼ teaspoon ground bay leaf
⅛ teaspoon celery seed
2 teaspoons toasted onion flakes

1 teaspoon garlic powder
1 teaspoon herbes de Provence or thyme
1 teaspoon Hungarian paprika
¼ teaspoon crushed red pepper or chilli powder
¼ teaspoon dry mustard

1. Blend all ingredients in blender until granulated and powdery. (If you do not have a blender, try a pestle and mortar.)
2. Store in a screw-top jar in a cool, dark, dry place.

To Use: This snappy seasoning is appropriate for salads, vegetables, fish and poultry, and can be used in cooking wherever vegetable seasoning is indicated.

Variation: Add 1 teaspoon toasted sesame seeds, ground ginger or dill weed to vary the flavour.

Per serving: 3 calories; 0.1 gm protein; 0 gm fat; 0.4 gm carbohydrate; 0.1 gm fibre; 0 mg cholesterol; 0.3 mg iron; 1 mg sodium; 6 mg calcium; 3 mg phosphorus; 171 IU Vitamin A; 0 mg thiamine; 0.01 riboflavin; 1 mg Vitamin C; 11 mg potassium; 0 mg zinc; 0 mg niacin; 2 mcg Vitamin B_6; 0 mcg Vitamin B_{12}; 1 mcg folic acid

Seasoned Breadcrumbs

Yield: approx. 100 g/4 oz (1 tablespoon = 1 serving)

Try making your own seasoned breadcrumbs. Simply combine one tablespoon of your favourite unsalted herb seasoning with 100 g/4 oz of dried breadcrumbs. Or for a more interesting and zesty flavour, prepare the following recipe. Store it in the refrigerator to preserve its freshness. If you read the label on commercial breadcrumbs carefully, you will note that in most circumstances they have fat, salt and sodium preservatives, and sugar added. With this in mind, it behooves us to prepare our own—besides you can also economize by using up stale bread.

100 g/4 oz dried fine bread-crumbs (preferably made from whole wheat bread)
Freshly ground pepper
Few grains crushed red pepper
½ teaspoon Hungarian paprika
1 teaspoon low-sodium vegetable seasoning (see page 24)

¼ teaspoon dried savory, crushed
½ teaspoon dried basil, crushed
½ teaspoon dried thyme, crushed
2 tablespoons grated Sap Sago cheese, toasted (see page 16)

1. Combine all ingredients in a small bowl. Mix well.
2. Store in refrigerator in an airtight container or freeze for future use.

Per serving: 16 calories; 3.7 gm protein; 0.3 gm fat; 2.0 gm carbohydrate; 0.2 gm fibre; 0 mg cholesterol; 0.3 mg iron; 35 mg sodium; 24 mg calcium; 12 mg phosphorus; 147 IU Vitamin A; 0.03 mg thiamine; 0.02 mg riboflavin; 0 mg Vitamin C; 19 mg potassium; 0 mg zinc; 0.2 mg niacin; 1 mcg Vitamin B_6; 0 mcg Vitamin B_{12}; 0 mcg folic acid

Basic White Sauce

Yield: about 600 ml/1 pint (3 tablespoons = 1 serving)

A sauce is meant to heighten the flavour of the food it covers. This basic white sauce or Béchamel, as it is sometimes called, is delicate in flavour, yet makes an interesting addition on occasion to already wonderful, crisp steamed vegetables.

3 our Stock Cubes (see page 21) or 3 tablespoons our Chicken or Vegetable stock (see pages 22, 49)	5 tablespoons dry nonfat milk
	1 bay leaf
	½ teaspoon thyme, crushed
	½ teaspoon white pepper
3 tablespoons unbleached flour	1 teaspoon vegetable seasoning
1 slice onion or 1 teaspoon chopped shallots	2 tablespoons dry sherry, sauterne, or vermouth
450 ml/¾ pint nonfat milk	(optional)

1. Melt stock cubes in a nonstick saucepan over moderate heat. Add flour and onion; blend with a wooden spoon or whisk.

2. Simmer over low heat for several minutes, *stirring constantly. Do not allow to brown.*

3. Remove from heat, add milks, bay leaf, thyme, white pepper and vegetable seasoning. Return to heat, stirring constantly until mixture coats the spoon. If desired, add wine and simmer 5 minutes more to evaporate alcohol.

4. Remove onion and bay leaf.

5. Cover and store until used, or place in an airtight container and refrigerate for several days, or freeze for future use.

Serving Suggestions: This sauce may be used over 1 kg/2 lb steamed vegetables such as broccoli florets, diced potatoes, quartered mushrooms, peas, asparagus or sliced carrots. To serve, place vegetables in a shallow, ovenproof serving dish. Drizzle sauce over vegetables, sprinkle with 2 tablespoons Parmesan or Sap Sago cheese or with Hungarian paprika, and place under grill to brown lightly before serving.

Variations: Instead of sprinkling cheese on top of vegetables, you may add 2 tablespoons Parmesan cheese to the white sauce and heat for 5 minutes. This is called a Mornay sauce. You may also substitute 150 ml/¼ pint of vegetable stock for 150 ml/¼ pint of nonfat liquid milk. Proceed as in recipe.

Per serving: 34 calories; 2.7 gm protein; 0.1 gm fat; 5.5 gm carbohydrate; 0.1 gm fibre; 1 mg cholesterol; 0.3 mg iron; 36 mg sodium; 90 mg calcium; 71 mg phosphorus; 97 IU Vitamin A; 0.05 mg thiamine; 0.11 mg riboflavin; 1 mg Vitamin C; 126 mg potassium; 0.28 mg zinc; 0.2 mg niacin; 26 mcg Vitamin B_6; 0.27 mcg Vitamin B_{12}; 3 mcg folic acid

Appetizers
and Hors d'Oeuvres

Spicy Bean Dip
Broccoli Dip
Cottage Cheese Caper
Spicy Pink Dip
Tuna Dip Tapénade
Herbed Yogurt Dip
Queso con Salsa
Homemade Crisps
Caponata
Marinated Chicken
  Drumsticks

Chicken Rumaki
Liptauer Cheese
Marinated Mushrooms
Petite Meatballs on Toast
Spinach-Stuffed Mushrooms
Salmon Steak Tartare
Seviche
Tomato Aspic Supreme with
  Cucumber Sauce
Salmon Pâté
Tuna Pâté

It has always been my contention that appetizers should be something special—a savoury treat. As is so frequently the case, the French have a word for it—*"amuse gueule"*: that which amuses the palate. It implies that appetizers are to be served to heighten the pleasure of eating. This may be accomplished by simply presenting fresh, unpeeled vegetables as crudités with a dipping sauce or by choosing a dramatic presentation, such as an antipasto or an attractively garnished seviche. Vegetables such as green and red peppers, aubergines, or cooked artichokes can be hollowed to form edible containers for cheese mixtures or dips. Our Cream Cheese (see page 23) may be flavoured to be served with crackers and crispbreads or moulded into a log or ball and coated with freshly chopped parsley, herbs, chives or Hungarian paprika.

Perhaps hot hors d'oeuvres, painstakingly prepared, are more to your liking. Whatever your choice may be, try to make it look and taste special —if not, forget it!

Spicy Bean Dip

Yield: about 600 ml/1 pint (1 tablespoon = 1 serving)

425-g/15-oz can chilli beans
1 clove garlic
120 ml/4 fl oz nonfat yogurt
120 ml/4 fl oz tomato sauce
½ small red onion, quartered
2–3 tablespoons green chilli
  sauce or to taste

1 whole red or green pepper
  for serving
2 tablespoons chopped tomato
  for garnish
1 tablespoon chopped fresh
  coriander for garnish

1. Place beans, garlic, yogurt and tomato sauce in blender or food processor. Blend until smooth.
2. Add onion and blend until chopped.
3. Add sauce to taste and blend briefly.
4. Chill several hours before serving to let flavours blend.
To Serve: Place in hollowed red or green pepper garnished with chopped tomato and chopped coriander and surround with our Homemade Crisps (see page 32).

Per serving: 43 calories; 2.1 gm protein; 2 gm fat; 3.9 gm carbohydrate; 0.1 gm fibre; 0 mg cholesterol; 0.1 mg iron; 91 mg sodium; 10 mg calcium; 3 mg phosphorus; 96 IU Vitamin A; 0.01 mg thiamine; 0.02 mg riboflavin; 1 mg Vitamin C; 5 mg potassium; 0.01 mg zinc; 0.1 mg niacin; 3 mcg Vitamin B$_6$; 0 mcg Vitamin B$_{12}$; 1 mcg folic acid

Broccoli Dip
(Almost Mimosa)

Yield: about 600 ml/1 pint (1 tablespoon = 1 serving)

1 275-g/10-oz packet
  frozen chopped broccoli,
  cooked, drained and cooled
50 g/2 oz skim-milk ricotta
  cheese
175 ml/6 fl oz nonfat yogurt
½ teaspoon thyme
½ teaspoon marjoram
1 tablespoon toasted onion
  flakes

3 spring onions
3 hard-boiled eggs, whites only
  (reserve 1 for garnish)
20 g/¾ oz fresh parsley
1 teaspoon low-sodium
  vegetable seasoning (see
  page 24)
2 tablespoons fresh dill

1. Squeeze out excess moisture from broccoli and combine with cheese, yogurt, thyme, marjoram, onion flakes, spring onions, 2 egg whites, parsley, vegetable seasoning and dill in blender or food processor.

2. Blend until finely chopped.

3. Chill several hours before serving to let flavours blend.

To Serve: Place dip in bowl, garnish with grated egg white, and surround with your choice of assorted raw vegetables, such as radishes, tomatoes, cauliflower, mange tout peas, peppers, carrots, cucumber, courgettes or mushrooms.

Per serving: 35 calories; 3.9 gm protein; 0.6 gm fat; 4.2 gm carbohydrate; 0.6 gm fibre; 2 mg cholesterol; 1.0 mg iron; 41 mg sodium; 81 mg calcium; 38 mg phosphorus; 1126 IU Vitamin A; 0.05 mg thiamine; 0.13 mg riboflavin; 26 mg Vitamin C; 149 mg potassium; 0.09 mg zinc; 0.5 mg niacin; 6 mcg Vitamin B_6; 0.03 mcg Vitamin B_{12}; 2 mcg folic acid

Cottage Cheese Caper

Yield: about 300 ml/½ pint (1 tablespoon = 1 serving)

This dip can also be used as a salad dressing.

225 g/8 oz Weight Watchers cottage cheese, rinsed and drained

4 tablespoons buttermilk, strained to remove fat globules

1 clove garlic

2 spring onions, chopped

1 tablespoon capers, rinsed and drained

2 tablespoons fresh lime juice

½ teaspoon low-sodium vegetable seasoning (see page 24)

Few grains cayenne pepper

Hungarian paprika for garnish

1. Whirl cottage cheese and buttermilk in blender or food processor until smooth.

2. Add garlic, spring onions, capers, lime juice, vegetable seasoning and cayenne. Blend until smooth.

3. Chill at least 1 hour to let flavours blend.

To Serve: If used as a dip, place in a bowl, sprinkle with Hungarian paprika, and serve with crackers or assorted raw vegetables.

Per serving: 29 calories; 3.9 gm protein; 0.3 gm fat; 2.4 gm carbohydrate; 0.2 gm fibre; 0 mg cholesterol; 0.3 mg iron; 75 mg sodium; 42 mg calcium; 12 mg

phosphorus; 136 IU Vitamin A; 0.03 mg thiamine; 0.09 mg riboflavin; 2 mg Vitamin C; 55 mg potassium; 0.01 mg zinc; 0.2 mg niacin; 0 mcg Vitamin B$_6$; 0 mcg Vitamin B$_{12}$; 0 mcg folic acid

Spicy Pink Dip

Yield: generous 600 ml/1 pint (1 tablespoon = 1 serving)

350 g/12 oz Weight Watchers cottage cheese, rinsed and drained

120 ml/4 fl oz salt-free tomato sauce

1 small onion, quartered

2 tablespoons horseradish, or to taste

1 100-g/14-oz can diced green chillies

1. Place the first 4 ingredients in food processor or blender. Process until smooth.
2. Pour into a bowl and fold in chillies.
3. Cover with cling film and chill.

To Serve: Serve with our Homemade Crisps (see page 32) or assorted crisp raw vegetables.

Per serving: 10 calories; 0.9 gm protein; 0.3 gm fat; 0.8 gm carbohydrate; 0.1 gm fibre; 0 mg cholesterol; 0.1 mg iron; 19 mg sodium; 8 mg calcium; 2 mg phosphorus; 38 IU Vitamin A; 0 mg thiamine; 0.02 mg riboflavin; 0 mg Vitamin C; 11 mg potassium; 0.01 mg zinc; 0.1 mg niacin; 3 mcg Vitamin B$_6$; 0 mcg Vitamin B$_{12}$; 1 mcg folic acid

Tuna Dip Tapénade

Yield: scant 600 ml/1 pint (2 tablespoons = 1 serving)

100 g/4 oz Weight Watchers cottage cheese, rinsed and drained

120 ml/4 fl oz nonfat yogurt

1 215-g/7½-oz can salt-free tuna in water, well drained

2 tablespoons lemon juice

¼ small onion

½ teaspoon Hungarian paprika

½ teaspoon salt-free mustard

1 tablespoon capers, rinsed and drained

1 whole red or green pepper for serving

1 tablespoon chopped fresh parsley for garnish

1. Place the first 7 ingredients in blender or food processor. Blend until mixture is smooth.

2. Add capers and process slightly.

3. Taste, and adjust seasonings.

To Serve: Remove stem and seeds from nicely shaped red or green pepper. Place tapénade in hollowed pepper. Sprinkle with parsley and surround with assorted crisp, raw vegetables, crackers, or our Homemade Crisps (see page 32).

Per serving: 38 calories; 6.7 gm protein; 0.3 gm fat; 1.8 gm carbohydrate; 0.2 gm fibre; 11 mg cholesterol; 0.4 mg iron; 36 mg sodium; 27 mg calcium; 37 mg phosphorus; 158 IU Vitamin A; 0.02 mg thiamine; 0.07 mg riboflavin; 13 mg Vitamin C; 86 mg potassium; 0.01 mg zinc; 2.6 mg niacin; 25 mcg Vitamin B_6; 0 mcg Vitamin B_{12}; 1 mcg folic acid

Herbed Yogurt Dip

Yield: scant 600 ml/1 pint (1 tablespoon = 1 serving)

450 ml/¾ pint nonfat yogurt
3 tablespoons chopped fresh dill
¼ teaspoon celery seed
¼ teaspoon caraway seed
1 tablespoon grated onion

1 steamed artichoke or 1 whole red or green pepper for serving
Chopped fresh dill for garnish

1. Combine yogurt with dill, celery and caraway seeds and onion.

2. Chill several hours or overnight to develop flavours.

To Serve: For a particularly attractive presentation, instead of a bowl, place yogurt in centre of a chilled steamed artichoke, choke removed, or a hollowed-out red or green pepper. (The artichoke is especially nice because its leaves may be used for dipping and the heart eaten when the dip is finished.) Sprinkle with dill. Place container with dip in centre of large platter or basket and surround with crisp, raw vegetables, such as cauliflower, broccoli florets, mange tout peas, peppers, swede, turnip, celery, cucumber, fresh fennel, cherry tomatoes, red radishes, spring onions, and courgettes.

Per serving: 8 calories; 1 gm protein; 0 gm fat; 2 gm carbohydrate; 0 gm fibre; 0 mg cholesterol; 0.5 mg iron; 10 mg sodium; 35 mg calcium; 7 mg phosphorus; 47 IU Vitamin A; 0 mg thiamine; 0 mg riboflavin; 4 mg Vitamin C; 34 mg potassium; 0 mg zinc; 0 mg niacin; 9 mcg Vitamin B_6; 0 mcg Vitamin B_{12}; 0 mcg folic acid

Queso con Salsa

(Cheese with Chilli Sauce)

Yield: about 300 ml/½ pint yogurt cheese (2 tablespoons = 1 serving)

Our Yogurt Cheese, from 450
ml/¾ pint nonfat yogurt
(see page 205)

300 ml/½ pint canned chilli
sauce

Unmould cheese onto a serving plate and spoon sauce over
and around cheese.

To Serve: Surround with crackers and crisp toasted pita bread.

Per serving: 33 calories; 4.0 gm protein; 0.2 gm fat; 4 gm carbohydrate; 0.5 gm
fibre; 0 mg cholesterol; 0.3 mg iron; 33 mg sodium; 86 mg calcium; 19 mg
phosphorus; 380 IU Vitamin A; 0.10 mg thiamine; 0.19 mg riboflavin; 11 mg
Vitamin C; 80 mg potassium; 0 mg zinc; 0.5 mg niacin; 0 mcg Vitamin B$_6$; 0 mcg
Vitamin B$_{12}$; 0 mcg folic acid

Homemade Crisps

Yield: 96 chips (4 chips = 1 serving)

It is difficult to find commercial crisps that are not high in
sodium because of added salt or preservatives, or high in fat
because of deep-frying. The following recipe gives you a
low-sodium, low-fat snack that can be prepared in large
amounts and frozen for future use. Serve with dips, soups or
salads.

12 salt-free corn tortillas, or 1
packet (6) whole wheat pita
bread
2 tablespoons mild soy sauce
120 ml/4 fl oz water, our
Chicken Stock (see page 22),
or our Vegetable Stock (see
page 49)

Onion powder (optional
seasoning)
Garlic powder (optional)
Herbal bouquet (optional)
Hungarian paprika (optional)
Low-sodium vegetable season-
ing (see page 24), optional

1. Cut through entire stack of 12 tortillas at once, making 4

cuts through centre to make 96 crisps or cut 6 whole wheat pita breads in 4 cuts and separate.

2. Lay wedges on nonstick baking sheets in single layers; avoid overlapping.

3. Combine soy sauce and water or stock in a plastic spray bottle and spray the wedges; this helps seasoning stick to chips.

4. Sprinkle with seasoning of your choice.

5. Bake in a preheated 200°C, 400°F, Gas Mark 6 oven until lightly browned and sufficiently crisp—approximately 8 minutes.

6. Cool. Store in airtight plastic bags or freeze for future use.

Variation: Crisps may be sprinkled with grated Sap Sago cheese (see page 16)—or Parmesan if your diet permits—before baking.

Per serving: 25 calories; 0.8 gm protein; 0.3 gm fat; 6 gm carbohydrate; 0 gm fibre; 0 mg cholesterol; 0.3 mg iron; 20 mg sodium; 1 mg calcium; 14 mg phosphorus; 33 IU Vitamin A; 0.2 mg thiamine; 0.01 mg riboflavin; 0 mg Vitamin C; 3 mg potassium; 0.12 mg zinc; 0 mg niacin; 0 mcg Vitamin B_6; 0 mcg Vitamin B_{12}; 0 mcg folic acid

Caponata
(An Aubergine Appetizer)

Serves: 10–12

675 g/1½ lb aubergine, halved
1 teaspoon low-sodium vegetable seasoning (see page 24)
3 tablespoons our Chicken Stock (see page 22)
1 stalk celery, chopped
1 medium onion, chopped
2 cloves garlic, finely chopped
½ green pepper, chopped
6 mushrooms, cleaned, stalks removed, and quartered
350-g/12-oz canned tomatoes, drained (sauce reserved) and chopped, or 2 large ripe tomatoes, peeled, seeded and chopped

5 tablespoons red wine vinegar
1 tablespoon unsweetened apple juice concentrate
3 tablespoons chopped fresh parsley
1 tablespoon capers, rinsed and drained
3 tablespoons salt-free tomato paste, mixed with 120 ml/4 fl oz water
5 tablespoons drained sauce from tomatoes, or canned tomato sauce if using fresh tomatoes
Freshly ground pepper
1 teaspoon Italian herb seasoning, crushed

1. Place halved aubergine on nonstick baking tin. Add 5 mm/¼ inch water. Bake in a preheated 200°C, 400°F, Gas Mark 6 oven for 15 to 20 minutes.

2. Cool, peel, and cube aubergine. Season with vegetable seasoning and place in colander to drain.

3. Place stock in a nonstick frying pan. Add chopped celery. Sauté 5 minutes. Add onion, garlic and green pepper. Sauté 10 minutes more. Add mushrooms, sauté 5 minutes more.

4. Add drained aubergine cubes and sauté until lightly browned, stirring with a wooden spoon. (If the mixture starts to stick, add a little tomato sauce.)

5. Add tomatoes, vinegar and apple juice concentrate. Cook 5 minutes.

6. Add parsley, capers, tomato paste mixed with water, tomato sauce, pepper and Italian herb seasoning.

7. Cook, uncovered, about 20 minutes, or until thick. Stir from time to time.

8. Adjust seasoning, cool, and chill in refrigerator container several hours or overnight before serving.

To Serve: Bring to room temperature, place in a bowl, and surround with toasted pita bread.

Variation: My friend Gracie tops each helping of Caponata with a dab of Hummus (see page 209); a wonderful combination of flavours with the welcome addition of the protein from the garbanzo beans.

Per serving: 43 calories; 1.8 gm protein; 0.9 gm fat; 8.4 gm carbohydrate; 1.7 gm fibre; 0 mg cholesterol; 1.4 mg iron; 8 mg sodium; 31 mg calcium; 43 mg phosphorus; 657 IU Vitamin A; 0.08 mg thiamine; 0.09 mg riboflavin; 21 mg Vitamin C; 289 mg potassium; 0.09 mg zinc; 1.1 niacin; 110 mcg Vitamin B_6; 0 mcg Vitamin B_{12}; 13 mcg folic acid

Marinated Chicken Drumsticks

675 g/1½ lb chicken drumsticks, skinned

150 ml/¼ pint our Italian Dressing (see page 13)

1½ teaspoons Italian herb seasoning, crushed

1½ teaspoons Hungarian paprika

1½ tablespoons green chilli sauce

1 tablespoon raspberry wine vinegar

Shredded lettuce for serving

Chopped fresh parsley for garnish

1. Place skinned chicken drumsticks in saucepan with remaining ingredients. Stir to combine.

2. Bring to the boil over medium heat, lower to simmering, and cook, covered, for about 20 to 30 minutes.

3. Taste, and adjust seasonings.

4. Place in refrigerator and chill 4 to 6 hours or overnight before serving.

To Serve: Arrange chicken drumsticks on a bed of shredded lettuce in a spokelike design. Sprinkle with parsley and serve.

Per serving: 41 calories; 6.7 gm protein; 1.1 gm fat; 0.7 gm carbohydrate; 0.1 gm fibre; 24 mg cholesterol; 0.7 mg iron; 54 mg sodium; 7 mg calcium; 58 mg phosphorus; 237 IU Vitamin A; 0.02 mg thiamine; 0.06 mg riboflavin; 2 mg Vitamin C; 94 mg potassium; 0 mg zinc; 2.5 mg niacin; 1 mcg Vitamin B_6; 0 mcg Vitamin B_{12}; 0 mcg folic acid

Chicken Rumaki

Serves: 12 (2 rumaki = 1 serving)

12 whole canned water
   chestnuts, drained
12 fresh or canned un-
   sweetened pineapple chunks
275 g/10 oz slightly frozen
   skinned and boned chicken
   breasts, thinly sliced across
   grain into 24 slices
2½ tablespoons mild soy
   sauce
4 tablespoons water

2 tablespoons frozen un-
   sweetened pineapple juice
   concentrate
2 tablespoons dry sherry
   or sake
1 teaspoon garlic powder
1 teaspoon ground ginger

2 tablespoons salt-free Chinese
   mustard or Dijon mustard
   for serving (optional)

1. Wrap each of the water chestnuts and each of the pineapple chunks with a slice of chicken. Secure with wooden cocktail sticks.

2. Combine soy sauce, water, pineapple juice, sherry, garlic powder and ginger in a plastic bag.

3. Add wrapped chestnuts and pineapple to bag. Marinate in refrigerator several hours or overnight.

4. Drain, place on grill pan, and grill on high about 2 minutes. Turn over, baste with sauce, and grill 2 minutes more. Baste again with sauce.

To Serve: Serve hot, with Chinese mustard or Dijon mustard on the side for dipping if you like.

Per serving: 48 calories; 5.98 gm protein; 0.33 gm fat; 4.4 gm carbohydrate; 0.14 gm fibre; 14 mg cholesterol; 0.29 mg iron; 163 mg sodium; 6 mg calcium; 53 mg phosphorus; 12 IU Vitamin A; 0.04 mg thiamine; 0.04 mg riboflavin; 3 mg Vitamin C; 122 mg potassium; 0.2 mg zinc; 2.76 mg niacin; 136 mcg Vitamin B_6; 0.09 mcg Vitamin B_{12}; 1.3 mcg folic acid

Liptauer Cheese

Yield: about 350 g/12 oz (2 tablespoons = 1 serving)

225 g/8 oz skim-milk ricotta
5 tablespoons nonfat yogurt
1 clove garlic, finely chopped
1 tablespoon capers, rinsed and drained
2 teaspoons Hungarian paprika
1½ teaspoons caraway seeds
½ teaspoon salt-free Dijon mustard

1 teaspoon low-sodium vegetable seasoning (see page 24)
Few grains crushed red pepper
1 teaspoon mild soy sauce
2 tablespoons chopped spring onions

1. Blend ricotta cheese in blender or food processor until smooth.

2. Add yogurt and process until smooth.

3. Add garlic, capers, paprika, caraway seeds, mustard, vegetable seasoning, crushed red pepper, soy sauce and spring onions. Process until well blended.

4. Taste, and adjust seasonings.

5. Pack in 3 individual soufflé dishes or ramekins, cover with cling film wrap and foil, and store in refrigerator 24 hours before using so that flavours may develop. Unused portion keeps well for about 1 week.

To Serve: Serve with unsalted whole wheat or rye crackers.

Per serving: 33 calories; 2.7 gm protein; 1.6 gm fat; 2.2 gm carbohydrate; 0.2 gm fibre; 6 mg cholesterol; 0.4 mg iron; 41 mg sodium; 67 mg calcium; 40 mg phosphorus; 420 IU Vitamin A; 0.02 mg thiamine; 0.06 mg riboflavin; 1 mg Vitamin C; 48 mg potassium; 0.26 mg zinc; 0.2 mg niacin; 4 mcg Vitamin B_6; 0.05 mcg Vitamin B_{12}; 0 mcg folic acid

Marinated Mushrooms

Serves: 12 (4 mushrooms = 1 serving)

250 ml/8 fl oz our Chicken
Stock (see page 22)
4 tablespoons water
150 ml/¼ pint red wine
vinegar
4 cloves garlic, crushed
2 tablespoons chopped fresh
parsley
2 teaspoons crushed herbes de
Provence
2 teaspoons salt-free Dijon
mustard

1 50-g/2-oz jar chopped
pimento, drained
450 g/1 lb small mushrooms,
wiped clean and stalks
removed

Radicchio leaves for serving
1 bunch spring onions finely
chopped, or 1 red onion,
finely chopped, for garnish

1. Place stock, water, vinegar, garlic, parsley, herbs, mustard
and pimento in jar. Shake to blend well.
2. Place mushrooms in bowl, pour over marinade. Cover bowl
and chill in refrigerator overnight.
To Serve: Arrange crisp radicchio leaves on a platter and cover
with drained mushrooms. Sprinkle mushrooms with chopped
spring onions or chopped red onion. This can also be served on a
cold buffet surrounded by beefsteak tomato slices and red onion
slices.

Helpful Hint: Save mushroom stalks for Mushroom Sauce from
Cuisine Minceur (page 214), soups or Duxelles (page 14).

Per serving: 28 calories; 1.8 gm protein; 0.3 gm fat; 5.5 gm carbohydrate; 1.5 gm
fibre; 0 mg cholesterol; 1.2 mg iron; 10 mg sodium; 33 mg calcium; 58 mg
phosphorus; 450 IU Vitamin A; 0.05 mg thiamine; 0.19 mg riboflavin; 11 mg
Vitamin C; 257 mg potassium; 0.07 mg zinc; 1.7 mg niacin; 69 mcg Vitamin B$_6$;
0 mcg Vitamin B$_{12}$; 16 mcg folic acid

Petite Meatballs on Toast

Serves: 24 (2 meatballs = 1 serving)

It is always such a hassle to prepare hors d'oeuvres on the day of
a party that I find these a joy to serve because they can be
prepared at my convenience and frozen for future use.

Thinly sliced whole wheat or
rye bread, cut into 48
4 cm/1½ inch circles
2 tablespoons nonfat yogurt
1 teaspoon salt-free Dijon
mustard
2 tablespoons nonfat milk
1 slice whole wheat bread,
crust removed, pulled into
crumbs
450 g/1 lb extra-lean minced
beef, or minced turkey
3 tablespoons chopped fresh
parsley

3 tablespoons grated onion
1 clove garlic, finely chopped
1 tablespoon salt-free tomato
juice
1 teaspoon Worcestershire
sauce
1 teaspoon low-sodium
vegetable seasoning (see
page 24)
Freshly ground pepper
50 g/2 oz salt-free tomato
sauce or tomato purée
1 tablespoon chopped fresh
basil

1. Place bread circles on baking sheet and toast lightly on both
sides under grill.

2. Mix yogurt and mustard together. Spread lightly on 1 side of
toasted circles.

3. Pour nonfat milk over whole wheat breadcrumbs. Let stand
until milk is completely absorbed.

4. Combine meat, parsley, onion, garlic, tomato juice, Worcestershire sauce, vegetable seasoning, ground pepper and soaked
bread mixture. Mix thoroughly with a fork.

5. Roll in 48 balls approximately 2.5 cm/1 inch in diameter
(wetting hands with cold water in between to prevent sticking).

*6. Place balls on toasted bread circles. Make an indentation,
about 5 mm/¼ inch deep, in the centre of each ball with the tip of
your little finger.

7. Grill about 3 to 4 minutes.

8. Fill centre with a dab of tomato sauce and basil.

To Serve: Serve hot. For an elegant look, place a doily on a
serving platter with either parsley, watercress, or a lovely flower
from your garden in the centre and surround with meatballs and a
few tomatoes.

*To Freeze for Future Use:*Prepare through step 6. Place finished
meatballs uncooked on a shallow baking sheet or foil pan and
flash-freeze. Cover with cling film or foil; seal tightly. Can be
stored 2 to 3 months (label pack with the date of freezing). For
serving, frozen meatballs should be at least partially defrosted
before grilling. If not completely defrosted, grill 5 to 6 minutes.

Per serving: 60 calories; 6 gm protein; 2.4 gm fat; 3.6 gm carbohydrate; 0.2 gm fibre; 18 mg cholesterol; 1 mg iron; 44 mg sodium; 14 mg calcium; 48 mg phosphorus; 1.06 IU Vitamin A; 0.04 mg thiamine; 0.06 mg riboflavin; 2 mg Vitamin C; 134 mg potassium; 0 mg zinc; 1.4 mg niacin; 2 mcg Vitamin B_6; 0 mcg Vitamin B_{12}; 2 mcg folic acid

Spinach-Stuffed Mushrooms

Serves: 12 (2 mushrooms = 1 serving)

2 275-g/10-oz packets frozen chopped spinach
100 g/4 oz low-fat ricotta cheese
1 clove garlic, finely chopped
1 teaspoon mild soy sauce
Few grains crushed red pepper
2 egg whites
450 g/1 lb or 25 medium-to-large

mushrooms, wiped clean and stalks removed
Low-sodium vegetable seasoning (see page 24)
100 g/4 oz salt-free tomato sauce
2 tablespoons grated Sap Sago cheese, toasted (see page 16)
Hungarian paprika

1. Thaw spinach and squeeze dry.
2. Mix spinach with a fork, adding ricotta, garlic, soy sauce, crushed red pepper and egg whites.
3. Sprinkle mushroom caps with vegetable seasoning and stuff with spinach mixture.
4. Place in baking dish spread with tomato sauce. Bake, uncovered, in a preheated 180°C, 350°F, Gas Mark 4 oven for 20 to 25 minutes, or until firm to touch.
5. Sprinkle with cheese and paprika.
To Serve: Serve hot as an hors d'oeuvre, or as an accompaniment or garnish to a main course dish.

Variation: Use frozen chopped broccoli instead of spinach.

Helpful Hint: Save mushroom stalks for Mushroom Sauce from Cuisine Minceur (page 214), soups or Duxelles (page 14).

Per serving: 46 calories; 4.6 gm protein; 0 gm fat; 4.6 gm carbohydrate; 1.4 gm fibre; 1 mg cholesterol; 1.4 mg iron; 68 mg sodium; 84 mg calcium; 84 mg phosphorus; 2708 IU Vitamin A; 0.08 mg thiamine; 0.28 mg riboflavin; 14 mg Vitamin C; 236 mg potassium; 1.2 mg zinc; 1.8 mg niacin; 48 mcg Vitamin B_6; 0.04 mcg Vitamin B_{12}; 8 mcg folic acid

Salmon Steak Tartare

Serves: 8 (50 g/2 oz = 1 serving)

This variation of beef tartare is even more pleasing than the recipe from which it is derived and, of course, better for your health.

450 g/1 lb *very fresh* salmon, finely chopped
3 tablespoons capers, rinsed, drained and chopped
1 teaspoon lemon juice
2 tablespoons salt-free Dijon mustard with herbs
2 tablespoons chopped fresh parsley

Radicchio leaves for serving
2 175 g/6 oz new potatoes, boiled, cooled, peeled and diced, for garnish
3 small beetroot, baked or boiled, cooled, peeled and diced, for garnish
3 tablespoons finely chopped red onion for garnish

Mix salmon, capers, lemon juice, mustard and parsley together. Chill to allow flavours to blend.

To Serve: Arrange salmon mixture in a flat mound on a serving plate covered with radicchio leaves. Score top of salmon with metal spatula into diamond-shaped pattern and garnish attractively with rows of diced potato, beetroot and red onion. Serve with slices of whole wheat bread cut into quarters.

Variation: If capers are omitted in this recipe, the sodium content will be reduced to 40 mg per serving. Either 1 tablespoon Worcestershire sauce or 2 tablespoons cognac may be used instead.

Helpful Hint: Chop salmon with a sharp knife or the chopping blade of a food processor. If using a food processor, be careful to process only until chopped, not puréed.

Per serving: 165 calories; 12.1 gm protein; 4.2 gm fat; 8.3 gm carbohydrate; 1.5 gm fibre; 19 mg cholesterol; 0.9 mg iron; 229 mg sodium; 56 mg calcium; 198 mg phosphorus; 182 IU Vitamin A; 0.1 mg thiamine; 0.15 mg riboflavin; 9 mg Vitamin C; 401 mg potassium; 0.14 mg zinc; 4.5 mg niacin; 90 mcg Vitamin B_6; 0 mcg Vitamin B_{12}; 7 mcg folic acid

Seviche

Serves: 10 (40 g/1½ oz = 1 serving); (as main course, serves 5)

Seviche is a cold, marinated fish dish that makes an elegant presentation served as an hors d'oeuvre in the living room, as a first course at the table, or as one of the main dishes on a hot-weather buffet.

2 shallots, finely chopped
120 ml/4 fl oz dry white wine or vermouth
450 g/1 lb halibut, cut in 2.5 cm/1 inch cubes
2 cloves garlic, finely chopped
3 tablespoons raspberry wine vinegar
2 dashes Tabasco sauce
1 tablespoon fresh orange juice or lime juice
Few grains crushed red pepper
1 tablespoon mild soy sauce
2 tablespoons capers, rinsed and drained

1 275-g/10-oz can quartered artichoke hearts, rinsed and drained
1 red onion, thinly sliced
1 green pepper, diced
1 red pepper, diced, or 1 50-g/2-oz jar chopped pimento, drained

2 ripe tomatoes, peeled, seeded and diced, for garnish
3 tablespoons chopped fresh parsley or coriander for garnish

1. Bring shallots and wine to the boil; add fish and blanch 1 minute (until fish turns opaque). Drain, *saving liquid.**

2. Combine remaining ingredients, except tomatoes and parsley, in a glass or stainless steel bowl.

3. Add drained fish with 2 tablespoons blanching liquid and marinate at least 4 hours in refrigerator before serving.

To Serve: Place on individual plates or in a serving bowl and top with diced tomato and chopped parsley. When served on a buffet or as a main dish, slices of cold steamed corn on the cob or cooked sweet potato may be added to the garnish before serving.

Variation: If your diet allows, as a treat use half scallops, half fish. Remember, however, that the scallops will raise the cholesterol level in the recipe.

***Helpful Hint:** Blanching liquid may be refrigerated or frozen and used at another time as a poaching liquid for fish.

Per serving: 83 calories; 11.2 gm protein; 0.8 gm fat; 7.8 gm carbohydrate; 1.6 gm fibre; 23 mg cholesterol; 1.2 mg iron; 91 mg sodium; 34 mg calcium; 136 mg phosphorus; 815 IU Vitamin A; 0.09 mg thiamine; 0.08 mg riboflavin; 31 mg Vitamin C; 452 mg potassium; 0.10 mg zinc; 4.3 mg niacin; 77 mcg Vitamin B_6; 0 mcg Vitamin B_{12}; 7 mcg folic acid

Tomato Aspic Supreme with Cucumber Sauce

Serves: 12

For a pleasant change in texture, I like to serve moulded salads occasionally. This aspic may be served as a first course or as a buffet or luncheon dish.

Juice of 1 lemon or lime
1 litre/1¾ pints salt-free tomato juice
Few drops Tabasco
15 g/½ oz powdered gelatine
75 g/3 oz celery, diced
75 g/3 oz green pepper, diced
50 g/2 oz spring onions, chopped
1 tablespoon horseradish (no preservatives, creaming agent, or oil added)
350 g/12 oz poached halibut,* drained, flaked

and chilled
1 cucumber, chopped, grated and squeezed dry
250 ml/8 fl oz nonfat yogurt
1 teaspoon garlic powder
1 teaspoon unsweetened apple juice concentrate
1 tablespoon grated onion (optional)
2 ripe tomatoes, peeled, seeded and diced, for garnish
3 tablespoons chopped fresh dill for garnish

1. Combine lemon or lime juice, tomato juice and Tabasco in a small saucepan and bring to the boil.

2. Place gelatine in a large bowl. Add boiling juice and stir until gelatine is completely dissolved.

3. Chill mixture until it becomes the consistency of unbeaten egg whites.

4. Add celery, green pepper, spring onion, horseradish and chilled, flaked fish. Mix gently to combine.

* To poach halibut, bring 450 ml/¾ pint dry white wine, 1 sliced onion, 1 sliced carrot, 1 bay leaf, a few grains crushed red pepper, and 2 sprigs fresh dill or parsley to the boil. Add fish fillet and poach 10 minutes, or until fish flakes. Remove fish, drain, and cool.

5. Place in an attractive glass serving bowl and chill until firm, or overnight (I use an old, treasured cut-glass bowl).

6. *To make sauce:* Grate and squeeze cucumbers. Combine with yogurt, garlic powder, apple juice concentrate and, if desired, grated onion, just before serving.

To Serve: Sprinkle diced tomato over aspic. Garnish with dollops of cucumber sauce and sprinkle with freshly chopped dill. When served on a buffet or as a luncheon dish, accompany with a green salad.

Per serving: 77 calories; 9.6 gm protein; 0.6 gm fat; 9.3 gm carbohydrate; 1.2 gm fibre; 14 mg cholesterol; 1.7 mg iron; 49 mg sodium; 80 mg calcium; 96 mg phosphorus; 1173 IU Vitamin A; 0.11 mg thiamine; 0.14 mg riboflavin; 32 mg Vitamin C; 488 mg potassium; 0.06 mg zinc; 3.5 mg niacin; 47 mcg Vitamin B$_6$; 0 mcg Vitamin B$_{12}$; 3.4 mcg folic acid

Salmon Pâté

Serves: 20 (2 tablespoons = 1 serving)

This attractive pâté can be used in many interesting ways and freezes beautifully.

1 435 g/15½ oz can red salmon, drained, skin and bones removed, or 550 g/ 1¼ lb fresh salmon, poached in court bouillon,* drained, skinned, boned and flaked

120 ml/4 fl oz our Sour Cream (see page 23) or skim-milk ricotta

3 artichoke hearts, rinsed and drained

1 spring onion

3 tablespoons chopped fresh dill

3 drops Tabasco sauce

1 teaspoon salt-free Dijon mustard

1 tablespoon fresh lemon juice, or to taste

1 tablespoon chopped fresh tarragon

1 tablespoon chopped chives

3 tablespoons chopped fresh parsley

50 g/2 oz pimento, drained

1 tablespoon capers, rinsed and drained

* *To poach salmon:* Combine 250 ml/8 fl oz dry white wine, 1 teaspoon thyme, 1 small sliced carrot, ¼ onion, 1 bay leaf, few grains crushed red pepper and 250 ml/8 fl oz water. Simmer 10 minutes. Add salmon and poach about 10 minutes, or until fish flakes. Cool in poaching liquor.

1. Place salmon in a blender or food processor with our Sour Cream, artichokes, spring onion, dill, Tabasco, mustard and lemon juice. Blend well.

2. Add tarragon, chives, parsley, pimento and capers. Blend until specks of each still appear.

3. Chill in covered refrigerator container for several hours or overnight to permit flavours to blend.

To Serve: Serve as an hors d'oeuvre or on a cold buffet. Mound pâté onto a scallop shell or flat serving dish and serve chilled with assorted crisp raw vegetables or crackers. For an elegant presentation just before serving, layer on thinly sliced cucumber to simulate scales of a fish and sprinkle with chopped fresh dill.

Variations: Pâté may be used to stuff eggs (see page 74), tiny tomatoes, or artichoke bottoms for a cold buffet or a salade composée.

To make a moulded salmon mousse, soak 7 g/¼ oz powdered gelatine in 4 tablespoons poaching liquid. Dissolve over low heat and stir into salmon mixture. Pour into a fish mould sprayed with non-stick spray. Chill 4 to 6 hours or overnight. Unmould onto a bed of salad greens and garnish with cucumber as in pâté.

Helpful Hints: Drain liquid from canned salmon through muslin or a triple-mesh strainer. Remember, if you use the drained canned salmon liquid in making the pâté, it will raise the sodium level considerably!

Reserve drained poaching liquid for use in making moulded salmon mousse (see Variations).

Per serving: 47 calories; 5.4 gm protein; 2.2 gm fat; 1.4 gm carbohydrate; 0.2 gm fibre; 8 mg cholesterol; 0.8 mg iron; 76 mg sodium; 76 mg calcium; 84 mg phosphorus; 208 IU Vitamin A; 0.02 mg thiamine; 0.07 mg riboflavin; 4 mg Vitamin C; 127 mg potassium; 0 mg zinc; 1.7 mg niacin; 1 mcg Vitamin B$_6$; 0 mcg Vitamin B$_{12}$; 0.5 mcg folic acid

Tuna Pâté

Serves: 20 (2 tablespoons = 1 serving; as a main course, serves 10)

1 375-g/13-oz can salt-free tuna in water, drained and flaked

175 g/6 oz Weight Watchers

cottage cheese, rinsed and drained

3 spring onions

1 tablespoon lemon juice

1 tablespoon green chilli sauce
2 tablespoons chopped green
  chillies
Freshly ground pepper
½ teaspoon herbes de
  Provence
1 50-g/2-oz jar chopped
  pimento, drained

2 tablespoons capers, rinsed
  and drained
2 tablespoons chopped fresh
  parsley for garnish
1 small green pepper, seeded
  and cut into 1 cm/½ inch
  strips, for garnish
4 tiny tomatoes, halved, for
  garnish

1. Place tuna, cottage cheese, spring onions, lemon juice, sauce, chillies, pepper and herbs in blender or food processor and process until smooth.

2. Add pimento and capers; process until chopped (flecks of pimento and capers remain).

3. Spoon mixture into a 750 ml/1¼ pint terrine or loaf tin that has been sprayed with nonstick spray.

4. Cover with cling film and chill in refrigerator 24 hours or overnight.

To Serve: Several hours before serving, run a knife around pâté and unmould onto a serving platter. At serving time, garnish pâté with chopped parsley, green pepper strips, and halved tomatoes. As an hors d'oeuvre, surround with crackers, crispbreads or small slices of rye bread. As an individual first course, place 1 slice of pâté on a lettuce leaf with a dab of Dijon mustard, several tomatoes, and strips of warm whole wheat toast. Tuna Pâté can also be served as a summer luncheon dish.

Per serving: 35 calories; 6.3 gm protein; 0.3 gm fat; 1.3 gm carbohydrate; 0.2 gm fibre; 12 mg cholesterol; 0.6 mg iron; 41 mg sodium; 17 mg calcium; 39 mg phosphorus; 217 IU Vitamin A; 0.02 mg thiamine; 0.05 mg riboflavin; 12 mg Vitamin C; 96 mg potassium; 0.01 mg zinc; 2.6 mg niacin; 18 mcg Vitamin B$_6$; 0 mcg Vitamin B$_{12}$; 1 mcg folic acid

❧ Soups ☙

Some Basic Stocks

Basic Turkey Stock
Basic Fish Stock

Basic Vegetable Stock

Hot Soups

Basic Broccoli Soup
Purée of Cauliflower Soup
Fresh Mushroom Soup
Split Pea or Lentil Soup
Chinese Hot and Sour Soup

Mediterranean Fish Soup
French Country Winter
 Vegetable Soup
Quick Cream of Leftover
 Vegetable Soup

Cold Soups

Gazpacho
Jellied Fish Consommé

Quick Cold Cucumber Soup
Fresh Strawberry Soup

Whether you are huddled by a roaring fire on a cold winter's evening or pausing at the end of a hot summer's day, you will find that a good soup—a hearty country vegetable soup or a cup of chilled gazpacho—will have a comforting and soothing effect on the psyche as well as the appetite. Soups, served hot or cold, add variety to our meals.

General Information for Freezing Soups

1. Cool soup, uncovered, at room temperature.

2. Chill overnight in refrigerator and remove any visible congealed fat before freezing.

3. Freeze in suitable plastic freezer containers or jars, leaving 2.5 cm/1 inch head space for expansion. (At this time you will want to remember to freeze in portion sizes that suit your family and life-style. I like to freeze single 250 ml/8 fl oz portions—I may want split pea soup when my partner has been looking forward to mushroom-barley!)

4. Cover containers tightly. (If soup is not tightly sealed, it will lose much of its flavour.)

5. Label with content and date.

6. To serve frozen soup, thaw to room temperature and reheat or put container of frozen soup in the microwave oven for 12 to 15 minutes, depending upon the amount.

Helpful Hints: Always use cold water to start a soup. Hot water seals the flavour into the bones and meat instead of allowing it to flow into the soup.

Do not put hot soup in the refrigerator. It makes the motor work too hard to cool it down.

SOME BASIC STOCKS

These basic stocks should be prepared when you have time. They may be frozen for future use. For Basic Chicken Stock, see Six Easy Basics, page 22.

Basic Turkey Stock

Yield: 1.8–2.25 litres/3–4 pints (250 ml/8 fl oz = 1 serving)

2.75 litres/5 pints cold water
Entire carcass of roast turkey with skin, meat scraps and giblets (not liver)*
1 large onion stuck with 4 cloves
3 medium carrots, cut in chunks
2 stalks celery with leaves, cut in chunks

2 large leeks, split and well washed
1 parsnip, cut in chunks
1 tomato, coarsely chopped
1 bouquet garni (4 sprigs parsley, ½ teaspoon crushed red pepper, 2 bay leaves, 1 teaspoon thyme, 1 tablespoon dried soup greens or similar)

1. Break up turkey carcass and place in a large saucepan with bones, skin and meat scraps. Cover with cold water.

2. Bring to the boil, remove scum, and add remaining ingredients.

* Any chicken backs, necks or skins you have on hand may also be added.

3. Bring to the boil again and reduce heat to barely simmer.

4. Half cover the pan and simmer 3 hours.

5. Strain stock through triple-mesh stainless steel strainer. Let cool, then cover and refrigerate.

6. Remove hardened fat before using or freezing. Keeps in refrigerator 3 to 4 days. For longer storage, freeze according to instructions on page 46.

To Use: Reheat and serve as a stock.

Variation: Serve as a *turkey-vegetable stock* by adding 1 560 g/20 oz packet frozen mixed vegetables, 2 chopped tomatoes, and 150 g/5 oz Steamed Brown Rice (see page 174). Bring to the boil, reduce to simmer, and cook 15 minutes before adding 3 tablespoons chopped fresh parsley or fresh basil.

Per serving: 34 calories; 2.6 gm protein; 0 gm fat; 5.5 gm carbohydrate; 0 gm fibre; 0 mg cholesterol; 0 mg iron; 5 mg sodium; 0 mg calcium; 0 mg phosphorus; 0 IU Vitamin A; 0 mg thiamine; 0 mg riboflavin; 0 mg Vitamin C; 0 mg potassium; 0 mg zinc; 0 mg niacin; 0 mcg Vitamin B_6; 0 mcg Vitamin B_{12}; 0 mcg folic acid

Basic Fish Stock

Yield: approx. 2.25 litres/4 pints (250 ml/8 fl oz = 1 serving)

1–1.4 kg/2–3 lb fish bones with skin and head,* washed
450 ml/¾ pint dry white wine
2.75 litres/5 pints cold water
2 onions, coarsely chopped
2 stalks celery with leaves, chopped
2 large carrots, chopped
1 leek (white part only), split, well washed and chopped
1 lemon, sliced
1 bouquet garni (4 sprigs parsley, 2 bay leaves, ½ teaspoon crushed red pepper, 1 teaspoon thyme, 1 tablespoon dried soup greens or similar)

1. Place bones in a large saucepan. Add wine and simmer on high heat 5 minutes.

2. Add remaining ingredients and simmer 1 hour.

3. Strain, cool and store in refrigerator or freezer (see instructions for freezing, page 46). Stock may be stored safely in refrigerator for 3 to 5 days.

* Do not use scales or gills. Do not use salmon or mackerel bones; they are too oily.

To Use: Use as a poaching liquid for fish or as a base for fish soup or bouillabaisse.

Per serving: 29 calories; 0 gm protein; 0 gm fat; 1.5 gm carbohydrate; 0 gm fibre; 0 mg cholesterol; 0.1 mg iron; 2 mg sodium; 3 mg calcium; 4 mg phosphorus; 0 IU Vitamin A; 0 mg thiamine; 0 mg riboflavin; 0 mg Vitamin C; 33 mg potassium; 0 mg zinc; 0 mg niacin; .14 mcg Vitamin B_6; 0 mcg Vitamin B_{12}; 0 mcg folic acid

Basic Vegetable Stock

Yield: 2.75 litres/4 pints (250 ml/8 fl oz = 1 serving)

120 ml/4 fl oz dry white wine
2 onions, chopped
2 shallots, chopped
2 leeks, split, well washed and chopped
4 carrots, chopped
1 turnip, chopped
1 swede, chopped
1 kohlrabi, chopped
1 parsnip, chopped
3 tomatoes, chopped
2 stalks celery with leaves, chopped
2 tablespoons dried soup

greens or similar
2.75 litres/ 5 pints cold water
1 bouquet garni (6 sprigs parsley, ½ teaspoon crushed red pepper, 2 bay leaves, 2 teaspoons herbes de Provence and 1 teaspoon thyme)
1 teaspoon low-sodium vegetable seasoning (see page 24)
Any leftover cooked or raw vegetables or vegetable liquid

1. Place wine in a large saucepan. Heat to boiling and add onions, shallots, leeks, carrots, turnips, swede, kohlrabi, parsnip, tomatoes and celery.

2. Simmer vegetables about 10 minutes, stirring from time to time.

3. Add dried soup greens, cold water, bouquet garni, vegetable seasoning and leftover vegetables or liquids.

4. Bring to the boil, lower to simmer, and simmer gently 2½ to 3 hours.

5. Strain through a stainless steel triple-mesh strainer. (Press vegetables to release their juices.)

6. Cool and freeze according to instructions on page 46.

To Use: Use in preparing any of our soups or sauces or as a hot beverage.

Per serving: 37 calories; 2 gm protein; 0 gm fat; 5.1 gm carbohydrate; 0 gm fibre; 0 mg cholesterol; 0.05 mg iron; 4 mg sodium; 1 mg calcium; 1 mg phosphorus; 0 IU Vitamin A; 0 mg thiamine; 0 mg riboflavin; 0 mg Vitamin C; 11 mg potassium; 0 mg zinc; 0 mg niacin; 4 mcg Vitamin B_6; 0 mcg Vitamin B_{12}; 0 mcg folic acid

HOT SOUPS

Basic Broccoli Soup

Serves:6 (175 ml/6 fl oz = 1 serving)

**450 ml/¾ pint our Chicken
Stock (see page 22)
450 g/1 lb fresh broccoli,* cut
in 2.5 cm/ 1 inch pieces**

**1 slice onion
½ teaspoon herbal bouquet
½ cup instant nonfat dry milk
(optional)**

1. Place chicken stock, broccoli, onion and herbs in a saucepan.
2. Bring to the boil and simmer until broccoli is tender.
3. Remove from heat, cool and purée in food processor or blender.
4. At this point, add milk for a creamed soup if you like. Soup may be frozen for future use according to instructions on page 46.

To Serve: Reheat before serving. Soup also may be served chilled.

Variations: Instead of broccoli, you may use other fresh or leftover cooked vegetables such as carrots, courgettes or peas.

Add ½ teaspoon curry powder, or to taste. This version is particularly good chilled.

Per serving: 29 calories; 2.6 gm protein; 0.2 gm fat; 5.2 gm carbohydrate; 2.2 gm fibre; 0 mg cholesterol; 0.9 mg iron; 10 mg sodium; 46 mg calcium; 33 mg phosphorus; 1411 IU Vitamin A; 0.04 mg thiamine; 0.06 mg riboflavin; 30 mg Vitamin C; 136 mg potassium; 0.01 mg zinc; 0.3 mg niacin; 93 mcg Vitamin B_6; 0 mcg Vitamin B_{12}; 29 mcg folic acid

---

* Broccoli stalks alone may be used, saving the florets for use as a vegetable dish at another time. You could use a few small florets for garnishing the soup at time of serving.

Purée of Cauliflower Soup

Serves:8 (175 ml/6 fl oz = 1 serving)

1 litre/1¾ pints nonfat milk
1 slice onion
1 bay leaf
1 medium head cauliflower
  (about 450 g/1 lb), cored
  and broken into florets
1 teaspoon low-sodium

vegetable seasoning (see
  page 24)
1 teaspoon powdered
  horseradish (optional)
Chopped chives, watercress or
  Hungarian paprika for
  garnish

1. In a large saucepan, bring milk to the boil with onion and bay
leaf. Add cauliflower and cook, partially covered, until tender
when pierced with a fork.

2. Remove bay leaf and place drained cauliflower and onion
slice into blender or food processor. Purée until smooth.

3. Return purée to milk in saucepan; whisk thoroughly until
smooth. Add vegetable seasoning to taste. If you prefer a zippier
flavour, add horseradish. Soup may be frozen according to
instructions on page 46.

To Serve: Serve in mugs or soup bowls garnished with chopped
chives, watercress or Hungarian paprika. Soup may also be served
chilled.

Per serving: 57 calories; 5.6 gm protein; 0.3 gm fat; 8.7 gm carbohydrate; 1 gm
fibre; 2 mg cholesterol; 0.6 mg iron; 69 mg sodium; 165 mg calcium; 140 mg
phosphorus; 57 IU Vitamin A; 0.11 mg thiamine; 0.26 mg riboflavin; 28 mg
Vitamin C; 285 mg potassium; 0.5 mg zinc; 0.5 mg niacin; 53 mcg Vitamin B_6;
0.49 mcg Vitamin B_{12}; 2 mcg folic acid

Fresh Mushroom Soup

Serves:8 (175 ml/6 fl oz = 1 serving)

550 g/1¼ lb mushrooms,
  wiped clean
2 bunches spring onions
3 our Stock Cubes, melted
  (see page 21), or 3
  tablespoons our Chicken
  Stock (see page 22)
Freshly ground pepper

½ teaspoon thyme
½ teaspoon herbes de
  Provence
Few grains freshly ground
  nutmeg
1 litre/1¾ pints our Chicken
  Stock

1. Mince mushrooms in food processor or blender.
2. Mince spring onions in food processor or blender.
3. Place melted stock cubes or stock in a large saucepan. Add mushrooms and onions and sauté 10 minutes.
4. Add freshly ground pepper, thyme, herbs and nutmeg.
5. Add 1 litre/1¾ pints stock, bring to the boil, and simmer 30 minutes.

This soup may also be frozen (see instructions page 46).

Variation: Add 1 tablespoon dry sherry to the mushrooms and spring onions while they are sautéing.

Per serving: 42 calories; 3.5 gm protein; 0.3 gm fat; 7 gm carbohydrate; 2.1 gm fibre; 0 mg cholesterol; 1.1 mg iron; 14 mg sodium; 19 mg calcium; 87 mg phosphorus; 164 IU Vitamin A; 0.08 mg thiamine; 0.33 mg riboflavin; 4 mg Vitamin C; 321 mg potassium; 0.02 mg zinc; 3 mg niacin; 89 mcg Vitamin B_6; 0 mcg Vitamin B_{12}; 18 mcg folic acid

Split Pea or Lentil Soup

Serves:14 (250 ml/8 fl.oz = 1 serving)

2.75 litres/5 pints our Chicken Stock (see page 22) or water
450 g/1 lb beef bones (optional)
450 g/1 lb green or yellow split peas or lentils or a combination of the three
1 bouquet garni (2 bay leaves, ½ teaspoon thyme, a few parsley sprigs and celery leaves, and a few grains red pepper)

1 clove garlic, chopped
6 small carrots, chopped
3 stalks celery with leaves, chopped
1 onion, chopped
1 leek, split, well-washed and chopped
1 turnip, chopped
1 teaspoon thyme

Whole wheat croûtons or chopped fresh parsley for garnish

1. Combine the stock, soup bones (if desired), peas, bouquet garni and garlic and cook in a large saucepan for 30 minutes
2. Add the carrots, celery, onion, leek, turnip and thyme and cook an additional hour.
3. Remove the bouquet garni and bones.
4. Purée all vegetables in food processor or blender and return to stock.

5. Reheat thoroughly before serving. May be frozen for future use (see instructions page 46).

To Serve: Place in warm soup bowls and garnish with whole wheat croûtons or chopped parsley.

Variations: Add 250 ml/8 fl oz nonfat evaporated milk after soup has been puréed to make a cream soup.

For a heartier soup, add 165 g/5½ oz Steamed Brown Rice (see page 174) after puréeing.

Diced cooked carrots and celery may be added to soup after soup has been puréed.

Per serving: 158 calories; 10.6 gm protein; 0.4 gm fat; 28.7 gm carbohydrate; 5 gm fibre; 0 mg cholesterol; 2.1 mg iron; 36 mg sodium; 28 mg calcium; 102 mg phosphorus 2418 IU Vitamin A; 0.26 mg thiamine; 0.11 mg riboflavin; 4 mg Vitamin C; 411 mg potassium; 1.15 mg zinc; 1.2 mg niacin; 89 mcg Vitamin B_6; 0 mcg Vitamin B_{12}; 21 mcg folic acid

Chinese Hot and Sour Soup

Serves:8 (250 ml/8 fl oz = 1 serving)

Generous 1.75 litres/3 pints our Chicken Stock (see page 22)

1 225-g/8 oz chicken breast, skinned, boned and thinly sliced

10 dried mushrooms (preferably Chinese), soaked in 250 ml/8 fl oz hot water 30 minutes, rinsed well, squeezed dry and thinly sliced*

1 215-g/7½-oz can bamboo shoots, thinly sliced

5 tablespoons white wine vinegar or brown rice vinegar

2 tablespoons mild soy sauce

Freshly ground pepper

1 tablespoon cornflour

120 ml/4 fl oz water

Dash Tabasco sauce

2 egg whites, lightly beaten

3 spring onions, finely chopped

100 g/4 oz mangetout peas

1. Bring stock to the boil in a large saucepan; add chicken and mushrooms. Bring to the boil again and simmer for 10 minutes.

2. Add bamboo shoots and simmer for 10 minutes.

3. Add vinegar, soy sauce and pepper.

4. Mix cornflour with water and add to soup. Return to the boil.

5. Add Tabasco and lightly beaten egg white to soup and stir.

6. Add spring onions and mangetout peas. Soup may be refrigerated and reheated and served several days later.

Variations: If your diet allows, add 1 tablespoon sesame oil in step 6. Add 50 g/2 oz finely dice tofu (Chinese bean curd) in step 6 for additional protein.

*Helpful Hint: Strain and save mushroom liquid to add to soup.

Per serving: 105 calories; 12.1 gm protein; 1.1 gm fat; 11.8 gm carbohydrate; 0.8 gm fibre; 19 mg cholesterol; 0.9 mg iron; 159 mg sodium; 14 mg calcium; 107mg phosphorus; 167 IU Vitamin A; 0.11 mg thiamine; 0.14 mg riboflavin; 5 mg Vitamin C; 347 mg potassium; 0.01 mg zinc; 4 mg niacin; 16 mcg Vitamin B_6; 0.01 mcg Vitamin B_{12}; 4 mcg folic acid

Mediterranean Fish Soup

Serves:12 (250 ml/8 fl oz = 1 serving)

Mediterranean Fish Soup is found on the menu frequently in both Italy and France. Each soup is slightly different, reflecting the taste and the supplies of the cook preparing it. Try it my way first —then vary to suit your palate.

4 tablespoons our Fish Stock (see page 48) or dry white wine

100 g/4 oz onion, finely chopped

100 g/4 oz carrots, finely chopped

1 bulb fennel, finely chopped, or 1 teaspoon fennel seed, crushed

100 g/4 oz leek (white part only), well-washed and finely chopped

4 cloves garlic, crushed

4 large ripe tomatoes, peeled, seeded and chopped, or 6 canned tomatoes, chopped

1 slice dried orange peel

1 bay leaf

1 teaspoon thyme or savory, crushed

1 teaspoon dried basil, crushed

Few grains crushed red pepper

½ teaspoon powdered saffron, or 2 pinches saffron threads

4 tablespoons Pernod or dry white wine

250 ml/8 fl oz salt-free tomato sauce

2.25 litres/4 pints our Fish Stock

450 g/1 lb haddock, snapper, sole or sea bass (if possible, use at least 2 different fishes for better flavour) cut into 1 cm/½ inch cubes

1. Place the 4 tablespoons fish stock in a large saucepan. Add onion, carrots, fennel, leek and garlic. Sauté 5 minutes or until soft, stirring constantly.

2. Add tomatoes, orange peel, bay leaf, thyme, basil, crushed red pepper and saffron. Cook 5 minutes more.

*3. Add Pernod or wine, tomato sauce and fish stock. Simmer, uncovered, for 1 hour.

4. Add cubed fish and cook 15 minutes before serving.

To Serve: Serve from a heated tureen at the table or in individual warmed bowls from the kitchen. Top each serving with a slice of French bread dried in the oven and rubbed with a clove of garlic, or place a slice of garlic-flavoured dried bread in each bowl first and ladle soup over it. This may be followed by a crisp green salad and fresh fruit.

Variation: For a heartier soup, add 300 g/11 oz Steamed Brown Rice (see page 174) to soup before serving, or serve over a spoonful of rice.

Helpful Hints: If you have no fish stock in your freezer, use 2.25 litres/4 pints water and 1 kg/2 lb fresh fish trimmings. (Do not use scales or gills. Do not use any trimmings from salmon or mackerel; they are too oily.) Be sure to remove trimmings by straining stock before the final 15 minutes of cooking with the added fish. Return strained vegetables to stock.

Per serving: 114 calories; 10.5 gm protein; 2 gm fat; 13.1 gm carbohydrate; 1.7 gm fibre; 19 mg cholesterol; 1.2 mg iron; 39 mg sodium; 36 mg calcium; 111 mg phosphorus; 1849 IU Vitamin A; 0.09 mg thiamine; 0.07 mg riboflavin; 19 mg Vitamin C; 391 mg potassium; 0.19 mg zinc; 1.5 mg niacin; 88 mcg Vitamin B_6; 0 mcg Vitamin B_{12}; 9 mcg folic acid

Borscht

Serves: 12 (250 ml/8 fl oz = 1 serving)

1 small green cabbage, finely shredded

2 onions, thinly sliced

6 large, fresh beetroot, peeled and grated

1 stalk celery, thinly sliced

3 shallots, finely chopped

3 ripe tomatoes, peeled, seeded and chopped, or 4 drained canned tomatoes, chopped

* Soup may be frozen for future use after step 3.

1.8 litres/3¼ pints our
  Chicken Stock (see page
  22)
1 bouquet garni (4 sprigs
  parsley, 2 bay leaves, 1
  teaspoon thyme, several
  celery leaves, few grains
  crushed red pepper)
1 tablespoon frozen
  unsweetened apple juice
  concentrate
Juice of ½ lemon
120 ml/4 fl oz vermouth or

dry white wine
Freshly ground pepper
1 teaspoon low-sodium
  vegetable seasoning (see
  page 24)
3 tablespoons chopped fresh
  dill, or 1 teaspoon dry dill
  weed

Our Sour Cream (see page 23)
  or nonfat yogurt and
  chopped fresh dill for
  garnish

1. Place green cabbage, onions, beetroot, celery, shallots, tomatoes, stock and bouquet garni in a large saucepan. Bring to the boil, cover and simmer 1 hour or until cabbage is tender.

2. Add apple juice concentrate, lemon juice, vermouth, freshly ground pepper, vegetable seasoning and dill. Cover and simmer 40 minutes.

3. Taste and adjust seasonings.

4. Soup tastes even better served the next day and reheated. May also be frozen for future use (see page 46); it keeps well for 3 or 4 months in the freezer.

To Serve: Serve piping hot with dollops of our Sour Cream and chopped dill for a garnish. Heavy whole wheat or seven-grain bread makes a wonderful accompaniment.

Per serving: 76 calories; 4.2 gm protein; 0.3 gm fat; 13.8 gm carbohydrate; 3.3 gm fibre; 0 mg cholesterol; 0.9 mg iron; 42 mg sodium; 49 mg calcium; 42 mg phosphorus; 358 IU Vitamin A; 0.07 mg thiamine; 0.07 mg riboflavin; 34 mg Vitamin C; 335 mg potassium; 0.32 mg zinc; 0.6 mg niacin; 133 mcg Vitamin B_6; 0 mcg Vitamin B_{12}; 23 mcg folic acid

French Country Winter Vegetable Soup

Serves:12 (250 ml/8 fl oz = 1 serving)

3 our Stock Cubes, melted
  (see page 21)
1 red onion, very finely
  chopped

3 cloves garlic, crushed
1 tablespoon very finely
  chopped shallot
1 leek, split, well washed and

very finely chopped
1 carrot, very finely chopped
1 large potato, very finely chopped
2 celery stalks, very finely chopped
1/4 small green cabbage, very finely chopped
4 mushrooms, very finely chopped
3 ripe tomatoes, peeled, seeded and very finely chopped
1 parsnip, very finely chopped (if available)
1 kohlrabi, very finely chopped (if available)
1 turnip, very finely chopped

(if available)
1 swede, very finely chopped (if available)
1 small celeriac, very finely chopped (if available)
1/2 fresh fennel bulb, very finely chopped (if available)
15 g/1/2 oz fresh sorrel or fresh basil
3 bay leaves
2 teaspoons herbes de Provence
Any very finely chopped leftover cooked vegetables, stock or defatted gravy
1 litre/1 3/4 pints our Chicken Stock (see page 22)
1 litre/1 3/4 pints water

1. Place stock cubes in large saucepan. Add onion, garlic, shallot and leek and sauté until transparent.

2. Add remaining vegetables, sorrel or basil, bay leaves, herbs and any leftover cooked vegetables, stock or defatted gravy to pan. Cook 5 minutes, stirring constantly.

3. Add chicken stock and water and cook until vegetables are tender —about 30 minutes.

4. If a finer texture is desired, purée entire mixture in food processor or blender in batches.

5. Taste and season with additional herbs such as thyme, basil or low-sodium vegetable seasoning (see page 24) if desired. This soup may also be frozen for future use (see page 46).

Variations: Use 2 litres/3 1/2 pints water instead of half water, half stock.

For a spicy tomato-vegetable soup, add 1 100 g/4 oz can salt-free tomato paste and 1 teaspoon of your favourite curry powder after step 4. Heat 10 minutes before serving, and garnish with chopped fresh parsley or coriander.

Per serving: 63 calories; 3.0 gm protein; 0.4 gm fat; 13.5 gm carbohydrate; 3.2 gm fibre; 0 mg cholesterol; 2.5 mg iron; 21 mg sodium; 111 mg calcium; 61 mg phosphorus; 1428 IU Vitamin A; 0.08 mg thiamine; 0.07 mg riboflavin; 28 mg

Vitamin C; 438 mg potassium; 0.18 mg zinc; 1.1 mg niacin; 83 mcg Vitamin B_6; 0 mcg Vitamin B_{12}; 11 mcg folic acid

Quick Cream of Leftover Vegetable Soup

Serves:10 (175 ml/6 fl oz = 1 serving)

1 medium onion, finely chopped

1 stalk celery with leaves, finely chopped

2 spring onions, finely chopped

120 ml/4 fl oz our Chicken Stock (see page 22) or Vegetable Stock (see page 49)

1 leftover baked potato, or 225 g/8 oz mashed or steamed potatoes

450 ml/¾ pint our Chicken Stock or leftover vegetable soup liquid

½ teaspoon low-sodium

vegetable seasoning (see page 24)

1 bay leaf

225 g/8 oz leftover cooked vegetables (broccoli, carrots, peas, beans, corn, cauliflower, ratatouille, or whatever you have)

450 ml/¾ pint nonfat milk

25 g/1 oz nonfat dry milk powder

120 ml/4 fl oz tomato purée (optional)

1 teaspoon curry powder (optional)

3 tablespoons fresh chopped parsley for garnish

1. Sauté onion, celery and spring onions in the 120 ml/4 fl oz stock in saucepan. Stir until transparent.

2. Add potato, the 450 ml/¾ pint stock, vegetable seasoning, bay leaf and all leftover vegetables.

3. Bring to the boil and simmer 2 minutes.

4. Remove all vegetable solids with a slotted spoon or strainer and purée.

5. Return purée to liquids in saucepan. Stir in nonfat milk and nonfat dry milk until well blended.

6. Simmer 5 minutes. If tomato purée and/or curry are desired, add them here. Taste and adjust seasonings.

To Serve: Serve hot with chopped parsley garnish.

Per serving: 76 calories; 4.3 gm protein; 0.2 gm fat; 15.1 gm carbohydrate; 1.5 gm fibre; 1 mg cholesterol; 1.2 mg iron; 57 mg sodium; 83 mg calcium; 96 mg phosphorus; 2522 IU Vitamin A; 0.11 mg thiamine; 0.13 mg riboflavin; 15 mg Vitamin C; 321 mg potassium; 0.3 mg zinc; 1 mg niacin; 79 mcg Vitamin B_6; 0.16 mcg Vitamin B_{12}; 9 mcg folic acid

COLD SOUPS

Gazpacho

Serves:10 (250 ml/8 fl oz = 1 serving)

This cold soup is an important part of the hot-weather cuisine in the south of Spain. The proportions may be varied to suit your taste.

5 large, ripe tomatoes, peeled and seeded
1 cucumber, roughly chopped
1 green or red pepper
½ red or white onion
2 shallots
1 large clove garlic
3 slices fresh whole wheat bread, crusts removed, cut into eighths
250 ml/8 fl oz our Chicken
Stock (see page 22) or water
2 275-g/10-oz cans salt-free tomato juice
Pinch cayenne pepper
5–8 tablespoons red wine vinegar
1 teaspoon Hungarian paprika
1 teaspoon dried oregano, or 1 tablespoon fresh oregano

1. Purée tomatoes, cucumber, pepper, onion, shallots and garlic in food processor or blender.
2. Add bread to the vegetable sauce and process.
3. Place puréed vegetables in a large bowl and add chicken stock, tomato juice, cayenne, vinegar, paprika and oregano.
4. Blend thoroughly. Chill several hours; adjust seasonings before serving. (Note that chilled soups need heavy seasoning.) Soup may be frozen for future use (see page 46).

To Serve: Serve as is, or garnish with the following diced vegetables: green pepper, red pepper, cucumber, spring onion, peeled seeded tomato, and our bite-sized garlic croûtons, toasted (see page 15). May also be served with a dollop of our Sour Cream (see page 23) or nonfat yogurt and freshly chopped dill. Gazpacho makes a different and delicious first course at a luncheon or a barbecue.

Per serving: 58 calories; 2.5 gm protein; 0.5 gm fat; 12.5 gm carbohydrate; 2 gm fibre; 0 mg cholesterol; 1.4 mg iron; 28 mg sodium; 25 mg calcium; 44 mg

phosphorus; 1460 IU Vitamin A; 0.11 mg thiamine; 0.08 mg riboflavin; 44 mg Vitamin C; 420 mg potassium; 0.19 mg zinc; 1.3 mg niacin; 119 mcg Vitamin B$_6$; 0 mcg Vitamin B$_{12}$; 9 mcg folic acid

Jellied Fish Consommé

Serves:8

Jellied Fish Consommé must be prepared the day before serving.

1.5 kg/3½ lbs fish bones and heads (choose from flounder, sole, bass, halibut, haddock, turbot, whiting, or any *fresh, nonoily* white fish—see note page 48)

1 large onion, chopped

1 leek (white part only), well washed and chopped

4 mushrooms, chopped

1 carrot, chopped

1 shallot, chopped

1 celery stalk, chopped

2 tomatoes, chopped

½ small stalk fennel, chopped

120 ml/4 fl oz dry white wine or vermouth

1.8 litres/3¼ pints *cold* water

1 bouquet garni (4 sprigs parsley, 1 strip orange rind, ½ teaspoon crushed red pepper, ½ teaspoon thyme and 1 bay leaf)

Our Sour Cream (see page 23) and chopped chives for garnish

1. Wash fish trimmings in cold water. Drain and place in a large saucepan, preferably stainless steel.

2. Add chopped vegetables to trimmings. Add white wine and boil 15 minutes.

3. Add cold water and bouquet garni, and bring to the boil. Reduce heat and simmer slowly for 30 minutes. Skim off scum periodically as it rises to the surface.

4. Continue to simmer over low heat for about 3 to 3½ hours, or until reduced by half. Skim during this time as often as necessary.

*5. Line a stainless steel triple-mesh strainer with muslin and strain consommé into a container for storage. (Press down lightly to remove juices from vegetables and bones.)

6. Cool, cover and refrigerate for use the next day. It will

* If you wish to clarify the consommé at this point so that it has a clear, jewel-like appearance, see instructions on page 14.

become jellied as it chills. Remove any fat that may surface and harden before serving.

To Serve: Spoon jellied consommé into chilled glass serving bowls, garnish with a dollop of our Sour Cream, and sprinkle with chives. This makes an elegant first course at a formal dinner party.

Per serving: 46 calories; 2.7 gm protein; 0 gm fat; 6.1 gm carbohydrate; 0 gm fibre; 0 mg cholesterol; 0.1 mg iron; 6 mg sodium; 1 mg calcium; 1 mg phosphorus; 0 IU Vitamin A; 0 mg thiamine; 0 mg riboflavin; 0 mg Vitamin C; 14 mg potassium; 0 mg zinc ; 0 mg niacin; 6 mcg Vitamin B_6; 0 mcg Vitamin B_{12}; 0 mcg folic acid

Quick Cold Cucumber Soup

Serves:10 (175 ml/6 fl oz = 1 serving)

2 large cucumbers
4 spring onions
15 g/½ oz fresh parsley
1 clove garlic
3 tablespoons chopped fresh dill, or 1 tablespoon dill weed
250 ml/8 fl oz nonfat yogurt
250 ml/8 fl oz our Chicken Stock (see page 22)

450 ml/¾ pint buttermilk, strained
2 drops Tabasco sauce
Juice of ½ lemon (optional)
½ green pepper, ½ red pepper, ½ cucumber and 2 tomatoes, all diced for garnish
Nonfat yogurt and chopped fresh dill for garnish

1. Cut up cucumber lengthwise and in eighths crosswise.
2. Place cucumber, spring onion and parsley in food processor or blender.
3. While puréeing mixture, add garlic, dill and yogurt. Blend well.
4. Place mixture in a bowl, add chicken stock, buttermilk and Tabasco. Add lemon juice, if desired.
5. Chill 4 to 6 hours or overnight before serving.

To Serve: Serve from chilled tureen and garnish with diced vegetables and, if desired, a dollop of yogurt. Sprinkle with freshly chopped fresh dill.

Variation: Sometimes I just combine all the diced garnish vegetables with the puréed cucumber soup and serve in chilled bowls with a little yogurt on top.

Per serving: 51 calories; 4 gm protein; 0.2 gm fat; 9 gm carbohydrate; 1.5 gm fibre; 1 mg cholesterol; 0.8 mg iron; 85 mg sodium; 120 mg calcium; 71 mg phosphorus; 990 IU Vitamin A; 0.08 mg thiamine; 0.2 mg riboflavin; 39 mg Vitamin C; 283 mg potassium; 0.06 mg zinc; 0.7 mg niacin; 45 mcg Vitamin B_6; 0 mcg Vitamin B_{12}; 5 mcg folic acid

Fresh Strawberry Soup

Serves:6 (175 ml/6 fl oz = 1 serving)

This cold fruit soup, with its beautiful deep pink colour, is lovely to serve as a first course at a summer luncheon.

550 g/1¼ lb fresh sweet, ripe strawberries, washed, hulled and cut in halves
1 tablespoon cornflour
250 ml/8 fl oz fresh orange juice

250 ml/8 fl oz red wine
4 tablespoons frozen unsweetened apple juice concentrate, or to taste
250 ml/8 fl oz nonfat yogurt
Fresh mint leaves for garnish

1. Purée half of the strawberries in a blender or food processor. Add remaining berries and purée.

2. Blend cornflour with 4 tablespoons of the orange juice in a large saucepan. Add remaining orange juice, the red wine, apple juice concentrate and puréed strawberries.

3. *Heat just to boiling* over medium heat, *stirring frequently*; remove from heat. Cool.

4. Stir in nonfat yogurt with a whisk.

5. Cover and refrigerate 2 to 4 hours before serving. This soup may be frozen (see page 46).

To Serve: This beautiful deep pink soup makes a dramatic presentation. Serve in chilled glass or elegant white china bowls garnished with whole or chopped fresh mint leaves and a stemmed whole strawberry.

Per serving: 107 calories; 2.6 gm protein; 0.5 gm fat; 17.1 gm carbohydrate; 1.5 gm fibre; 0 mg cholesterol; 1 mg iron; 25 mg sodium; 76 mg calcium; 26 mg phosphorus; 213 IU Vitamin A; 0.08 mg thiamine; 0.15 mg riboflavin; 60 mg Vitamin C; 225 mg potassium; 0.01 mg zinc; 1 mg niacin; 69 mcg Vitamin B_6; 0 mcg Vitamin B_{12}; 7 mcg folic acid

❧ Salads ❧

Antipasto à la Roma
Bean Sprout, Spinach and
　Mushroom Salad
Green Bean Salad
Cabbage, Apple and Raisin
　Slaw
Chinese Cabbage Salad
Chef's Salad
Chinese Chicken in Lettuce
　Leaves
Calico Corn Salad
Tabouli
Gingered Cucumbers
Cucumber, Spring Onion and
　Yogurt Salad

Heavenly Stuffed Eggs
Hearts of Palm and
　Watercress Salad
Roasted Pepper and
　Mushroom Vinaigrette
Crunchy Pea Salad
Potato Salad with Yogurt
　Dressing
Orange and Onion Salad
Confetti Rice Salad
Special Salmon Mousse
Two-Way Tomatoes
Tuna Vinaigrette
Turkey and Orange Salad
Courgette "Coleslaw"

A Few Salad Dressings

Buttermilk Dressing
Herb Dressing
Cucumber Yogurt Dressing

Zesty Buttermilk Dressing
My Favourite Russian
　Dressing

Somehow, when we think of salads we think of all the wonderful fresh vegetables that spring and summer bring. However, there are many salads equally tasty that can be prepared year-round, even when the selection of fresh produce is limited, using dried peas and beans, cucumbers, onions, spring onions, green peppers, carrots, cabbages, potatoes and selected salt-free frozen vegetables.

The French have traditionally served their salads *after* the main course. Many years ago, Californians started serving their salads as a separate course before the main course instead of with or after the main course. This custom has become widely accepted in the United States. It is advantageous to serve a salad as a first course, because this is when we are most hungry and larger amounts of food are eaten. A salad will therefore help satisfy this hunger while supplying us with vitamins, minerals and fibre. The need for larger portions of a main course is decreased and the result is a diet lower in calories yet nourishing and satisfying.

Antipasto à la Roma

Serves: 10–12

Antipastos lead the procession in all fine Italian meals. You could serve a salmon pâté with crackers alone, or a more elaborate platter of assorted vegetables and mixtures. Here we have a simple assortment—try it once, then add your own individual interpretation.

1 425-g/ 15-oz can garbanzo beans

1 215-g/7½-oz can salt-free tuna in water, drained and flaked

120 ml/4 fl oz our Italian Dressing (see page 13)

1 300-g/10-oz can quartered artichoke hearts, rinsed and well drained

1 50-g/2-oz jar chopped pimento, drained

120 ml/4 fl oz our Italian Dressing

100 g/4 oz small mushrooms, cleaned and stalks removed

1 225-g/8-oz can salt-free tomato sauce

1 teaspoon Italian herb seasoning, crushed

3 tablespoons chopped fresh parsley

1 lettuce, washed and dried

1 green pepper, sliced in rings

1 red pepper, sliced in rings

2 heads chicory, sliced lengthwise

2 tablespoons capers, rinsed and drained

3 tablespoons chopped fresh parsley

1. Drain beans. Add tuna and the first 120 ml/4 fl oz Italian dressing and marinate in refrigerator for 4 hours.

2. Combine artichokes with pimento and the second 120 ml/4 fl oz Italian dressing and marinate for 4 hours.

3. Combine mushrooms, tomato sauce, herb seasoning and parsley, and marinate for 4 hours.

4. Arrange dry lettuce leaves in bottom of a shallow salad bowl or platter. Arrange drained bean mixture, drained artichoke hearts and mushrooms in groups on lettuce. Intersperse pepper rings and chicory slices attractively on platter. Sprinkle with capers and chopped parsley.

5. Platter may be prepared several hours in advance and covered with cling film.

To Serve: This appetizer is suitable to be served to guests in the living room before an Italian-style dinner. To complete the menu, serve a pasta dish, hot crusty Italian bread, and Strawberries with Strawberry Sauce (page 191) or cheesecake for dessert. Antipasto also could be served as a luncheon dish. Salt-free breadsticks or crusty rolls are a good complement.

Variation: Omit tuna and add turkey slices rolled and placed intermittently on platter.

Per serving: 209 calories; 15.7 gm protein; 4.2 gm fat; 30.5 gm carbohydrate; 6.7 gm fibre; 13 mg cholesterol; 4.7 mg iron; 95 mg sodium; 114 mg calcium; 223 mg phosphorus; 2357 IU Vitamin A; 0.21 mg thiamine; 0.28 mg riboflavin; 52 mg Vitamin C; 708 mg potassium; 0 mg zinc; 4.8 mg niacin; 50 mcg Vitamin B_6; 0 mcg Vitamin B_{12}; 22 mcg folic acid

Bean Sprout, Spinach and Mushroom Salad

Serves:8

450 g/1 lb fresh bean sprouts, rinsed and drained

1 bunch fresh spinach (450 g/1 lb) washed and drained, stalks removed

175 g/6 oz mushrooms, cleaned and sliced

1 50-g/2-oz jar chopped pimento, drained

1 shallot, finely chopped

2 tablespoons red wine or brown rice vinegar

Juice of 1 lemon

1 tablespoon mild soy sauce

1 teaspoon salt-free Dijon mustard

1 teaspoon Hungarian paprika

120 ml/4 fl oz our Chicken Stock (see page 22)

Freshly ground pepper

1 small red onion, thinly sliced (optional)

1. In a large salad bowl, combine bean sprouts, spinach, mushrooms and pimento. Cover with cling film and refrigerate.

2. *To make salad dressing*, combine shallot, vinegar, lemon juice, soy sauce, mustard, paprika, chicken stock and pepper in a screw-top jar. Shake well.

3. At serving time, add well-blended salad dressing to chilled vegetables. If desired, add red onion at this time. Mix well but gently with 2 forks.

Per serving: 40 calories; 3.6 gm protein; 0.3 gm fat; 6.7 gm carbohydrate; 13.6 gm fibre; 0 mg cholesterol; 1.6 mg iron; 79 mg sodium; 27 mg calcium; 69 mg phosphorus; 1482 IU Vitamin A; 0.11 mg thiamine; 0.2 mg riboflavin; 26 mg Vitamin C; 303 mg potassium; 0.11 mg zinc; 1.4 mg niacin; 66 mcg Vitamin B_6; 0 mcg Vitamin B_{12}; 16 mcg folic acid

Green Bean Salad

Serves:8

½ cucumber, thinly sliced
1 550 g/1¼ lb frozen cut green beans, thawed, cooked 2 minutes and drained
1 425-g/15-oz can garbanzo beans, rinsed and drained
½ pepper, seeded and finely chopped
½ small red onion, finely chopped
1 50-g/2-oz jar pimentos, drained
1 clove garlic, crushed
150 ml/¼ pint our Italian Dressing (see page 13)
15 g/½ oz fresh parsley, chopped
1 teaspoon dried basil*, crushed
Radicchio leaves for serving
Peeled, seeded tomato wedges and chopped fresh parsley, for garnish

1. Combine all ingredients except radicchio and tomato wedges in salad bowl and mix thoroughly.

2. Allow to marinate in refrigerator several hours before serving. *To serve*: Line a serving platter with radicchio leaves. Mound vegetable mixture lightly on platter. Garnish with peeled, seeded tomato wedges dipped in chopped fresh parsley.

Per serving: 134 calories; 7.7 gm protein; 1.5 gm fat; 24.5 gm carbohydrate; 5.6 gm fibre; 0 mg cholesterol; 3.2 mg iron; 52 mg sodium; 89 mg calcium; 129 mg phosphorus; 1016 IU Vitamin A; 0.16 mg thiamine; 0.14 mg riboflavin; 33 mg Vitamin C; 445 mg potassium; 0.02 mg zinc; 1.0 mg niacin; 33 mcg Vitamin B_6; 0 mcg Vitamin B_{12}; 4 mcg folic acid

* 15 g/½ oz chopped fresh basil may be substituted for the parsley and dried basil.

Cabbage, Apple and Raisin Slaw

Serves: 8

This salad is high in Vitamins A and C and potassium. When buying cabbage, choose firm, crisp green ones.

1 small green cabbage
(approx. 675 g/1½ lb),
finely shredded
3 carrots, coarsely grated
2 stalks celery, thinly sliced
1 teaspoon low-sodium
vegetable seasoning (see
page 24)
50 g/2 oz seeded raisins
2 crisp green apples (Pippin or
Granny Smith), peeled,

cored and sliced
1½ tablespoons white wine or
raspberry vinegar
2 tablespoons unsweetened
apple juice concentrate
120–150 ml/4–5 fl oz nonfat
yogurt

1 sprig fresh parsley and
thinly sliced red apple for
garnish

1. Cut cabbage in quarters, remove core and shred.
2. Add grated carrots and sliced celery.
3. Season with vegetable seasoning and ground pepper.
4. Add raisins and apples.
5. Combine vinegar, apple juice concentrate and yogurt. Add to cabbage mixture. Mix with a fork until salad is well blended. Taste and adjust seasonings.
6. Place in a serving bowl and garnish with a sprig of fresh parsley in centre of salad and thin apple slices (with red skin up) in spokelike fashion around the parsley. Cover with cling film and chill several hours before serving to blend flavours.

To Serve: This is a wonderful salad to serve with grilled fish, steamed peas and new potatoes.

Variation: Substitute about 100 g/4 oz drained, crushed unsweetened pineapple or fresh chopped pineapple for the apples and 3 tablespoons frozen unsweetened pineapple juice concentrate for the apple juice concentrate.

Per serving: 82 calories; 2.2 gm protein; 0.3 gm fat; 19.7 gm carbohydrate; 4.6 gm fibre; 0 mg cholesterol; 1 mg iron; 46 mg sodium; 77 mg calcium; 44 mg phosphorus; 3265 IU Vitamin A; 0.09 mg thiamine; 0.1 mg riboflavin; 36 mg Vitamin C; 368 mg potassium; 0.38 mg zinc; 0.7 mg niacin; 168 mcg Vitamin B$_6$; 0 mcg Vitamin B$_{12}$; 25 mcg folic acid

Chinese Cabbage Salad

Serves: 6

Chinese cabbage is a mild-tasting vegetable that is delicious served raw or braised in chicken stock until crisp. When shopping for this salad, make certain that your Chinese cabbage is long, straight, slightly green, and crisp—if not, choose another salad.

About 350 g/12 oz Chinese
  cabbage, shredded
100 g/4 oz cucumber, diced
1 red pepper, thinly sliced
150 ml/¼ pint our Vegetable
  Stock (see page 49) or
  Chicken Stock (see page
  22)
2 tablespoons red wine
vinegar
2 tablespoons brown rice
  vinegar
½ teaspoon salt-free Dijon
  mustard
Freshly ground pepper
½ small red onion, finely
  chopped

1. Place shredded cabbage, cucumber and red pepper slices in a bowl.

2. *To make vinaigrette dressing*, combine stock, vinegar, mustard, pepper and chopped red onion in a jar. Shake thoroughly.

3. Add dressing to vegetables in bowl, toss thoroughly, and serve.

To Serve: This is a crisp salad, the flavour of which complements Marinated Steak (page 131).

Per serving: 23 calories; 1.3 gm protein; 0.2 gm fat; 5.1 gm carbohydrate; 1 gm fibre; 0 mg cholesterol; 0.5 mg iron; 14 mg sodium; 25 mg calcium; 28 mg phosphorus; 802 IU Vitamin A; 0.04 mg thiamine; 0.04 mg riboflavin; 46 mg Vitamin C; 188 mg potassium; 0.03 mg zinc; 0.4 mg niacin; 11 mcg Vitamin B_6; 0 mcg Vitamin B_{12}; 2 mcg folic acid

Chef's Salad

Serves 6

A hot-weather meal-in-one, and a delightful way to use leftover turkey.

1 450-g/1-lb packet frozen carrots, cauliflower and cut green beans, cooked and cooled

1 275-g/10-oz packet frozen artichoke hearts, cooked and cooled, or canned

4 mushrooms, cleaned and sliced

2 spring onions, thinly sliced

150 ml/¼ pint our Vinaigrette or Italian Dressing (see page 13)

½ Cos lettuce, washed, dried and shredded

350 g/12 oz roast turkey breast, shredded

175 g/6 oz defrosted frozen peas

1 tomato, seeded and cut into wedges, for garnish

1. Combine cooked and cooled vegetables and artichoke hearts with mushrooms and spring onions.

2. Add vinaigrette dressing and marinate 1 hour in refrigerator.

3. Combine lettuce, turkey and peas in a salad bowl. Add marinated vegetables with dressing and toss lightly.

To Serve: Serve immediately, garnished with tomato wedges and accompanied by crisp rolls, French or Italian bread.

Per serving: 165 calories; 23gm protein; 2.7 gm fat; 9.8 gm carbohydrate; 2.3 gm fibre; 44 mg cholesterol; 2.1 mg iron; 167 mg sodium; 55 mg calcium; 219 mg phosphorus; 1216 IU Vitamin A; 0.17 mg thiamine; 0.25 mg riboflavin; 18 mg Vitamin C; 698 mg potassium; 1.38 mg zinc; 7.7 mg niacin; 76 mcg Vitamin B$_6$; 0 mcg Vitamin B$_{12}$; 30 mcg folic acid

Chinese Chicken in Lettuce Leaves

Serves: 8

900 g/2 lb cooked chicken,* shredded or chopped in food processor

4 dried black mushrooms, soaked in 250 ml/8 fl oz hot water for 30 minutes, rinsed well, squeezed dry and chopped

250 ml/8 fl oz dry sherry

4 tablespoons our Chicken Stock (see page 22)

1 tablespoon mild soy sauce

1 teaspoon juice from grated ginger

1 tablespoon unsweetened pineapple juice concentrate

1 teaspoon Chinese Five Spices powder

* Any cooked chicken can be used, but leftover roast or grilled chicken is best.

1 tablespoon sesame seeds
1 200 g/7 oz can water
  chestnuts, rinsed, drained
  and chopped

6 spring onions, sliced
Freshly ground pepper

8 cold, crisp lettuce leaves

1. Marinate chopped chicken and mushrooms in sherry for about 1 hour.

2. Blend chicken stock, soy sauce, ginger juice, pineapple juice and Five Spices with sherry drained from chicken. Mix well.

3. Heat dry pan and toast sesame seeds quickly and lightly.

4. Combine drained chicken and mushrooms and chopped chestnuts with soy sauce mixture. Heat about 5 minutes, or until heated through.

5. Add sliced spring onions and pepper.

To Serve: Mound mixture on a heated platter surrounded by cold crisp lettuce leaves, and sprinkle with toasted sesame seeds. Each person may spoon some of the mixture into a lettuce leaf, roll it up, and savour the flavour.

Variation: If your diet allows, 1 teaspoon sesame oil may be added to the soy sauce mixture in step 2.

Per serving: 176 calories; 17.7 gm protein; 4 gm fat; 8.9 gm carbohydrate; 0.8 gm fibre; 61 mg cholesterol; 1.7 mg iron; 116 mg sodium; 21 mg calcium; 172 mg phosphorus; 280 IU Vitamin A; 0.09 mg thiamine; 0.21 mg riboflavin; 5 mg Vitamin C; 404 mg potassium; 0.1 mg zinc; 6.6 mg niacin; 11 mcg Vitamin B_6; 0 mcg Vitamin B_{12}; 5 mcg folic acid

Calico Corn Salad

Serves: 10

1 450-g/16-oz packet frozen
  sweetcorn kernels, cooked
  and cooled in cooking
  liquid
1 100-g/4-oz jar pimento,
  sliced
15 g/½ oz fresh parsley,
  chopped
1 bunch spring onions,
  chopped
1 green pepper, chopped
1 red pepper, chopped

1 215-g/7½-oz can hearts of
  palm, rinsed, drained and
  cut in 5 mm/¼ inch rounds
20 small tomatoes, halved
3–4 tablespoons white wine
  vinegar
1 teaspoon dried tarragon,
  crushed, or 1 tablespoon
  chopped fresh tarragon
1 teaspoon dry mustard
Freshly ground white pepper

1. Drain sweetcorn and save cooking liquid.

2. Combine corn, pimento, parsley, spring onions, green and red peppers, hearts of palm and halved tomatoes.

3. *To make salad dressing*, combine remaining ingredients and 250 ml/8 fl oz liquid from cooked corn. Blend well.

4. Mix salad dressing with corn mixture and marinate 2 to 4 hours before serving.

To Serve: Serve in a large glass bowl or on bed of green, leafy lettuce.

Variation: If your diet allows, 1 tablespoon safflower oil may be added to the salad dressing.

Per serving: 75 calories; 2.3 gm protein; 0.5 gm fat; 12.9 gm carbohydrate; 1.2 gm fibre; 0 mg cholestrol; 1.2 mg iron; 9 mg sodium; 24 mg calcium; 91 mg phosphorus; 1577 IU Vitamin A: 0.08 mg thiamine; 0.08 mg riboflavin; 60 mg Vitamin C; 614 mg potassium; 0.06 mg zinc; 1.1 mg niacin; 53 mcg Vitamin B$_6$; 0 mcg Vitamin B$_{12}$; 5 mcg folic acid

Tabouli

(Cracked Wheat Salad)

Serves: 8

Bulgur, or cracked wheat, is a grain commonly used in the Middle East. Tabouli is a Lebanese dish. If you like, you may substitute buckwheat groats, commonly called kasha, for the bulgar wheat.

Scant 225 g/8 oz cracked
    wheat
1.4 litres/2⅓ pints boiling
    water
120 ml/4 fl oz lemon juice
5 tablespoons our Chicken
    stock (see page 22)
1 tablespoon mild soy sauce
1 teaspoon low-sodium
    vegetable seasoning (see
    page 24)
Freshly ground crushed red
    pepper
15 g/½ oz fresh mint,

chopped
100 g/4 oz red onion,
    chopped, or 1 bunch spring
    onions, chopped
25 g/1 oz fresh parsley, finely
    chopped
½ aubergine, peeled, diced
    and steamed
100 g/4 oz radishes, sliced
½ cucumber, diced
2 ripe tomatoes, peeled,
    seeded and diced
1 lettuce, washed and crisped,
    for serving

1 small green pepper, cut into
   rings, for garnish
1 275-g/10-oz can artichoke

quarters, rinsed and
drained, for garnish

1. Combine cracked wheat with boiling water and let stand 45 minutes, or until firm but not crunchy and the liquid is absorbed.

2. Combine lemon juice, chicken stock, soy sauce, vegetable seasoning, crushed red pepper and mint. Mix.

3. Add drained cracked wheat, onion, parsley and aubergine to lemon mixture. Mix thoroughly, cover and chill several hours.

4. When ready to serve, add radishes, cucumber and tomatoes. Mix gently with a fork.

To Serve: Mound salad mixture on a serving platter surrounded with lettuce leaves. Place a row of green pepper rings down centre of salad and garnish with artichokes. Additional chopped parsley may be sprinkled on top.

Per serving: 139 calories; 5 gm protein; 0.7 gm fat; 30.2 carbohydrate; 2.6 gm fibre; 0 mg cholesterol; 3.4 mg iron; 75 mg sodium; 70 mg calcium; 129 mg phosphorus; 2417 IU Vitamin A; 0.17 mg thiamine; 0.12 mg riboflavin; 56 mg Vitamin C; 452 mg potassium; 0.13 mg zinc; 2mg niacin; 86 mcg Vitamin B$_6$; 0 mcg Vitamin B$_{12}$; 13 mcg folic acid

Gingered Cucumbers

Serves: 8

120 ml/4 fl oz white wine
   vinegar
4 tablespoons water
1 tablespoon mild soy sauce
1½ teaspoons grated fresh
   ginger
2 tablespoons frozen

unsweetened apple juice
   concentrate
1 cucumber, thinly sliced
1 large carrot, grated
3 spring onions, sliced
2 tablespoons chopped fresh
   parsley

1. Combine vinegar, water, soy sauce, ginger and apple juice concentrate. Blend well.

2. Add cucumber, carrot, spring onions and parsley. Toss and cover.

3. Refrigerate 1 to 2 hours. Toss again before serving.

To Serve: This salad is particularly tasty served with grilled or barbecued chicken.

Per serving: 36 calories; 0.8 gm protein; 0.1 gm fat; 7.1 gm carbohydrate; 1.5 gm fibre; 0 mg cholesterol; 0.3 mg iron; 71 mg sodium; 22 mg calcium; 11 mg phosphorus; 1524 IU Vitamin A; 0.01 mg thiamine; 0.02 mg riboflavin; 11 mg Vitamin C; 185 mg potassium; 0.06 mg zinc; 0.3 mg niacin; 20 mcg Vitamin B_6; 0 mcg Vitamin B_{12}; 2 mcg folic acid

Cucumber, Spring Onion and Yogurt Salad

Serves: 8

1 cucumber, halved lengthwise and thinly sliced
½ green pepper, diced
6 spring onions, chopped
3 tablespoons chopped fresh dill
Freshly ground pepper
250 ml/8 fl oz nonfat yogurt

3 tablespoons frozen unsweetened apple juice concentrate

1 ripe tomato, seeded and chopped, for garnish
Chopped fresh parsley or dill for garnish

1. Squeeze cucumber dry to remove excess liquid, and place in a bowl with green pepper, spring onions, fresh dill and ground pepper. Mix with a fork.

2. Cover with cling film and chill until 1 hour before serving.

3. Add yogurt and frozen apple juice concentrate to cucumber mixture. Mix thoroughly with a fork and place in a serving bowl and chill. (This hour of marinating gives flavours a chance to blend—but is not so long that mixture will become watery.)

4. Garnish with chopped tomato and chopped parsley or dill before serving.

Per serving: 48 calories; 2 gm protein; 0.1 gm fat; 7.7 gm carbohydrate; 1.4 gm fibre; 0 mg cholesterol; 0.4 mg iron; 20 mg sodium; 62 mg calcium; 20 mg phosphorus; 270 IU Vitamin A; 0.03 mg thiamine; 0.09 mg riboflavin; 26 mg Vitamin C; 164 mg potassium; 0.02 mg zinc; 0.4 mg niacin; 33 mcg Vitamin B_6; 0 mcg Vitamin B_{12}; 2 mcg folic acid

Heavenly Stuffed Eggs

Serves: 12 (2 egg halves and approx. 2 teaspoons pâté = 1 serving)

12 size 1/large eggs
½ recipe Salmon Pâté (see
   page 43) for stuffing
Coarsely chopped fresh dill,
   or 2 tablespoons chopped

fresh parsley mixed with 1
teaspoon dill weed
2–3 bunches watercress
Tiny tomatoes and carrot
sticks for garnish

1. Hard boil the eggs in simmering water for 20 minutes.
2. Cool eggs quickly in cold water, *crack* shells, and let cool in cold water.*
3. Peel eggs, cut in half lengthwise or crosswise, and remove the yolks (Your dog will love them.)
4. Stuff whites with pâté and sprinkle with freshly chopped dill.
To Serve: To serve as a salad, for each serving place 2 stuffed egg whites on a bed of watercress and garnish with tiny tomatoes with stalks and carrot sticks. The eggs may also be placed on a platter and served as hors d'oeuvres or part of a buffet.

*Helpful Hint: Adding ice cubes to the water hastens chilling of eggs and allows eggs to be peeled more readily. It also *prevents* the formation of a dark ring around the yolk formed by iron in the white and sulphur in the yolk.

Per serving: 76 calories; 10.4 gm protein; 2.5 gm fat; 4 gm carbohydrate; 0.7 gm fibre; 7 mg cholesterol; 1.2 mg iron; 123 mg sodium; 57 mg calcium; 92 mg phosphorus; 2067 IU Vitamin A; 0.03 mg thiamine; 0.17 mg riboflavin; 18 mg Vitamin C; 280 mg potassium; 0.07 mg zinc; 2.5 mg niacin; 26 mcg Vitamin B_6; 0.05 mcg Vitamin B_{12}; 2 mcg folic acid

Hearts of Palm and Watercress Salad

Serves: 12

1½ tablespoons of finely
   chopped shallots
1 clove garlic, finely chopped
1 teaspoon mild soy sauce

2 teaspoons salt-free Dijon
   mustard
Freshly ground pepper
Juice of ½ lemon

3 tablespoons red wine vinegar or raspberry wine vinegar

5 tablespoons our Chicken Stock (see page 22)

½ tablespoon chopped fresh parsley

1 tablespoon chopped chives

3 tablespoons finely diced green pepper

½ teaspoon low-sodium vegetable seasoning (see page 24)

2 400-g/14-oz cans hearts of palm, rinsed and drained

1 50-g/2-oz jar chopped pimento, drained

2 lettuces, leaves separated, washed and well drained

1 bunch watercress, washed, tough stems removed

Tiny tomatoes for garnish (optional)

1. *To make vinaigrette dressing*, combine first 12 ingredients in a screw-top jar and shake vigorously. Chill 1 hour.

2. Cut hearts of palm into 5 mm/¼ inch circles or into strips and place in a bowl. Add pimento and vinaigrette dressing. Mix lightly and marinate in refrigerator for 1 hour.

To Serve: Arrange lettuce leaves on a large serving platter. Place hearts of palm and pimento mixture on lettuce and top with watercress. Garnish with tiny tomatoes.

Per serving: 31 calories; 2.5 gm protein; 0.4 gm fat; 5.9 gm carbohydrate; 0.8 gm fibre; 0 mg cholesterol; 1.3 mg iron; 26 mg sodium; 36 mg calcium; 56 mg phosphorus; 877 IU Vitamin A; 0.14 mg thiamine; 0.08 mg riboflavin; 21 mg Vitamin C; 491 mg potassium; 0 mg zinc; 0.6 mg niacin; 7 mcg Vitamin B_6; 0 mcg Vitamin B_{12}; 8 mcg folic acid

Roasted Pepper and Mushroom Vinaigrette

Serves: 8

A bright red pepper is a fully matured, ripe green pepper. It is sweeter and has about fourteen times as much Vitamin A as a green pepper. Unfortunately, it is not always available, is quite perishable, and because of its late harvest, is more expensive. Try using it raw in salads or stuffed, and for a delicious change, roast it before using (see steps 2, 3, and 4 below).

2 tablespoons lemon juice

2 tablespoons red wine vinegar

2 tablespoons white wine

vinegar or brown rice
vinegar
2 cloves garlic, finely chopped
Freshly ground pepper
1 tablespoon chopped fresh
basil, or 1 teaspoon dried
basil crushed
150 ml/¼ pint our Chicken
Stock (see page 22) or
Vegetable Stock (see page
49)

3 red peppers
3 green peppers
450 gm/1 lb mushrooms,
cleaned, stalks removed,
and sliced
1 red onion, thinly sliced

Lettuce leaves for serving
Chopped fresh parsley or
chopped fresh basil for
garnish

1. *To make vinaigrette dressing*, combine the first 7 ingredients in a screw-top jar and shake thoroughly. Adjust flavours to your taste.

2. *To roast peppers* lay them on grill pan close to grill and scorch skin on all sides. Watch closely so peppers do not get too burned.

3. Remove roasted peppers to brown paper bag or wrap in kitchen paper towel and "sweat" for 10 or 15 minutes.

4. Scrape off charred skins and remove stalks and seeds.

5. Cut into strips.

6. Combine sliced peppers with vinaigrette dressing and chill several hours.

7. An hour before serving, add mushrooms and red onion. Mix lightly and refrigerate.

8. Drain salad before serving.

To Serve: Line a large platter or individual salad plates with lettuce and mound with salad mixture. Sprinkle with chopped parsley.

Other uses for Roasted Red or Green Peppers: Plain sliced roasted peppers are a wonderful ingredient in preparing a pipérade (a mixture of tomatoes, onions and peppers used with fish or chicken). Marinated sliced roasted peppers are delicious as an addition to a green salad, as a low-calorie snack, or as part of a relish tray or antipasto. *To marinate the roasted pepper slices*, sprinkle them with 1 tablespoon olive oil, 2 tablespoons red wine vinegar, and 1 crushed clove garlic, and store, covered, in refrigerator. They'll keep this way for 1 week. (Plain roasted pepper slices should be used the same day.)

Per serving: 45 calories; 3 gm protein; 0.4 gm fat; 9.1 gm carbohydrate; 2.8 gm fibre; 0 mg cholesterol; 1.5 mg iron; 19 mg sodium; 27 mg calcium; 94 mg phosphorus; 1443 IU Vitamin A; 0.12 mg thiamine; 0.32 mg riboflavin; 90 mg Vitamin C; 447 mg potassium; 0.06 mg zinc; 2.8 mg niacin; 157 mcg Vitamin B_6; 0 mcg Vitamin B_{12}; 25 mcg folic acid

Crunchy Pea Salad

Serves: 8

275 g/10 oz frozen petits pois, defrosted in strainer under spray of cold water, or 275 g/10 oz fresh peas, steamed and chilled
1 200-g/7-oz can water chestnuts, drained and sliced
3 stalks celery,* thinly sliced
100 g/4 oz carrots, grated
4 spring onions, thinly sliced
2 tablespoons salt-free tomato juice
2 tablespoons red wine vinegar
1 tablespoon mild soy sauce
1 teaspoon salt-free Dijon mustard
1 clove garlic, finely chopped
1 teaspoon Hungarian paprika
1 teaspoon frozen unsweetened apple juice concentrate

1. Combine peas, water chestnuts, celery, carrots and spring onions.

2. *To make the marinade*, mix the remaining ingredients and beat well.

3. Pour over salad; blend well.

4. Cover and chill for about 1 hour.

5. Drain excess marinade before serving.

To Serve: May be served as is or with the addition of 1 teaspoon non-fat yogurt per serving as a garnish. A sliced tomato wedge and chopped parsley may also be added to each serving. Delightful with cold grilled chicken for a summer picnic.

Variation: Add 100 g/4 oz fresh bean sprouts.

Per serving: 60 calories; 2.8 gm protein; 0.3 gm fat; 12.4 gm carbohydrate; 1.7 gm fibre; 0 mg cholesterol; 1.1 mg iron; 131 mg sodium; 19 mg calcium; 60 mg phosphorus; 1958 IU Vitamin A; 0.17 mg thiamine; 0.1 mg riboflavin; 11 mg Vitamin C; 284 mg potassium; 0.07 mg zinc; 1.1 mg niacin; 78 mcg Vitamin B_6; 0 mcg Vitamin B_{12}; 12 mcg folic acid

* Celery can be omitted to lower the sodium content.

Potato Salad with Yogurt Dressing

Serves: 10

1.4 kg/3 lb potatoes, steamed, cooled, skinned and diced
½ cucumber, peeled, seeded and diced
3 hard-boiled egg whites, coarsely grated
100 g/4 oz celery, diced
50 g/2 oz green pepper, diced
50 g/2 oz spring onions, chopped
3 tablespoons fresh parsley finely chopped
½ teaspoon Italian seasoning
1 teaspoon low-sodium vegetable seasoning (see page 24)
Freshly ground white pepper
150 ml/¼ pint nonfat yogurt
1–2 tablespoons tarragon vinegar
1 tablespoon frozen unsweetened apple juice concentrate
2 teaspoons salt-free Dijon mustard
½ teaspoon celery seed, crushed

1. Toss diced potatoes with cucumber, grated egg whites, celery, green pepper, spring onions, parsley, Italian seasoning, vegetable seasoning and white pepper.

2. Combine remaining ingredients and pour over vegetables. Toss to mix.

3. Chill for several hours before serving to allow flavours to blend.

To Serve: Serve with cold chicken, cold sliced turkey, or leftover chilled Meat Loaf (page 133).

Variation: Cold steamed cauliflower may be substituted for the potatoes for fewer calories.

Per serving: 114 calories; 5 gm protein; 0.3 gm fat; 23.8 gm carbohydrate; 3.5 gm fibre; 0 mg cholesterol; 1.4 mg iron; 46 mg sodium; 56 mg calcium; 72 mg phosphorus; 442 IU Vitamin A; 0.16 mg thiamine; 0.13 mg riboflavin; 39 mg Vitamin C; 514 mg potassium; 0.43 mg zinc; 2 mg niacin; 267 mcg Vitamin B_6; 0.01 mcg Vitamin B_{12}; 12 mcg folic acid

Orange and Onion Salad

Serves: 6

1 Cos lettuce
6 navel oranges
1 large red or white onion
4 tablespoons our Chicken
    Stock (see page 22) or
    water
2 tablespoons raspberry wine
    vinegar or red wine vinegar
1 clove garlic, finely chopped

1 teaspoon low-sodium
    vegetable seasoning (see
    page 24)
½ teaspoon dry mustard
1 tablespoon frozen
    unsweetened apple juice
    concentrate
Few grains crushed red pepper

1. Wash and dry lettuce leaves. Arrange in a salad bowl or on a platter.
2. Using a sharp, serrated knife, peel the oranges (removing all white pith). Slice thinly.
3. Peel onion and slice into thin rings, or chop.
4. Arrange orange slices and onion in salad bowl.
*5. *To make salad dressing*, combine the remaining ingredients in a screw-top jar. Shake thoroughly.
6. Just before serving, pour dressing over salad.
To Serve: This salad makes a colourful and flavourful accompaniment for a stuffed cabbage or a meat loaf.

Variations: Red pomegranate seeds make an attractive and tasty garnish. Spinach leaves may be substituted for lettuce.

*Helpful Hint: Salad and dressing may be prepared separately, covered, and refrigerated early in the day. Combine just before serving.

Per serving: 85 calories; 2.4 gm protein; 0.5 gm fat; 20.3 gm carbohydrate; 3.3 gm fibre; 0 mg cholesterol; 1.4 mg iron; 8 mg sodium; 86 mg calcium; 49 mg phosphorus; 935 IU Vitamin A; 0.17 mg thiamine; 0.09 mg riboflavin; 69 mg Vitamin C; 389 mg potassium; 0.45 mg zinc; 0.8 mg niacin; 128 mcg Vitamin B_6; 0 mcg Vitamin B_{12}; 25 mcg folic acid

Confetti Rice Salad

Serves: 8

300 g/11 oz Steamed Brown
  Rice (see page 174), cooled
175 g/6 oz frozen or cooked
  fresh green peas
½ green pepper, finely diced
½ red pepper, finely diced, or
  1 100-g/4-oz can chopped
  pimento, drained
50 g/2 oz spring onions, finely
  chopped
15 g/½ oz fresh parsley, finely
  chopped
120 ml/4 fl oz our Vinaigrette
  Dressing (see page 13)
2 tablespoons nonfat yogurt
½ teaspoon salt-free Dijon
  mustard
Lettuce leaves for serving
1 275-g/10-oz can artichoke
  hearts, rinsed, drained, and
  rolled in chopped fresh
  parsley, for garnish

1. Combine cooled rice with peas, green pepper, red pepper, spring onions and parsley.

2. Mix vinaigrette dressing with yogurt and Dijon mustard. Add to rice mixture and combine gently with a fork.

3. Chill 2 to 3 hours or overnight until ready to serve.

To Serve: Place chilled rice mixture in a lettuce-lined bowl and garnish with parsleyed artichoke hearts. This is lovely served as an accompaniment for luncheon or dinner with Turkey Tonnato (page 129) or cold grilled chicken.

Variations: This rice salad may be used for stuffing 8 small tomatoes. To serve as a main-dish salad, add 450 g/1 lb diced leftover roast chicken.

Per serving: 89 calories; 3.1 gm protein; 0.5 gm fat; 18.4 gm carbohydrate; 2.3 gm fibre; 0 mg cholesterol; 1.2 mg iron; 30 mg sodium; 36 mg calcium; 66 mg phosphorus; 1123 IU Vitamin A; 0.13 mg thiamine; 0.07 mg riboflavin; 38 mg Vitamin C; 167 mg potassium; 0.04 mg zinc; 1.3 mg niacin; 49 mcg Vitamin B_6; 0 mcg Vitamin B_{12}; 9 mcg folic acid

Special Salmon Mousse

Serves: 12

1 450-g/16-oz can red
  salmon, drained, skinned
  and bones removed
120 ml/4 fl oz nonfat yogurt
50 g/2 oz Weight Watchers
  cottage cheese, rinsed and
  drained
1 tablespoon lemon juice
½ teaspoon dry horseradish
1 teaspoon dry mustard or
  salt-free Dijon mustard
  with herbs
Few grains cayenne pepper

15 g/½ oz powdered gelatine
350 ml/12 fl oz our Chicken
  Stock (see page 22)
250 ml/8 fl oz skimmed
  evaporated milk *well
  chilled*
50 g/2 oz Cos lettuce, finely
  shredded
Radicchio for serving
6 limes or lemons for garnish
100-g/4-oz jar chopped
  pimento, drained and
  chopped, for garnish

1. Combine salmon, yogurt, cottage cheese, lemon juice, horseradish, mustard and cayenne in blender or food processor. Blend until smooth. (*Do not overmix.*)

2. Soften gelatine in 120 ml/4 fl oz of the cool chicken stock. Liquefy over hot water or heat and add to salmon with the remaining chicken stock.

3. Whip thoroughly chilled milk in chilled bowl until stiff. Fold salmon mixture and lettuce into whipped milk.

4. Spray a fish mould with nonstick spray and turn salmon mixture into mould. Cover with cling film.

5. Chill overnight or until firm.

To Unmold and Serve: Unmould onto a platter lined with radicchio leaves. (To facilitate unmoulding, loosen around edges with a metal spatula, invert mould over platter, and shake gently until unmoulded.) Cut limes in half with saw-tooth edges and top with chopped pimento. If necessary, slice off ends of limes so that they stand straight. Surround mould with lime cups. Complete luncheon menu with Cucumber, Spring Onion and Yogurt Salad (page 73), Pickled Beetroot (page 211), crisp rolls, and pineapple or melon in Strawberry Sauce (page 186) for dessert.

Per serving: 120 calories; 14.9 gm protein; 5.4 gm fat; 6.4 gm carbohydrate; 0.1 gm fibre; 20 mg cholesterol; 1 mg iron; 159 mg sodium; 176 mg calcium; 181 mg phosphorus; 569 IU Vitamin A; 0.05 mg thiamine; 0.18 mg riboflavin; 21 mg Vitamin C; 291 mg potassium; 0.16 mg zinc; 3 mg niacin; 21 mcg Vitamin B$_6$; 0.03 mcg Vitamin B$_{12}$; 4 mcg folic acid

Two-Way Tomatoes

Serves: 4

The same ingredients give you two different recipes—a cold soup and a salad—either of which is lovely served with grilled fish.

4 large ripe tomatoes, peeled, seeded, and cut into wedges
350 ml/12 fl oz nonfat yogurt
1 large clove garlic, crushed
Dash Tabasco sauce

15 fresh mint leaves, chopped
Radicchio leaves (for serving salad)
2 tablespoons chopped fresh dill for garnish

To Make Salad:
1. Put sliced tomatoes in a bowl.
2. Combine yogurt, garlic, Tabasco and chopped mint. Pour over tomatoes and toss gently with a fork.
3. Chill several hours.
To Serve: Place on small platter lined with radicchio leaves and sprinkle with chopped dill.

To Make Soup:
1. Combine all ingredients except radicchio (use the dill) and process in blender or food processor.
2. Chill and serve as soup the next day. If mixture is too thick, add a little more yogurt or tomato juice.
To Serve: Serve in chilled bowls.

Per serving: 78 calories; 5.8 gm protein; 0.4 gm fat; 14.5 gm carbohydrate; 2.7 gm fibre; 0 mg cholesterol; 1.3 mg iron; 57 mg sodium; 160 mg calcium; 52 mg phosphorus; 2051 IU Vitamin A; 0.16 mg thiamine; 0.28 mg riboflavin; 47 mg Vitamin C; 463 mg potassium; 0.34 mg zinc; 2.1 mg niacin; 176 mcg Vitamin B$_6$; 0 mcg Vitamin B$_{12}$; 15 mcg folic acid

Tuna Vinaigrette

Serves: 6

5 tablespoons raspberry wine
vinegar
150 ml/¼ pint our Chicken
Stock (see page 22)
½ teaspoon low-sodium
vegetable seasoning (see
page 24)
Freshly ground pepper
½ teaspoon oregano, crushed
½ teaspoon chervil, crushed
1 tablespoon chopped fresh
parsley
2 tablespoons chopped
pimento
1 clove garlic, finely chopped
1 375-g/13-oz can salt-free
tuna in water, rinsed,
drained and flaked
2 450-g/16-oz cans quartered

artichoke hearts, rinsed and
drained
8 mushrooms, cleaned and
sliced
175 g/6 oz frozen petits pois,
defrosted or fresh peas,
steamed and chilled
3 hard-boiled egg whites,
coarsely chopped
½ green pepper, diced
½ cucumber, peeled, seeded
and diced

2 tablespoons toasted sesame
seeds for garnish
12 tiny tomatoes for garnish
1 bunch watercress, washed
and tough stalks removed,
for garnish

1. *To make vinaigrette dressing*, combine the first 9 ingredients in a screw-top jar. Shake well to blend.

*2. Place tuna, artichokes, mushrooms, peas, egg whites, green pepper and cucumber in a salad bowl.

3. Add salad dressing to salad ingredients; toss with 2 forks.

To Serve: Sprinkle with toasted sesame seeds and arrange tomatoes and sprigs of watercress on top.

*Helpful Hint: The salad may be prepared through step 2 early in the day and combined with the salad dressing later on for serving.

Per serving: 185 calories; 26.7 gm protein; 2.8 gm fat; 18.5 gm carbohydrate; 3.1 gm fibre; 39 mg cholesterol; 3.1 mg iron; 173 mg sodium; 88 mg calcium; 278 mg phosphorus; 1672 IU Vitamin A; 0.26 mg thiamine; 0.49 mg riboflavin; 51 mg Vitamin C; 863 mg potassium; 0.04 mg zinc; 11.2 mg niacin; 91 mcg Vitamin B_6; 0.02 mcg Vitamin B_{12}; 12 mcg folic acid

Turkey and Orange Salad

Serves: 6

350 g/12 oz cooked turkey,
cubed
50 g/2 oz celery, sliced
50 g/2 oz water chestnuts,
sliced
120 ml/4 fl oz our Vinaigrette
Dressing (see page 13)
¼ teaspoon curry powder

(optional)
225 g/8 oz orange segments
1 small red onion, thinly
sliced

Radicchio leaves for serving
Chopped fresh parsley for
garnish

1. Marinate turkey, celery and water chestnuts in vinaigrette dressing (add curry to dressing if desired).
2. Add half the orange segments and the red onion just before serving.

To Serve: Arrange on radicchio leaves, garnish with parsley and the remaining orange segments.

Variation: Mix with 1 Cos lettuce, shredded, before serving.

Per serving: 133 calories; 16.3 gm protein; 3.1 gm fat; 10.4 gm carbohydrate; 1.9 gm fibre; 42 mg cholesterol; 1.7 mg iron; 86 mg sodium; 69 mg calcium; 151 mg phosphorus; 1160 IU Vitamin A; 0.1 mg thiamine; 0.15 mg riboflavin; 47 mg Vitamin C; 418 mg potassium; 1.15 mg zinc; 4.1 mg niacin; 61 mcg Vitamin B_6; 0 mcg Vitamin B_{12}; 12 mcg folic acid

Courgette "Coleslaw"

Serves: 6

The term "coleslaw" means a cabbage salad; however, there are many other vegetable combinations that can be used for a similar effect. If you have access to home-grown courgettes, it's especially delicious, but fresh courgettes from the market in season also makes a wonderful "slaw".

6 courgettes, trimmed and
coarsely grated
1 clove garlic, crushed
1 tablespoon grated onion
3 small carrots, grated

Freshly ground pepper
120 ml/4 fl oz our Chicken
Stock (see page 22)
3 tablespoons white wine
vinegar

1 shallot, finely chopped
½ teaspoon thyme, crushed
½ teaspoon chervil, crushed

½ teaspoon basil, crushed
½ teaspoon salt-free Dijon
mustard

1. Place grated courgettes on kitchen paper towels. Pat gently to remove moisture.

2. Turn courgettes into salad bowl with garlic, onions, carrots and ground pepper. Toss to blend.

3. *To make vinaigrette dressing*, place stock, vinegar, shallot, thyme, chervil, basil and mustard in screw-top jar. Shake vigorously.

4. Add dressing to courgette mixture and blend well.

5. Cover and chill in refrigerator for several hours until icy cold.

To Serve: Place in a chilled bowl or on a bed of greens with a garnish of crisp radishes or tiny tomatoes.

Per serving: 33 calories; 1.7 gm protein; 0.2 gm fat; 7.2 gm carbohydrate; 3.5 gm fibre; 0 mg cholesterol; 0.9 mg iron; 14 mg sodium; 44 mg calcium; 38 mg phosphorus; 3043 IU Vitamin A; 0.06 mg thiamine; 0.09 mg riboflavin; 19 mg Vitamin C; 283 mg potassium; 0.11 mg zinc; 1 mg niacin; 40 mcg Vitamin B_6; 0 mcg Vitamin B_{12}; 2 mcg folic acid

A FEW SALAD DRESSINGS

Buttermilk Dressing

Yield: 850 ml/1⅓ pints (1 tablespoon—1 serving)

250 ml/8 fl oz unsalted
tomato juice or tomato
sauce
120 ml/4 fl oz red wine
vinegar
1 teaspoon chervil

1 teaspoon basil
2 cloves garlic, finely chopped
450 ml/¾ pint buttermilk,
strained to remove fat
globules

Put all ingredients in a bowl, blend well with whisk, and store in screw-top container. Keeps well in refrigerator.

Per serving: 4 calories; 0.3 gm protein; 0 gm fat; 0.7 gm carbohydrate; 0 gm fibre; 0 mg cholesterol; 0.1 mg iron; 9 mg sodium; 9 mg calcium; 8 mg phosphorus; 29 IU Vitamin A; 0 mg thiamine; 0.01 mg riboflavin; 1 mg Vitamin C; 23 mg potassium; 0 mg zinc; 0 mg niacin; 0 mcg Vitamin B_6; 0 mcg Vitamin B_{12}; 0 mcg folic acid

Herb Dressing

Yield: 750 ml/1¼ pints (1 tablespoon = 1 serving)

250 ml/8 fl oz raspberry wine
  vinegar
½ tablespoon basil
1 tablespoon rosemary
1 tablespoon thyme

1 bay leaf
1 clove garlic, crushed
450 ml/¾ pint our Chicken
  Stock (see page 22), chilled
½ red onion, finely chopped

Put all ingredients in a bowl, blend well with whisk, and store in screw-top container. Keeps well in refrigerator.

Per serving: 3 calories; 0.1 gm protein; 0 gm fat; 0.7 gm carbohydrate; 0.1 gm fibre; 0 mg cholesterol; 0.2 mg iron; 0 mg sodium; 4 mg calcium; 1 mg phosphorus; 10 IU Vitamin A; 0 mg thiamine; 0 mg riboflavin; 0 mg Vitamin C; 9 mg potassium; 0 mg zinc; 0 mg niacin; 1 mcg Vitamin B_6; 0 mcg Vitamin B_{12}; 0 mcg folic acid

Cucumber Yogurt Dressing

Yield: 450 ml/¾ pint (1 tablespoon = 1 serving)

250 ml/8 fl oz nonfat yogurt
1 teaspoon lemon juice
1 clove garlic, finely chopped
1 tablespoon finely chopped
  fresh parsley
1 tablespoon chopped chives

Few grains red pepper
1 teaspoon salt-free Dijon
  mustard
100 g/4 oz cucumber, peeled
  and grated

Put all ingredients in a bowl, blend well with whisk, and store in screw-top container. Keeps well in refrigerator.

Per serving: 6 calories; 0.6 gm protein; 0 gm fat; 1 gm carbohydrate; 0 gm fibre; 0 mg cholesterol; 0 mg iron; 7 mg sodium; 19 mg calcium; 2 mg phosphorus; 82 IU Vitamin A; 0.01 mg thiamine; 0.03 mg riboflavin; 1 mg Vitamin C; 13 mg potassium; 0 mg zinc; 0.1 mg niacin; 0 mcg Vitamin B_6; 0 mcg Vitamin B_{12}; 0 mcg folic acid

Zesty Buttermilk Dressing

Yield: about 600 ml/1 pint (1 tablespoon = 1 serving)

250 ml/8 fl oz nonfat yogurt
250 ml/8 fl oz buttermilk,
 strained to remove fat
 globules
3 tablespoons fresh parsley
 chopped
1 tablespoon instant toasted
 onion flakes
1 large clove garlic, crushed
¼ teaspoon dried basil, or 1
 tablespoon fresh basil

¼ teaspoon dried oregano, or
 1 tablespoon fresh oregano
¼ teaspoon dried rosemary,
 or 1 tablespoon fresh
 rosemary
25 g/1 oz watercress leaves,
 chopped
½ teaspoon low-sodium
 vegetable seasoning (see
 page 24)

1. Blend yogurt and buttermilk in blender or food processor.
2. Add remaining ingredients and blend well.
3. Refrigerate for at least 1 hour before using so that flavours
may develop.

Per serving: 7 calories; 0.6 gm protein; 0 gm fat; 1 gm carbohydrate; 0 gm fibre; 0
mg cholesterol; 0.1 mg iron; 12 mg sodium; 20 mg calcium; 8 mg phosphorus; 141
IU Vitamin A; 0.01 mg thiamine; 0.03 mg riboflavin; 2 mg Vitamin C; 20 mg
potassium; 0 mg zinc; 0.1 mg niacin; 1 mcg Vitamin B_6; 0 mcg Vitamin B_{12}; 0 mcg
folic acid

My Favourite Russian Dressing

Yield: about 300 ml/½ pint (1 tablespoon = 1 serving)

250 ml/8 fl oz nonfat yogurt
4 tablespoons salt-free tomato
 sauce
2 hard-boiled egg whites,
 chopped
25 g/1 oz green pepper, diced

½ teaspoon onion powder
¼ teaspoon garlic powder
¼ teaspoon low-sodium
 vegetable seasoning (see
 page 24)
Dash Tabasco sauce

Place all ingredients into a bowl and blend well with whisk.

To Use: Especially good served over Cos lettuce salad, garnished with chopped pimento and freshly chopped parsley.

Per serving: 7 calories; 0.6 gm protein; 0.2 gm fat; 0.8 gm carbohydrate; 0 gm fibre; 0 mg cholesterol; 0 mg iron; 8 mg sodium; 11 mg calcium; 1 mg phosphorus; 50 IU Vitamin A; 0.01 mg thiamine; 0.03 mg riboflavin; 2 mg Vitamin C; 7 mg potassium; 0 mg zinc; 0.1 mg niacin; 3 mcg Vitamin B_6; 0 mcg Vitamin B_{12}; 0 mcg folic acid

❧Traditional Main Dishes❧

At the risk of not "beefing up" your diet, let us turn our attention to the preparation of main dishes. Main courses are commonly regarded as our principal source of protein, and traditionally they have included either fish, poultry, game or red meat. This chapter contains a wide variety of delectable recipes using those ingredients. In order to minimize the intake of cholesterol and fat, I limit the use of red meat to lean steak or lean minced round. Fatty fishes are used only occasionally. All shellfish except lobster are off limits. Poultry is used with skin and all visible fat removed. And the amount of meat in each serving is limited to 100 g/4 oz.

Other main courses using little or no meat or fish can be found in the chapters on Casseroles, Pastas and Grains, Soup and Salads.

FISH

Bouillabaisse
My Favourite Flounder Fillets
Filets de Poisson aux Tomates
Simply Baked Salmon Fillets
Five-Minute Fillet of Sole
Vegetable-Stuffed Fillet of
   Sole
Fillet of Sole in
   Tomato-Orange Sauce

Eva's Easy-Does-It Poached
   Salmon
Easy Summer Fish Casserole
Simple Poached Halibut
Sea Bass with Julienne
   Vegetables
Baked Salmon Loaf
Grilled Halibut Steaks
Sweet and Pungent Fish

Not too many years ago fish was considered an inexpensive meal. With the new national awareness of the importance of proper nutrition, fish—with its low-fat, low-cholesterol, high-protein content—has proved to be a high-quality main dish. The increased demand for and limited supply of fish has unfortunately also increased its cost.

Fish contains adequate amounts of Vitamin B and D and large amounts of phosphorus, potassium, iron and other trace minerals such as iodine and fluorine. A 100 g/4 oz serving of fish will supply approximately half of the total protein required by the body each day. The high-quality protein of fish is complemented by its low calories. The fat content of fish does vary, however, from under 1 percent to over 15 percent. The following fishes are listed in order of their approximate fat content—starting with those with a minimal fat content and progressing to those with a high fat content. If you are counting calories, you should of course choose from among those fishes considered lean or containing less than 3 percent fat. My overall suggestion is that you choose fish as a main course several times a week.

The following are considered lean fish:
3% fat—Cod
Haddock
Hake
Flat Fish, such as Sole, Flounder, Turbot, Plaice and Halibut
Red Snapper
Sea Bass
Sturgeon

The following are considered moderately fat fish:
Striped Bass
Carp
Swordfish
Tuna
Whiting

The following are considered fat fish:
Lake Trout
Mullet
Mackerel
15% fat—Salmon

There is a rule of thumb to be followed when cooking fish. Measure the fish at its thickest point and cook it 10 minutes for each measured 2.5 cm/1 inch. This rule of thumb applies to all cooking methods, whether it be baking, grilling or poaching.

Frozen fish (not thawed) takes twice the cooking time but ends up being overcooked on the outside while still cold on the inside. Frozen fish should therefore be thawed at room temperature and cooked immediately for best results; however, I recommend the use of frozen fish only as a last resort. When you think the fish has finished cooking, take a fork and gently flake it; if it passes the test, it's yours to serve and enjoy.

Fresh fish, properly prepared, will be a memorable main dish.

Bouillabaisse

(Fish Chowder)

Serves: 8

This easily prepared bouillabaisse, made with low-calorie white fish, can be made a day ahead or frozen for future use.

1 onion, very finely chopped
2 whole leeks, very finely chopped
1 carrot, very finely chopped
1 stalk celery, very finely chopped
3 cloves garlic, very finely chopped
250 ml/8 fl oz our Fish Stock (see page 48) or water
2 bay leaves
2 teaspoons thyme, crushed
½ teaspoon basil, crushed
3 tablespoons finely chopped fresh fennel, or ½ tablespoon dried fennel seed
150 ml/¼ pint dry white wine
3 potatoes, cut into 1 cm/½ inch cubes
1 800-g/28-oz can tomatoes, puréed
2 tomatoes, peeled, seeded and diced
1 450-g/16-oz can salt-free tomato sauce
1 7.5-cm/3-inch strip fresh orange rind
1 litre/1¾ pints water
Juice of 1 lemon
675 g–1 kg/1½–2 lb white fish (such as flounder, plaice, sole, halibut, turbot, cod), cut into 2.5 cm/1 inch cubes
3 tablespoons fresh chopped parsley
Few grains crushed red pepper
2 frozen 225 g/8 oz lobster tails, defrosted, cut into serving pieces with shell (optional)

1. Simmer finely chopped ingredients in fish stock or 250 ml/8 fl oz water for 10 minutes.

*2. Add bay leaves, thyme, basil, fennel, wine, potatoes, tomatoes, tomato sauce, orange rind and the 1 litre/1¾ pints water. Simmer for 30 minutes or until potatoes are tender.

3. While ingredients are simmering, squeeze lemon over fish cubes and let marinate for 30 minutes.

4. After chowder has simmered about 30 minutes, add fish, parsley and crushed red pepper. Continue to simmer 20 minutes more. (If you are adding the lobster, do so 5 minutes before serving.)

To Serve: This dish may be served in individual ramekins or soup plates with rounds of toasted French bread rubbed with fresh garlic. A roasted red pepper and mushroom salad is a delicious beginning, and Grapefruit Baked Alaska (page 187) a satisfying end.

Per serving: 262 calories; 23.2 gm protein; 6.3 gm fat; 25.5 gm carbohydrate; 3.5 gm fibre; 57 mg cholesterol; 3.6 mg iron; 234 mg sodium; 75 mg calcium; 312 mg phosphorus; 3446 IU Vitamin A; 0.22 mg thiamine; 0.17 mg riboflavin; 54 mg Vitamin C; 1053 mg potassium; 1.16 mg zinc; 4.3 mg niacin; 370 mcg Vitamin B_6; 1.36 mcg Vitamin B_{12}; 14 mcg folic acid

My Favourite Flounder Fillets

Serves: 4 (100 g/4 oz cooked fish = 1 serving)

On the day your local fishmonger has really fresh flounder, plaice or heavy sole, buy it and try this recipe. Its success depends solely (no pun intended) on the freshness of the fish.

4 thick flounder, plaice or sole fillets**, (500 g/1¼ lb fish)	vegetable seasoning (see page 24)
Juice of ½ lemon	Hungarian paprika
1 tablespoon mild soy sauce	2 tablespoons chopped fresh parsley for garnish
1 teaspoon onion powder	4 lemon wedges for garnish
1 teaspoon low-sodium	

*May be prepared a day ahead or frozen after step 2. See instructions for freezing soups, page 46.
**White fish may be substituted, but remember, it is higher in fat.

1. Wash fish in acidulated water (450 ml/¾ pint cold water with 1 tablespoon lemon juice added) and pat dry with kitchen paper towels.

2. Line grill pan with foil. Lay fillets on foil.

3. Sprinkle with lemon juice, soy sauce, onion powder and vegetable seasoning. Marinate at room temperature for 30 minutes.

4. Sprinkle with paprika and place in preheated grill, 15 cm/6 inches from flame.

5. Grill 10 minutes, or until fish flakes.

To Serve: Garnish with chopped parsley and lemon wedges. Serve with steamed potatoes and broccoli spears.

Variation: I like to double my recipe so that I can prepare cold fish salad for the next day. After grilling, wrap the remaining fish in cling film and refrigerate overnight. Serve cold the next day with our Herb Dressing (page 86) on a bed of greens. Garnish with a marinated cucumber salad, sliced beefsteak tomatoes and red onions sprinkled with chopped fresh basil.

Per serving: 130 calories; 24.6 gm protein; 1.3 gm fat; 4.3 gm carbohydrate; 0.3 gm fibre; 65 mg cholesterol; 1.9 mg iron; 235 mg sodium; 41 mg calcium; 291 mg phosphorus; 370 IU Vitamin A; 0.12 mg thiamine; 0.09 mg riboflavin; 21 mg Vitamin C; 573 mg potassium; 0.99 mg zinc; 2.6 mg niacin; 248 mcg Vitamin B_6; 1.7 mcg Vitamin B_{12}; 1 mcg folic acid

Filets de Poisson aux Tomates

(Fish Fillets with Tomato Purée)

Serves: 6

120 ml/4 fl oz dry white wine
450 g/1 lb fish bones*
450 ml/¾ pint water
Few slices leek (white part only)
1 bouquet garni (3 sprigs parsley, 1 teaspoon thyme, 1 bay leaf)
1 small onion stuck with 2

whole cloves
½ lemon, sliced
1 teaspoon crushed red pepper
1 large shallot, finely chopped
1 large onion, finely chopped
1 leek, chopped (green part only)
1 kg/2 lb ripe tomatoes,

*Do not use salmon or mackerel bones; they are too oily.

peeled, seeded and
chopped, or 1 800-g/28-oz
can tomatoes, drained and
chopped
1 teaspoon thyme
1 bay leaf
1 slice ginger root

Few grains crushed red pepper
1 kg/2 lb fish fillets (such as
plaice, flounder, sea bass,
cod, or trout)
Chopped fresh parsley and
lemon wedges or slices for
garnish

1. *To make court bouillon*:* Combine wine, fish bones, water, leek, bouquet garni, onion, lemon and crushed red pepper in non-aluminium saucepan.

2. Bring to the boil and simmer 30 minutes.

3. Strain and use for steaming the fish in step 6.

4. *To make sauce*: Combine shallot, onion, leek and tomatoes in a saucepan.

5. Add thyme, bay leaf, ginger root and pepper and cook slowly 30 minutes. Remove bay leaf and ginger root, then purée.

6. *To steam fish*: Place fish fillets on rack in frying pan or fish poacher and add about 5 cm/2 inches of steaming court bouillon.

7. Cover and let steam 5 minutes, or until fish flakes. (It takes about 10 minutes for each 2.5 cm/1 inch of thickness of fish.) Serve at once.

To Serve: Place several spoonfuls of purée on a hot plate and top with a fish fillet. Sprinkle fish with chopped parsley and top with a lemon wedge or slice. The meal is completed with a baked potato and chives and steamed green beans.

Per serving: 182 calories; 28.6 gm protein; 1.6 gm fat; 12.7 carbohydrate; 3 gm fibre; 76 mg cholesterol; 2.4 mg iron; 128 mg sodium; 52 mg calcium; 349 mg phosphorus; 1459 IU Vitamin A; 0.18 mg thiamine; 0.15 mg riboflavin; 38 mg Vitamin C; 951 mg potassium; 1.45 mg zinc; 3.7 mg niacin; 440 mcg Vitamin B$_6$; 1.82 mcg Vitamin B$_{12}$; 19 mcg folic acid

---

*This court bouillon may also be used as a poaching or steaming liquid for other fish. After cooking, it may be frozen for future use; see instructions for freezing soups on page 57.

Simply Baked Salmon Fillets

Serves: 4

4 150 g/5 oz salmon fillets, at
   room temperature
3 tablespoons lemon juice
1 tablespoon dry vermouth or
   white wine

1 teaspoon onion powder
½ teaspoon oregano, crushed
Freshly ground pepper
Hungarian paprika

1. Rinse fish in acidulated water (see page 93) and pat dry with kitchen paper towels.

2. Arrange fillets close together in a shallow baking dish sprayed with nonstick spray.

3. Stir together lemon juice, vermouth, onion powder and crushed oregano. Pour evenly over fish.

4. Sprinkle with freshly ground pepper and Hungarian paprika.

5. Bake in a preheated 180°C, 350°F, Gas Mark 4 oven about 10 to 15 minutes (depending upon the thickness of the fish), or until the fish flakes with a fork.

To Serve: Spoon the juices over the fish, garnish with chopped parsley and lemon wedges, and serve with steamed new potatoes, peas and a cucumber-yogurt salad.

Per serving: 304 calories; 29 gm protein; 11 gm fat; 1.9 gm carbohydrate; 0.2 gm fibre; 53 mg cholesterol; 1.6 mg iron; 144 mg sodium; 9 mg calcium; 446 mg phosphorus; 342 IU Vitamin A; 0.18 mg thiamine; 0.07 mg riboflavin; 5 mg Vitamin C; 509 mg potassium; 0 mg zinc; 10.5 mg niacin; 7 mcg Vitamin B_6; 0 mcg Vitamin B_{12}; 0 mcg folic acid

Five-Minute Fillet of Sole

Serves: 6 (100 g/4 oz cooked fish = 1 serving)

6 fillets of sole (1 kg/2 lb fish)
1½ teaspoons low-sodium
   vegetable seasoning (see
   page 24)
5 tablespoons nonfat yogurt
1½ tablespoons lemon juice

1 tablespoon salt-free Dijon
   mustard
1 tablespoon grated
   horseradish

Chopped fresh parsley for
   garnish

1. Wash fish in acidulated cold water (see page 93). Pat fish dry with kitchen paper towel and sprinkle with vegetable seasoning.

2. Combine yogurt, lemon juice, mustard and horseradish.

3. Place fish in grill pan and spread some of yogurt mixture over each fillet.

4. Grill 5 minutes, or until fish flakes. Serve immediately.

To Serve: Garnished with chopped parsley, this fish, served with Courgettes with Pasta Shells (page 173), presents a colourful yet quick dinner.

Per serving: 134 calories; 26.1 gm protein; 1.6 gm fat; 1.8 gm carbohydrate; 0.1 gm fibre; 76 mg cholesterol; 1.6 mg iron; 133 mg sodium; 48 mg calcium; 302 mg phosphorus; 80 IU Vitamin A; 0.12 mg thiamine; 0.11 mg riboflavin; 2 mg Vitamin C; 542 mg potassium; 1.06 mg zinc; 2.8 mg niacin; 260 mcg Vitamin B_6; 1.82 mcg Vitamin B_{12}; 0 mcg folic acid

Vegetable-Stuffed Fillet of Sole

Serves: 6(100 g/4 oz cooked fish = 1 serving)

24 slim, fresh asparagus
  spears, tough ends removed
24 green beans, ends removed
6 small carrots, quartered
  lengthwise
6 fillets of sole (1 kg/2 lb fish)
Juice of 1 lemon
8 crushed fennel seeds
1 teaspoon celery seed,
  crushed
1 teaspoon low-sodium
  vegetable seasoning (see
  page 24)
Freshly ground pepper
3 shallots, finely chopped, or
  3 spring onions, chopped
250 ml/8 fl oz dry white wine
  or vermouth

1. Steam vegetables until barely tender. Set aside.

2. Sprinkle both sides of fish fillets with lemon juice, crushed fennel, celery seed, vegetable seasoning and ground pepper.

3. Sprinkle bottom of a 33 × 23 × 5 cm/ 13 × 9 × 2-inch baking dish with chopped shallots or spring onions.

4. Divide vegetables into 6 portions* and place 1 portion across dark side of each fillet; roll up.

5. Place seam-side-down on shallots in baking dish and pour wine over fish.

*1 portion of vegetables equals 4 asparagus spears, 4 green beans and 4 carrot strips.

6. Place in a preheated 180°C, 350°F, Gas Mark 4 oven and bake for 20 minutes, or until fish flakes with a fork. *Serve immediately.*

To Serve: Since you already have your lovely vegetables included in the recipe, complete your meal with a baked potato, baked beetroot salad (see page 153) on crisp lettuce, and Yogurt Dessert Mould (page 191), for dessert.

Helpful Hint: Asparagus should be lightly peeled with a vegetable peeler to take off the tough outer coating.

Per serving: 205 calories; 28.1 gm protein; 1.7 gm fat; 12.6 gm carbohydrate; 3.6 gm fibre; 76 mg cholesterol; 3.1 mg iron; 148 mg sodium; 89 mg calcium; 374 mg phosphorus; 6191 IU Vitamin A; 0.26 mg thiamine; 0.25 mg riboflavin; 31 mg Vitamin C; 982 mg potassium; 1.26 mg zinc; 4.1 mg niacin; 352 mcg Vitamin B$_6$; 1.82 mcg Vitamin B$_{12}$; 4 mcg folic acid

Fillet of Sole in Tomato-Orange Sauce

Serves: 8 (75 g/3 oz cooked fish = 1 serving)

We seldom think of oranges and tomatoes as the right combination of sweet and savoury flavours, but here they are—elegant but easy.

8 sole fillets (1 kg/2 lb fish)
Juice of ½ lemon
1 teaspoon low-sodium vegetable seasoning (see page 24)
4 tablespoons dry vermouth or white wine
1 large onion, chopped
2 shallots, chopped
4 ripe, large tomatoes, peeled, seeded and chopped, or 6 canned tomatoes, drained
250 ml/8 fl oz fresh orange juice
2 tablespoons frozen unsweetened orange juice concentrate
2 tablespoons frozen unsweetened apple juice concentrate
Few grains crushed red pepper
½ teaspoon herbes de Provence for fish

Fresh parsley sprigs and orange slices for garnish

1. Season sole fillets with lemon juice and vegetable seasoning. Roll fillets, skin-side-inside, and place in a shallow baking dish sprayed with a nonstick spray.

2. *To make sauce*: Place vermouth in small saucepan and bring to the boil. Add onion and shallots and sauté until transparent.

3. Add tomatoes and simmer 10 minutes.

4. Add orange juice, apple juice and orange juice concentrates, red pepper and herbs and simmer 5 minutes.

5. Pour sauce over fish fillets in baking dish and bake in a preheated 180°C, 350°F, Gas Mark 4 oven for 25 to 30 minutes, or until fish flakes with a fork.

To Serve: Garnish fish with parsley sprigs and orange slices; to complete meal, serve steamed peas and mange tout peas with toasted sesame seeds and parsleyed brown rice.

Per serving: 151 calories; 20.7 gm protein; 1.3 gm fat; 12.7 gm carbohydrate; 1.7 gm fibre; 57 mg cholesterol; 2 mg iron; 95 mg sodium; 48 mg calcium; 262 mg phosphorus; 845 IU Vitamin A; 0.16 mg thiamine; 0.11 mg riboflavin; 42 mg Vitamin C; 714 mg potassium; 1.01 mg zinc; 2.7 mg niacin; 304 mcg Vitamin B_6; 1.36 mcg Vitamin B_{12}; 12 mcg folic acid

Eva's Easy-Does-It Poached Salmon

Serves: 2 (100 g/4 oz cooked fish = 1 serving)

250 ml/8 fl oz water
250 ml/8 fl oz dry white wine or vermouth
1 bay leaf
⅛ teaspoon freshly ground crushed red pepper
1 275 g/10 oz salmon steak or fillet
1 stalk celery, cut in 2.5 cm/1 inch pieces

2 small carrots, cut in 2.5 cm/1 inch pieces
4 slices onion
1 small green pepper, seeded and cut in 2.5 cm/1 inch pieces
4 sprigs fresh parsley or fresh dill
3 lemon slices

1. Place water, wine, bay leaf and crushed red pepper in a small frying pan. Bring to the boil.

2. Add salmon, celery, carrots, onions, green pepper and parsley.

3. Lay lemon slices on top of salmon.

4. Bring to the boil again, lower heat, cover pan and simmer 10 to 15 minutes, or until fish flakes with a fork. (Remember the rule of thumb is 10 minutes of cooking time for each 2.5 cm/1 inch thickness.)

5. Cool in cooking liquid.

To Serve: Serve with vegetables (they will be crisp) and lemon wedges. To complete your meal, add a sliced tomato salad with mustard-yogurt dressing and whole wheat bread, and finish with a serving of fresh fruit.

Helpful Hint: Save strained fish stock; store in refrigerator for up to 3 days, or freeze to use for poaching liquid for salmon at some future date.

Per serving: 319 calories; 33.1 gm protein; 11 gm fat; 7.7 gm carbohydrate; 1.6 gm fibre; 53 mg cholesterol; 2.3 mg iron; 144 mg sodium; 36 mg calcium; 292 mg phosphorus; 2759 IU Vitamin A; 0.29 mg thiamine; 1.16 mg riboflavin; 40 mg Vitamin C; 809 mg potassium; 0.15 mg zinc; 10.6 mg niacin; 87 mcg Vitamin B$_6$; 0 mcg Vitamin B$_{12}$; 11 mcg folic acid

Easy Summer Fish Casserole

Serves: 6 (75 g/3 oz cooked fish = 1 serving)

2 medium potatoes, washed and thinly sliced
1 teaspoon low-sodium vegetable seasoning (see page 24)
½ small onion, thinly sliced
225 g/8 oz mushrooms, cleaned and sliced
450 g/1 lb courgettes, thinly sliced
4 ripe tomatoes, peeled, seeded and chopped, or 6 canned tomatoes, drained and chopped
6 100 g/4 oz fillets of flounder, sole, plaice or snapper (675 g/1½ lb fish)

Juice of ½ lemon
1 teaspoon low-sodium vegetable seasoning (see page 24)
1 teaspoon thyme or herbes de Provence
1 tablespoon fresh basil, chopped, or 1 teaspoon dry basil, crushed
Hungarian paprika
3 spring onions, thinly sliced
2 tablespoons dry vermouth or white wine

6 thin lemon slices for garnish
2 tablespoons chopped fresh parsley for garnish

1. Spray a 2-litre/3½-pint shallow baking dish with nonstick spray.

2. Layer sliced potatoes in baking dish and season with the first teaspoon vegetable seasoning. Arrange sliced onion over potatoes and cover with foil. Bake in preheated 180°C, 350°F, Gas Mark 4 oven for 15 minutes.

*3. Place mushrooms, courgettes and tomatoes over partially cooked potato mixture. Arrange fish over vegetables. Sprinkle with lemon juice, the second teaspoon vegetable seasoning, thyme, basil and Hungarian paprika. Cut diagonal slices in fish and top with sliced spring onions and dry vermouth.

4. Bake 20 to 25 minutes more, *uncovered*, or until fish flakes with fork. If not sufficiently browned, place under grill for a minute or two before serving.

To Serve: Garnish with lemon slices and chopped parsley. Complete the meal with a beetroot and chicory salad.

Per serving: 189 calories; 23.6 gm protein; 1.5 gm fat; 20.5 gm carbohydrate; 6.7 gm fibre; 57 mg cholesterol; 3.5 mg iron; 102 mg sodium; 93 mg calcium; 358 mg phosphorus; 1438 IU Vitamin A; 0.29 mg thiamine; 0.37 mg riboflavin; 53 mg Vitamin C; 1223 mg potassium; 1.03 mg zinc; 6 mg niacin; 349 mcg Vitamin B_6; 1.36 Vitamin B_{12}; 20 mcg folic acid

Simple Poached Halibut

Serves: 6 (75 g/3 oz cooked fish = 1 serving)

Adding milk to your poaching liquid gives the fish a sweeter and milder taste.

6 2.5 cm/1 inch thick halibut fillets (675 g/1½ lb fish), skinned
750 ml/1¼ pints fish stock**

250 ml/8 fl oz nonfat milk
1 bay leaf
Lemon wedges and watercress for garnish

1. Place fish in frying pan
2. Heat stock with milk. Pour hot mixture over fish; add bay leaf.
3. Cover and *simmer gently* for about 10 minutes, or until fish flakes.

To Serve: Remove fish from pan carefully with a spatula, place on a warm platter, and surround with boiled potatoes, lemon wedges and watercress.

*The dish may be prepared through step 3, then covered with foil and placed in the refrigerator until you are ready to finish cooking sometime later in the day or even the next day. Hence, you could prepare it in the morning and then do the final baking in the evening just before serving dinner.
**If you have no fish stock, use all milk with 1 slice of onion and a bouquet garni (4 sprigs of parsley, 1 bay leaf, 1 teaspoon thyme, ½ teaspoon crushed red pepper).

Variation: *To make Halibut with Red Pepper Sauce*: Roast 675 g/ 1½ lb red peppers as described on page 76. In blender or food processor with steel blade, purée peppers. Add cayenne and freshly ground pepper to taste. Blend until smooth. Before removing fish from poaching liquid, place a layer of red pepper sauce on a platter; then top with fish and surround with boiled potatoes, steamed carrots, lemon wedges and watercress.

Per serving: 134 calories; 25.4 gm protein; 1.4 gm fat; 3.3 gm carbohydrate; 0 gm fibre; 57 mg cholesterol; 0.9 mg iron; 68 mg sodium; 26 mg calcium; 280 mg phosphorus; 510 IU Vitamin A; 0.08 mg thiamine; 0.1 mg riboflavin; 0 mg Vitamin C; 523 mg potassium; 0.03 mg zinc; 9.4 mg niacin; 4 mcg Vitamin B_6; 0.03 mcg Vitamin B_{12}; 0 mcg folic acid

Sea Bass with Julienne Vegetables

Serves: 6 (100 g/ 4 oz cooked fish = 1 serving)

If all the vegetables are cut ahead of time, this dish will only take about 20 to 25 minutes to prepare.

1 kg/2 lb sea bass or sole fillets
2 shallots, finely chopped
Dry white wine
1 teaspoon low-sodium vegetable seasoning (see page 24)
2 turnips, peeled and cut into julienne strips
4 carrots, peeled, and cut into julienne strips
8 green beans, cut into julienne strips

6 mushrooms, cleaned and cut into julienne strips
1 teaspoon herbes de Provence
5 tablespoons nonfat evaporated milk, or 5 tablespoons nonfat yogurt mixed with 1 teaspoon cornflour
Pinch cayenne pepper
Lemon juice
Chopped fresh parsley for garnish

1. Cut fish into 6 portions.
2. Sprinkle shallots on bottom of shallow casserole dish and lay fish in dish on top of shallots. Add white wine to barely cover fish. Sprinkle with vegetable seasoning.
3. Bake fish in a preheated 180°C, 350°F, Gas Mark 4 oven for 10 to 15 minutes, or until fish flakes.*

*Keep fish warm during remainder of preparation by covering with foil.

4. Sauté vegetables in 4 tablespoons liquid from fish; add herbs.

5. Pour off remaining liquid from fish; reduce by half.

6. Add nonfat evaporated milk or yogurt mixed with cornflour. Simmer slowly, stir, add pepper, sautéed vegetables and lemon juice to taste.

To Serve: This is an elegant meal-in-one, best served on individual plates. Place fish on a bed of *al dente* pasta shells, top with vegetables and sauce, and garnish with chopped parsley.

Per serving: 187 calories; 34.2 gm protein; 1 gm fat; 8.5 gm carbohydrate; 2.6 gm fibre; 83 mg cholesterol; 2.4 mg iron; 150 mg sodium; 132 mg calcium; 258 mg phosphorus; 5677 IU Vitamin A; 0.23 mg thiamine; 0.42 mg riboflavin; 10 mg Vitamin C; 840 mg potassium; 0.2 mg zinc; 5.6 mg niacin, 89 mcg Vitamin B$_6$; 0 mcg Vitamin B$_{12}$; 6 mcg folic acid

Baked Salmon Loaf

Serves: 6

1 courgette
1 small carrot
½ onion
1 175 g/6 oz potato, peeled, diced and cooked
2 egg whites
1 teaspoon Worcestershire sauce
Dash cayenne pepper
1 tablespoon lemon juice
1 450-g/16-oz can red

salmon, drained, bones and skin removed
50 g/2 oz fresh whole wheat bread crumbs
150 ml/¼ pint nonfat milk
1 teaspoon low-sodium baking powder
1 275-g/10-oz packet frozen mixed vegetables

Watercress for garnish

1. Place courgette, carrot and onion in food processor. Process until minced.

2. Add potato, egg whites, Worcestershire sauce, cayenne and lemon juice. Blend well.

3. Add flaked salmon, breadcrumbs and milk; process until just combined.

4. Add baking powder and blend briefly.

5. Spray a 23 × 13-cm/9 × 5-inch loaf tin with nonstick spray.

6. Place half of salmon mixture in tin, layer with frozen mixed vegetables, and top with remainder of salmon mixture.

7. Bake in a preheated 190°C, 375°F, Gas Mark 5 oven for 45 minutes, or until loaf is firm and lightly browned.

To Serve: Unmould onto a heated platter, slice, and garnish with watercress. To complete the meal, serve steamed asparagus, baked potatoes, and Cabbage, Apple and Raisin Slaw (see page 67).

Per serving: 257 calories; 21.8 gm protein; 8.9 gm fat; 22.5 gm carbohydrate; 2.4 gm fibre; 27 mg cholesterol; 2.3 mg iron; 172 mg sodium; 183 mg calcium; 302 mg phosphorus; 3532 IU Vitamin A; 0.24 mg thiamine; 0.22 mg riboflavin; 16 mg Vitamin C; 677 mg potassium; 0.27 mg zinc; 6.9 mg niacin; 88 mcg Vitamin B_6; 0.12 mcg Vitamin B_{12}; 6 mcg folic acid

Grilled Halibut Steaks

Serves: 4 (100 g/4 oz cooked fish = 1 serving)

1 tablespoon mild soy sauce
1 teaspoon garlic powder
Juice of ½ lemon
4 150-g/5-oz halibut or

swordfish steaks
Hungarian paprika
Lemon wedges and chopped
fresh parsley for garnish

1. Combine soy sauce, garlic powder and lemon juice.
2. Pour over fish in plastic bag and let marinate at least 30 minutes or several hours.
3. Drain fish (reserving marinade)* and place on grill pan, sprinkle with paprika, and grill 10 minutes, or until fish flakes. If fish seems to dry excessively while grilling, baste with reserved marinade. Serve immediately.

To Serve: Garnish with chopped parsley and lemon wedges. To round out the meal, serve steamed, frozen salt-free French-cut green beans and corn, crisp French bread and a lightly seasoned green salad. Top with a slightly chilled 120 ml/4 fl oz glass of California chardonnay wine.

***Helpful Hint:** The marinade may be refrigerated for about 10 days and used for basting other grilled fish dishes.

Per serving: 186 calories; 27.7 gm protein; 5.7 gm fat; 1.3 gm carbohydrate; 0.1 gm fibre; 62 mg cholesterol; 1.4 mg iron; 183 mg sodium; 28 mg calcium; 225 mg phosphorus; 1946 IU Vitamin A; 0.08 mg thiamine; 0.08 mg riboflavin; 3 mg Vitamin C; 657 mg potassium; 0 mg zinc; 9.1 mg niacin; 3 mcg Vitamin B_6; 0 mcg Vitamin B_{12}; 0 mcg folic acid

Sweet and Pungent Fish

Serves: 6 (100 g/4 oz cooked fish = 1 serving)

6 150-g/ 5-oz fillets of sole,
   halibut or haddock (1 kg/2
   lb fish)
Juice of ½ lemon
1 teaspoon low-sodium
   vegetable seasoning (see
   page 24)
5 tablespoons brown rice
   vinegar
1½ tablespoons cornflour
3 tablespoons frozen
   unsweetened apple juice

   concentrate
1 tablespoon mild soy sauce
½ tablespoon ground ginger
1 500-g/20-oz can
   unsweetened pineapple
   chunks with juice
1 green pepper, seeded and
   cut in strips
1 red pepper, seeded and cut
   in strips
1 medium onion, chopped
2 tablespoons dry sherry

1. Arrange fish fillets in a shallow glass or ceramic baking dish sprayed with nonstick spray and sprinkle with lemon juice and vegetable seasoning.

2. *To make sauce:* Combine vinegar, cornflour, apple juice concentrate, soy sauce and ginger in a saucepan.

3. Cook over moderate heat, stirring constantly, until thickened. *Do not overcook.*

4. Add pineapple chunks and juice, green and red pepper strips, onion and sherry. Blend.

5. Pour sauce over fish and bake in a preheated 180°C, 350°F, Gas Mark 4 oven for 30 minutes.

To Serve: Serve with Steamed Brown Rice (see page 174) and peas.

Variation: This pungent sauce is also delicious served over a whole steamed red snapper, as you frequently find it served in Chinese restaurants.

Per serving: 189 calories; 23.5 gm protein; 1.3 gm fat; 19.9 gm carbohydrate; 1.3 gm fibre; 66 mg cholesterol; 2 mg iron; 208 mg sodium; 45 mg calcium; 285 mg phosphorus; 884 IU Vitamin A; 0.20 mg thiamine; 0.13 mg riboflavin; 70 mg Vitamin C; 729 mg potassium; 1 mg zinc; 2.8 mg niacin; 361 mcg Vitamin B_6; 1.59 mcg Vitamin B_{12}; 6.8 mcg folic acid

POULTRY

In these times of rising food costs, the popularity of poultry is at an all-time high. This is not only because of its low cost per serving and low cholesterol content, but also because of the many different and delectable ways it can be prepared. Always remove all visible fat and skin and the wing tips (*including the double-bone portion* of the wings, because it is extremely difficult to skin; the first portion can remain) from poultry *before* preparing. Discard the fat, but the scraps of skin, the giblets, and the wing tips should be stored in a container in your freezer to use in preparing stock.

Orange-Glazed Chicken

Serves: 8 (½ chicken = 1 serving)

50 g/2 oz onion, finely chopped
1 shallot, finely chopped
1 large clove garlic, crushed
3 tablespoons finely chopped

fresh parsley
450 ml/¾ pint fresh orange juice
Grated rind of 1 orange
1 teaspoon mild soy sauce

4 small chickens, halved, wing tips and all visible fat removed
Juice of 1 lemon
1 teaspoon low-sodium vegetable seasoning (see page 24)
Freshly ground pepper
75 g/3 oz seeded raisins
50 g/2 oz chestnuts, chopped

1½ tablespoons cornflour
3 tablespoons cold water
450 g/1 lb Steamed Brown Rice (see page 174) or wild rice for serving
Watercress for garnish
3 navel oranges, peeled with sharp knife, all white removed, cut into 5 mm/¼ inch slices, for garnish

1. Combine onion, shallot, garlic, parsley, orange juice, rind and soy sauce in a large bowl.

2. Add chickens, mix, and marinate several hours at room temperature.

3. Remove chickens from marinade and place skin-side-up in a shallow casserole. Season with lemon juice, vegetable seasoning and pepper.

4. Place in top of a preheated 200°C, 400°F, Gas Mark 6 oven. Bake uncovered for 30 minutes.

5. Heat remaining marinade until boiling and pour over birds. Sprinkle with raisins and chestnuts.

6. Cover and bake 30 additional minutes. Remove chickens from casserole and keep warm.

7. Blend cornflour with the cold water. Blend into sauce in baking dish. Cook over medium heat until thickened.

To Serve: Place rice on a large, warm serving platter, arrange chickens on rice, and spoon sauce with raisins and chestnuts over chickens. Surround with watercress and orange slices and serve immediately.

Per serving: 512 calories; 55.1 gm protein; 12.9 gm fat; 41.4 gm carbohydrate; 3.4 gm fibre; 100 mg cholesterol; 4.1 mg iron; 125 mg sodium; 58 mg calcium; 348 mg phosphorus; 613 IU Vitamin A; 0.25 mg thiamine; 0.31 mg riboflavin; 38 mg Vitamin C; 797 mg potassium; 3.18 mg zinc; 18 mg niacin; 921 mcg Vitamin B_6; 0.72 mcg Vitamin B_{12}; 10 mcg folic acid

Irene's Chicken Supreme

Serves: 8 (½ chicken = 1 serving)

An evening of good food and good conversation shared with good friends is a memory to be cherished. My dear friend Irene served this delicious dish on one such occasion.

1 medium onion, chopped
1 shallot, chopped
1 carrot, chopped
4 our Stock Cubes, melted
  (see page 21), or 4
  tablespoons our Chicken
  Stock (see page 22)
2 small green cabbages (1.4
  kg/3 lb), shredded
1 teaspoon thyme or herbes de
  Provence
120 ml/4 fl oz dry white wine
  or vermouth

75 g/3 oz seeded raisins
4 small chickens or poussins,
  halved, wing tips and all
  visible fat removed
Juice of ½ lemon
2 teaspoons low-sodium
  vegetable seasoning (see
  page 24)
Hungarian paprika
4 tablespoons dry white wine
Chopped fresh parsley for
  garnish

1. Sauté onion, shallot and carrot in a sauté pan with stock cubes until they are transparent. Stir constantly.

2. Add shredded cabbage, thyme, the 120 ml/4 fl oz white wine and raisins. Cover and cook until softened (about 20 minutes).

3. Season halved chickens with lemon juice, vegetable seasoning and paprika. Place in flameproof casserole. Brown under grill about 7 minutes on each side.

4. Add cabbage mixture to casserole, lay browned chickens on top, and sprinkle with the 4 tablespoons dry white wine.

5. Cover and bake in a preheated 230°C, 450°F, Gas mark 8 oven for 10 minutes.

6. Remove cover and continue baking at 180°C, 350°F, Gas mark 4 until tender, about 20 to 30 minutes.

To Serve: Serve chicken and cabbage on an attractive serving platter, surrounded with grilled tomatoes and garnished with chopped parsley. Cooked pasta shells with peas make a nice accompaniment.

Per serving: 430 calories; 54 gm protein; 8.5 gm fat; 22.8 gm carbohydrate; 7.4 gm fibre; 107 mg cholesterol; 4.1 mg iron; 122 mg sodium; 136 mg calcium; 348 mg phosphorus; 1727 IU Vitamin A; 0.25 mg thiamine; 0.31 mg riboflavin; 85 mg Vitamin C; 1042 mg potassium; 3.92 mg zinc; 18 mg niacin; 1197 mcg Vitamin B_6; 0.72 mcg Vitamin B_{12}; 66 mcg folic acid

Baked Chicken Breasts Supreme

Serves 12 (100 g/4 oz cooked chicken = 1 serving)

This recipe uses seasoned yogurt as a marinade for chicken breasts, adding a piquant and interesting taste.

2 tablespoons lemon juice
3 cloves garlic, crushed
1½ tablespoons mild soy sauce, or 1 tablespoon Worcestershire sauce (it has ⅓ the sodium)
1 teaspoon Hungarian paprika
2 teaspoons celery seed
1 tablespoon salt-free mustard
Few grains crushed red pepper
250 ml/8 fl oz nonfat yogurt

6 whole chicken breasts (about 2.75 kg/6 lb chicken), skinned, boned, halved and flattened*
100 g/4 oz dry whole wheat breadcrumbs
Hungarian paprika

2 tablespoons chopped fresh parsley for garnish
Watercress for garnish
18 tiny tomatoes for garnish

1. Combine lemon juice, garlic, soy sauce, paprika, celery seed, mustard, crushed red pepper and yogurt in a bowl. Mix well.

2. Add chicken breasts to yogurt mixture and marinate overnight (24 to 48 hours).

3. Remove chicken breasts from yogurt mixture and arrange in rows in a shallow baking dish sprayed with nonstick spray.

4. Sprinkle with whole wheat breadcrumbs and paprika and bake in a preheated 180°C, 350°F, Gas Mark 4 oven for 45 to 55 minutes.

To Serve: Sprinkle with chopped parsley, arrange watercress and tomatoes attractively around chicken, and serve.

Variation: For variety in flavour, a bed of Duxelles (see page 14) may be placed in the bottom of the baking dish before the yogurt-marinated chicken is added.

*Helpful Hints: Many times, I skin chicken breasts but leave the bone. Meat cooked on the bone has an added flavour. The skin may be frozen and used in a future chicken stock preparation.

To flatten chicken breasts, place half breast between two pieces of greaseproof paper or cling film and pound until it is 5 mm/¼ inch thick.

Per serving: 190 calories; 24.2 gm protein; 3.6 gm fat; 7.8 gm carbohydrate; 0.7 gm fibre; 92 mg cholesterol; 2.1 mg iron; 118 mg sodium; 59 mg calcium; 245 mg phosphorus; 774 IU Vitamin A; 0.11 mg thiamine; 0.36 mg riboflavin; 12 mg Vitamin C; 429 mg potassium; 0.06 mg zinc; 7.9 mg niacin; 33 mcg Vitamin B_6; 0 mcg Vitamin B_{12}; 3 mcg folic acid

Chicken Breasts Supreme with Poached Cucumbers

Serves: 4 (100 g/4 oz cooked chicken = 1 serving

This recipe requires about 15 minutes of last-minute preparation. I suggest that you serve your salad at the end of the meal so that its vinegary flavour does not mask the delicate flavour of the sauce.

2 whole chicken breasts, skinned, boned, halved and flattened (see page 108)
1 teaspoon low-sodium vegetable seasoning (see page 24)
3 our Stock Cubes (see page 22)
2 cloves garlic, finely chopped
25 g/1 oz shallots, finely chopped
8 whole fennel seeds, crushed
250 ml/8 fl oz dry white wine

or vermouth
2 large cucumbers, peeled, cut in half, seeded, and cut into 5 mm/¼ inch crescents
1 50 ml/¼ pint nonfat yogurt
2 teaspoons cornflour
1 teaspoon salt-free Dijon mustard with herbs
4 tomatoes, diced, or 4 canned tomatoes, diced

2 tablespoons chopped fresh parsley for garnish

1. Season chicken with vegetable seasoning several hours before serving.
2. In a large sauté pan, melt 3 stock cubes. Add garlic, shallots and fennel seeds. Sauté 2 minutes over medium heat.
3. Add wine and bring to the boil.
4. Add chicken breasts, cover and poach 3 to 4 minutes per side.
5. Remove chicken to a heated platter and keep covered and warm.
6. Reduce pan liquid to about two thirds. Add cucumber crescents and poach, covered, about 5 minutes, until translucent but crisp. Arrange on heated platter around chicken.
7. Place yogurt in a small bowl and whisk in 2 teaspoons

cornflour. *Slowly* whisk hot pan juices into yogurt until well blended. Add mustard. Return sauce to sauté pan and stir 2 minutes over *low heat* until thickened. Taste, and adjust seasonings.

8. Add tomatoes and heat until warmed through.

To Serve: Pour sauce over chicken and cucumbers and sprinkle with chopped parsley. May be served with bulgur wheat or brown rice cooked in our Chicken Stock (see page 22).

Per serving: 227 calories; 25 gm protein; 3.4 gm fat; 13.1 gm carbohydrate; 1.6 gm fibre; 92 mg cholesterol; 2.7 mg iron; 98 mg sodium; 111 mg calcium; 273 mg phosphorus; 665 IU Vitamin A; 0.17 mg thiamine; 0.42 mg riboflavin; 18 mg Vitamin C; 624 mg potassium; 0.06 mg zinc; 8.2 mg niacin; 58 mcg Vitamin B_6; 0 mcg Vitamin B_{12}; 3 mcg folic acid

Chicken Breasts Italiano

Serves: 6 (100 g/4 oz cooked chicken = 1 serving)

The sauce in this recipe should be prepared several days before serving.

4 tablespoons our Chicken Stock (see page 22)
1 large red onion, finely chopped
675 g/1½ lb canned tomatoes, drained
4 tablespoons dry Marsala wine
2 cloves garlic, crushed
1 teaspoon basil, crushed
½ teaspoon oregano, crushed
1 teaspoon Italian seasoning, crushed
1 bay leaf
¼ teaspoon coriander seed
¼ teaspoon fennel seed, crushed

1 7.5 cm/3-inch piece orange rind
15 g/½ oz fresh parsley, finely chopped
3 whole chicken breasts (1.5 kg/3 lb chicken), skinned, boned, halved, and flattened (see page 108)
Juice of ½ lemon
1 teaspoon low-sodium vegetable seasoning (see page 24)
½ teaspoon garlic powder
Hungarian paprika
3 tablespoons grated Sap Sago cheese, toasted (see page 16)

1. *To make sauce:* Heat stock in a frying pan, add onion and sauté until lightly browned.

2. Stir in the next 10 ingredients; cover and simmer 1 hour.

3. Remove sauce from heat, adjust seasoning and add parsley.

4. Refrigerate or freeze sauce until needed. When ready to use, reheat.

5. Season flattened chicken breasts on both sides with lemon juice, vegetable seasoning, garlic powder and paprika.

6. Heat a nonstick frying pan or an iron frying pan sprayed with nonstick spray and sear breasts for 3 to 5 minutes on each side (or grill on each side).

7. Remove breasts to a heated ovenproof platter; cover with heated sauce and sprinkle with toasted Sap Sago cheese.

8. Heat under grill until sauce bubbles, and serve immediately.

To Serve: Complete the meal with parsleyed spaghettini with peas and carrots, and an Italian salad of crisp salad green and marinated garbanzo beans. Lila's Frozen Dessert (page 196) would end the meal on a light note.

Variation: If your diet permits, you may use grated Parmesan cheese instead of Sap Sago.

Per serving: 191 calories; 25.7 gm protein; 4.6 gm fat; 12 gm carbohydrate; 1.6 gm fibre; 92 mg cholesterol; 3.8 mg iron; 255 mg sodium; 118 mg calcium; 307 mg phosphorus; 1894 IU Vitamin A; 0.18 mg thiamine; 0.38 mg riboflavin; 39 mg Vitamin C; 748 mg potassium; 0.33 mg zinc; 8.5 mg niacin; 153 mcg Vitamin B_6; 0 mcg Vitamin B_{12}; 14 mcg folic acid

Company's-Coming Chicken, with Brown and Wild Rice

Serves: 8 (100 g/4 oz cooked chicken = 1 serving)

25 g/1 oz corn flakes (no salt or sugar added), crushed
1 teaspoon curry powder*
4 whole chicken breasts, skinned, boned, halved
250 ml/8 fl oz buttermilk, strained to remove fat globules
75 g/3 oz seeded raisins

4 tablespoons dry sherry, or 120 ml/4 fl oz pineapple juice (drained from canned, crushed pineapple below)
500 ml/18 fl oz our Vegetable Stock (see page 49), our Chicken Stock (see page 22), or water
90 g/3½ oz wild rice

*1 teaspoon low-sodium vegetable seasoning (see page 24) and ½ teaspoon garlic powder can be substituted for the curry.

90 g/3½ oz brown rice
100 g/4 oz crushed,
   unsweetened canned

pineapple, drained

Watercress for garnish

1. Crush corn flakes; add curry powder.
2. Dip chicken breasts in buttermilk, coating both sides; then roll breasts in seasoned corn flakes, coating evenly.
3. Place on a shallow nonstick baking tin and bake in a preheated 190°C, 375°F, Gas Mark 5 oven 45 to 60 minutes, or until tender. Prepare rice as follows while chicken is baking.
4. Plump raisins in warmed sherry or pineapple juice. Drain, reserving liquid.
5. Combine drained juice and stock in a large saucepan and bring to the boil. Add rice, bring to the boil again; *don't stir.*
6. Cover and simmer about 45 minutes, or until all liquid is absorbed. Keep covered, remove from heat, and allow to steam for about another 10 to 15 minutes.
7. Stir raisins and pineapple into rice with a fork before serving.
To Serve: Place a bed of rice on a large warmed serving platter; top with baked chicken breasts and garnish with watercress.

Per serving: 271 calories; 25.9 gm protein; 3.6 gm fat; 31.6 gm carbohydrate; 2 gm fibre; 93 mg cholesterol; 2.7 mg iron; 134 mg sodium; 68 mg calcium; 339 mg phosphorus; 268 IU Vitamin A; 0.22 mg thiamine; 0.46 mg riboflavin; 3 mg Vitamin C; 519 mg potassium; 0.46 mg zinc; 9 mg niacin; 98 mcg Vitamin B_6; 0 mcg Vitamin B_{12}; 10 mcg folic acid

Tandoori Chicken

Serves: 8 (100 g/4 oz cooked chicken = 1 serving)

Tandoori chicken is delicious either hot or cold.

2 1 kg/2 lb chickens,
   quartered and skinned,
   with wing tips removed, or
   4 whole chicken breasts,
   skinned and halved
450 ml/¾ pint nonfat yogurt
3 cloves garlic, crushed
1 tablespoon grated fresh
   ginger

4 tablespoons lime or lemon
   juice
½ teaspoon ground coriander
½ teaspoon cumin
4 tablespoons frozen
   unsweetened apple juice
   concentrate
Few drops Tabasco sauce
1 bunch spring onions (white

part only), chopped, or 25
g/1 oz onion, grated
2 tablespoons mild soy sauce

or 1 tablespoon
Worcestershire sauce

1. Cut small slits in each piece of chicken with the point of a sharp knife.
2. Combine remaining ingredients in a bowl and stir to blend.
3. Marinate quartered chicken in yogurt mixture 24 to 48 hours.
4. Remove chicken from marinade and grill or barbecue on grill until golden brown on both sides—about 15 to 20 minutes on each side.

To Serve: Serve on a bed of watercress, garnished with tomatoes, with Raita (page 212) as a condiment. Spinach, Cheese and Mushroom Squares (page 159), steamed carrots, toasted whole wheat pita bread, and the always enjoyed fresh fruit platter complete a delicious meal.

Helpful Hint: Remaining marinade may be stored in refrigerator and used to prepare additional chicken up to 10 to 12 days later.

Per serving: 160 calories; 23.7 gm protein; 3.2 gm fat; 8 gm carbohydrate; 0.2 gm fibre; 92 mg cholesterol; 1.8 mg iron; 145 mg sodium; 63 mg calcium; 240 mg phosphorus; 180 IU Vitamin A; 0.11 mg thiamine; 0.36 mg riboflavin; 8 mg Vitamin C; 407 mg potassium; 0.02 mg zinc; 7.7 mg niacin; 9 mcg Vitamin B$_6$; 0 mcg Vitamin B$_{12}$; 1 mcg folic acid

Barbecue-Style Grilled Chicken

Serves: 4 (100 g/4 oz cooked chicken = 1 serving)

1 1 kg/2 lb chicken, sectioned, skinned, and wing tips and all visible fat removed
1 teaspoon onion powder
Juice of 1 lemon
1 350 g/12 oz can salt-free tomato juice
Few drops Tabasco sauce
Juice of ½ lemon
50 g/2 oz fresh whole wheat
breadcrumbs
25 g/1 oz whole wheat flour
1 teaspoon Hungarian paprika
1 teaspoon garlic powder
½ teaspoon chilli powder
½ teaspoon thyme
½ teaspoon oregano
½ teaspoon sage (optional)

1. Sprinkle skinned chicken pieces with onion powder and half the lemon juice.

2. Combine tomato juice, Tabasco and remaining lemon juice.

3. Combine breadcrumbs, flour, paprika, garlic powder, chilli powder, thyme and oregano. Add sage if desired.

4. Dip chicken pieces in tomato juice mixture, then in seasoned breadcrumb mixture.

5. Place on nonstick shallow baking tin and bake towards the top of a preheated 180°C, 350°F, Gas Mark 4 oven for 45 to 60 minutes.

To Serve: For indoor or outdoor entertaining, this is lovely served with baked beans and a selection of raw vegetables for making your own salad. To complete the meal, serve a large platter of sliced fresh fruits.

Per serving: 270 calories; 31.9 gm protein; 4.8 gm fat; 23.9 gm carbohydrate; 0.8 gm fibre; 116 mg cholesterol; 4.1 mg iron; 165 mg sodium; 43 mg calcium; 325 mg phosphorus; 1272 IU Vitamin A; 0.21 mg thiamine; 0.45 mg riboflavin; 20 mg Vitamin C; 670 mg potassium; 0.05 mg zinc; 10.6 mg niacin; 10 mcg Vitamin B_6; 0 mcg Vitamin B_{12}; 1 mcg folic acid

Chicken and Vegetable Mousse

Serves: 12 (1 slice = 1 serving)

A little extra preparation the day before will produce a light and eye-appealing main course—or, if you choose, an elegant appetizer.

1–2 bunches fresh spinach or lettuce, well washed
2 spring onions chopped
675 g/1½ lb minced chicken*
1 teaspoon low-sodium vegetable seasoning (see page 24)
Few grains crushed red pepper
4 egg whites
2 courgettes** cut in 4 strips lengthwise

1 275-g/10-oz packet frozen broccoli spears or florets, or 450 g/1 lb fresh broccoli
3 small carrots, cut in 4 strips lengthwise
4 canned artichoke bottoms, cut in 4 strips
450 ml/¾ pint Fresh Tomato Sauce with Fresh Basil (see page 169)

* Preminced chicken is very fatty. It is better to make your own with a mincer or food processor, or have it done to order for you with the fat and skin removed.
** Fresh asparagus spears or whole green beans may be substituted for the courgettes.

1. Remove stalks from the spinach. Drop spinach or lettuce leaves into boiling water and blanch 30 seconds. Remove and pat dry with kitchen paper towels. (Handle leaves carefully.)

2. Spray a 23 × 13 × 10-cm/9 × 5 × 4-inch loaf tin with nonstick spray. Overlap spinach or lettuce leaves on bottom and sides of tin.

3. Place spring onions in blender or food processor and chop. Add chicken, vegetable seasoning, and crushed red pepper, and blend thoroughly. Add egg whites and blend until mixture is a fine paste.

4. Spread one-third of this mixture over spinach leaves. Pack down with a metal spatula, reaching into the corners of the pan.

5. Arrange half of the courgettes, broccoli, carrots and artichokes on top of the chicken purée, *placing vegetables lengthwise*.

6. Repeat, adding a layer of one-third of the chicken, then the remaining vegetables, and ending with chicken purée.

7. Press the mixture lightly with your hand to remove any air pockets.

8. Cover tin with foil and place in a baking tin with 2.5 cm/1 inch hot water.

9. Bake in preheated 180°C, 350°F, Gas Mark 4 oven 1 hour, or until a knife comes out clean.

10. Remove loaf tin from hot water and cool. At this point, if there is any excess liquid, pour it off, and then place covered loaf tin in refrigerator overnight to set.

To Unmould and Serve: Place a bed of tomato sauce on a serving platter and unmould the mousse on top of the sauce. To facilitate unmoulding, loosen around edges with spatula, invert mould over platter, and shake gently until unmoulded. This mousse makes a delicious luncheon dish served with a green salad and crisp rolls. Spoon some tomato sauce on top of each serving.

Per serving: 140 calories; 15 gm protein; 3.3 gm fat; 9.1 gm carbohydrate; 2.4 gm fibre; 46 mg cholesterol; 2.3 mg iron; 82 mg sodium; 65 mg calcium; 170 mg phosphorus; 5340 IU Vitamin A; 0.12 mg thiamine; 0.3 mg riboflavin; 38 mg Vitamin C; 475 mg potassium; 0.27 mg zinc; 4.6 mg niacin; 95 mcg Vitamin B$_6$; 0.01 mcg Vitamin B$_{12}$; 20 mcg folic acid

Onion Lover's Chicken with Onions

Serves: 4 (100 g/4 oz cooked chicken = 1 serving)

1 1 kg/2 lb chicken, skinned, all visible fat removed, with wing tips removed, and cut into 4 portions
Juice of ½ lemon
Freshly ground pepper
½ teaspoon garlic powder
Hungarian paprika
1 teaspoon herbal bouquet

1.25 kg/2½ lb onions, sliced
3 cloves garlic
250 ml/8 fl oz dry white wine
1 tablespoon red wine vinegar
1 bay leaf
1 teaspoon thyme, crushed, or 4 sprigs fresh thyme
3 tablespoons chopped fresh parsley for garnish

1. Season chicken with lemon juice, freshly ground pepper, garlic powder, paprika and herbal bouquet.

2. In a heavy nonstick frying pan, or one sprayed with nonstick spray, sear the chicken portions. (If they stick, add a touch of dry white wine.)

3. When chicken is browned, add onions, garlic, white wine, vinegar, bay leaf and thyme.*

4. Cover and simmer 30 to 40 minutes, until chicken juices run clear, stirring occasionally.

5. Taste, and adjust seasonings before serving.

To Serve: Remove chicken and onions to a warm platter, surround with steamed potatoes and carrots, and sprinkle with chopped parsley.

Per serving: 237 calories; 25.2 gm protein; 3.4 gm fat; 20.4 gm carbohydrate; 4.3 gm fibre; 92 mg cholesterol; 3.7 mg iron; 89 mg sodium; 97 mg calcium; 313 mg phosphorus; 573 IU Vitamin A; 0.14 mg thiamine; 0.38 mg riboflavin; 26 mg Vitamin C; 720 mg potassium; 0.59 mg zinc; 7.8 mg niacin; 230 mcg Vitamin B$_6$; 0 mcg Vitamin B$_{12}$; 48 mcg folic acid

* Can also be transferred to a casserole dish and baked in a preheated 190°C, 375°F, Gas Mark 5 oven for 30 to 40 minutes.

Addie's Grilled Chicken

Serves: 8 (100 g/4 oz cooked chicken = 1 serving)

250 ml/8 fl oz white wine
1 clove garlic, crushed
1 tablespoon mild soy sauce
1 teaspoon salt-free mustard
1 teaspoon low-sodium
vegetable seasoning (see
page 24)
1 teaspoon rosemary, crushed

Juice of ½ lemon
4 whole chicken breasts (1.75
kg/4 lb chicken; leave bone
in for flavour), skinned,
halved and all visible fat
removed
Hungarian paprika

1. Combine the first 7 ingredients in a bowl for marinade. Add chicken breasts to marinate.
2. Cover and refrigerate 4 to 6 hours or overnight.
3. Place chicken on grill rack and sprinkle with paprika. Grill 10 cm/4 inches from heat, about 20 minutes on each side, basting with remaining marinade from time to time.

To Serve: Serve from grill to table in order to savour the flavourful and juicy quality of the chicken. Can be accompanied by rice and Chopped Broccoli Chinese Style (page 154).

Helpful Hint: Leftover marinade can be refrigerated and used to marinate chicken for another meal.

Per serving: 152 calories; 22.2 gm protein; 3.2 gm fat; 2.2 gm carbohydrate; 0.1 gm fibre; 92 mg cholesterol; 1.9 mg iron; 129 mg sodium; 24 mg calcium; 238 mg phosphorus; 203 IU Vitamin A; 0.09 mg thiamine; 0.29 mg riboflavin; 2 mg Vitamin C; 369 mg potassium; 0 mg zinc; 7.4 mg niacin; 13 mcg Vitamin B_6; 0 mcg Vitamin B_{12}; 0 mcg folic acid

Chicken Breasts with Artichokes

Serves: 8 (100 g/4 oz cooked chicken = 1 serving)

4 whole chicken breasts,
skinned, halved and all
visible fat removed
Juice of ½ lemon
1 teaspoon low-sodium

vegetable seasoning (see
page 24)
1 teaspoon herbes de
Provence, crushed
½ teaspoon crushed red

pepper
Hungarian paprika
4 our Stock Cubes (see page 21)
225 g/8 oz mushrooms, thinly sliced
3 spring onions, chopped
2½ tablespoons unbleached flour
150 ml/¼ pint our Chicken Stock (see page 22)
3 tablespoons dry sherry
2 275-g/10-oz packets frozen artichoke hearts, or 2 275-g/10-oz cans artichoke hearts, rinsed and drained
3 tablespoons fresh parsley for garnish

1. Place chicken breasts in a flameproof casserole.
2. Sprinkle both sides with lemon juice, vegetable seasoning, herbs, crushed red pepper and paprika.
3. Grill chicken quickly, 5 minutes on each side.
4. Melt stock cubes in a sauté pan, add sliced mushrooms and spring onions, and sauté 3 minutes over medium high heat.
5. Sprinkle flour on top, stirring constantly to blend in flour.
6. Slowly add chicken stock and sherry. Stir constantly.
7. Simmer uncovered for 5 minutes, or until sauce thickens, stirring occasionally.
8. Add artichoke hearts to sauce. Stir well.
*9. Pour sauce over browned chicken and cover.
10. Bake in a preheated 180°C, 350°F, Gas Mark 4 oven for 40 to 45 minutes.

To Serve: Sprinkle with chopped parsley and serve with Steamed Brown Rice (see page 174) and steamed broccoli florets.

Per serving: 167 calories; 24.7 gm protein; 3.5 gm fat; 8.3 gm carbohydrate; 1.5 gm fibre; 92 mg cholesterol; 2.8 mg iron; 90 mg sodium; 54 mg calcium; 302 mg phosphorus; 666 IU Vitamin A; 0.16 mg thiamine; 0.49 mg riboflavin; 11 mg Vitamin C; 607 mg potassium; 0.08 mg zinc; 9.1 mg niacin; 50 mcg Vitamin B_6; 0 mcg Vitamin B_{12}; 9 mcg folic acid

Harold's Favourite Chicken with Cabbage

Serves: 4 (100 g/4 oz cooked chicken = 1 serving)

My husband, Harold, is a cabbage lover, and this quick recipe satisfies both his palate and my busy time schedule.

* May be prepared through step 9 in the morning and baked just before serving dinner.

1 tablespoon mild soy sauce
3 tablespoons lemon juice
2 cloves garlic, crushed
1 teaspoon grated fresh ginger
  root
2 whole chicken breasts (1 kg/
  2 lb chicken), skinned,

halved, and all visible fat
  removed
1 onion, sliced
1 teaspoon low-sodium
  vegetable seasoning (see
  page 24)
Hungarian paprika
½ cabbage, shredded

1. Combine soy sauce, lemon juice, garlic and ginger root.
2. Place in a plastic bag with the chicken breasts and marinate overnight or all day.
3. Place onion slices in a flameproof casserole. Lay chicken breasts on onions, pour marinade over chicken, and sprinkle with vegetable seasoning and paprika. Cover and roast 50 minutes in a preheated 180°C, 350°F, Gas Mark 4 oven.
4. Remove cover and grill chicken until lightly browned, about 5 minutes on each side.
5. Add shredded cabbage, cover, and return to oven for 30 additional minutes.

To Serve: Serve with Cracked Wheat Pilaf (see page 176) and parsleyed carrots.

Variation: Omit the Cracked Wheat Pilaf. Add 350 g/12 oz pasta shells after completing step 5. Cover and bake 15 additional minutes before serving.

Per serving: 166 calories; 24.1 gm protein; 3.4 gm fat; 9.9 gm carbohydrate; 3.4 gm fibre; 92 mg cholesterol; 2.5 mg iron; 207 mg sodium; 71 mg calcium; 277 mg phosphorus; 405 IU Vitamin A; 0.16 mg thiamine; 0.34 mg riboflavin; 43 mg Vitamin C; 608 mg potassium; 0.39 mg zinc; 7.8 mg niacin; 158 mcg Vitamin B_6;0 mcg Vitamin B_{12}; 32 mcg folic acid

Roast Chicken on a Bed of Vermicelli

Serves: 4 (100 g/4 oz cooked chicken = 1 serving)

1 1-kg/2-lb chicken,
  quartered, skinned, and
  wing tips and all visible fat
  removed

Juice of ½ lemon
1 teaspoon low-sodium
  vegetable seasoning (see
  page 24)

½ teaspoon garlic powder
½ teaspoon onion powder
Hungarian paprika
1 onion, thinly sliced
2 carrots, thinly sliced
1 clove garlic, crushed
120 ml/4 fl oz our Chicken
 Stock (see page 22)

225 g/8 oz vermicelli or whole
 wheat spaghettini
1 tablespoon dry sherry
1 tablespoon mild soy sauce
 or Worcestershire sauce
4 spring onions, sliced
2 tablespoons chopped fresh
 parsley for garnish

1. Season chicken pieces on both sides with lemon juice, vegetable seasoning, garlic powder, onion powder and paprika.

2. Place onion slices, carrot slices and garlic on bottom of small flameproof casserole. Lay seasoned chicken on top of onion mixture; add chicken stock.

3. Cover casserole and place in a preheated 180°C, 350°F, Gas Mark 4 oven for 45 minutes. While chicken is roasting, prepare pasta.

4. Cook vermicelli in boiling water according to package directions.

5. Drain pasta; return to pan and add sherry, soy sauce and spring onions.

6. When chicken is done, remove cover and brown chicken under grill for 5 minutes.

To Serve: Arrange pasta mixture on a large warmed platter or on individual plates. Cover pasta with vegetables and pan juices from casserole. Lay chicken pieces on top, sprinkle with chopped parsley, and serve immediately.

Per serving: 380 calories; 36.8 gm protein; 5.2 gm fat; 45.8 gm carbohydrate; 2.1 gm fibre; 92 mg cholesterol; 3.4 mg iron; 228 mg sodium; 53 mg calcium; 267 mg phosphorus; 4433 IU Vitamin A; 0.37 mg thiamine; 0.43 mg riboflavin; 13 mg Vitamin C; 556 mg potassium; 0.26 mg zinc; 9.2 mg niacin; 101 mcg Vitamin B_6; 0 mcg Vitamin B_{12}; 13 mcg folic acid

Chicken Paprika with Yogurt

Serves: 8 (100 g/4 oz cooked chicken = 1 serving)

2 large onions, finely chopped
1 large clove garlic, crushed
3 our Stock Cubes, melted
 (see page 21), or 4

tablespoons our Chicken
 Stock (see page 22)
1 1.5-kg/3-lb chicken,
 skinned, wing tips and all

visible fat removed, and cut into 8 serving pieces
1 teaspoon low-sodium vegetable seasoning (see page 24)
1 large ripe tomato, peeled, seeded, and chopped
1½–2 tablespoons Hungarian paprika

250 ml/8 fl oz our Chicken Stock
1 green pepper, seeded and sliced
1 bay leaf
1½ tablespoons cornflour or unbleached flour
4 tablespoons nonfat yogurt (optional)

1. In a large heavy casserole, sauté onions and garlic in melted stock cubes or stock.
2. Cook over medium heat until softened but not browned.
3. Add chicken, sprinkled with vegetable seasoning.
4. Cover and cook over low heat for 10 minutes.
5. Add diced tomato and coat pieces of chicken with paprika. Cover and cook 10 minutes over low heat.
*6. Add chicken stock, green pepper and bay leaf and cook over *very low heat* for about 25 minutes, or until the chicken is tender.
7. Remove chicken and peppers.
8. Combine cornflour or unbleached flour with 3 tablespoons cold water and add to onion mixture. Stir, bring to the boil, and cook mixture until thickened, stirring constantly.
9. Add yogurt,** and stir over *low heat* until well blended.
10. Return chicken and peppers to sauce and warm thoroughly. Adjust seasonings. Cover until ready to serve.

To Serve: Place on a warm serving platter and garnish with dollops of yogurt, if desired. The pungent sauce is delicious served over plain Steamed Brown Rice (see page 174). Cabbage, Apple and Raisin Slaw (page 67) is a wonderful accompaniment.

Per serving: 177 calories; 24.8 gm protein; 3.7 gm fat; 11.2 gm carbohydrate; 3 gm fibre; 92 mg cholesterol; 3.8 mg iron; 79 mg sodium; 75 mg calcium; 277 mg phosphorus; 4166 IU Vitamin A; 0.18 mg thiamine; 0.43 mg riboflavin; 59 mg Vitamin C; 628 mg potassium; 0.23 mg zinc; 8.4 mg niacin; 72 mcg Vitamin B_6; 0 mcg Vitamin B_{12}; 11 mcg folic acid

* May be prepared several hours ahead of time through step 6.
** You may omit yogurt entirely and serve chicken after sauce has been thickened with cornflour or flour.

Chicken and Vegetables Poached in White Wine

Serves: 4 (¼ chicken = 1 serving)

This chicken dish is an old favourite of the French in Provence—simple country cooking for a cold winter evening.

3 our Stock Cubes (see page 21), or 3 tablespoons white wine
2 carrots, chopped
1 medium onion, chopped
1 small turnip, chopped
1 leek (white part only), chopped
1 1-kg/2-lb chicken, quartered, skinned, and wing tips and all visible fat removed
1 teaspoon low-sodium vegetable seasoning (see page 24)

Freshly ground white or green peppercorns
250–350 ml/8–12 fl oz dry white wine or dry vermouth
450 ml/¾ pint our Chicken Stock (see page 22)
1 bouquet garni (½ teaspoon thyme, 1 bay leaf, 4 sprigs parsley, 4 celery leaves, 1 crushed clove garlic, ½ teaspoon tarragon, few grains crushed red pepper)

1. Melt stock cubes in flameproof casserole. Add chopped vegetables. Cook slowly in covered casserole for about 10 minutes, stirring frequently. *Do not allow to brown.*

2. Season chicken quarters with vegetable seasoning and freshly ground pepper.

3. Spread chicken over and around cooked vegetables. (Arrange white meat on top, as it cooks more rapidly.)

4. Add wine and chicken stock to barely cover.

5. Bury bouquet garni in vegetables; bring to simmering point. Taste, and adjust seasonings.

6. Cover casserole and simmer slowly in a preheated 160°C, 325°F, Gas Mark 3 oven about 25 to 35 minutes. When done, meat should feel tender when pressed with a fork and juices should run clear yellow, not pink. *Do not overcook.*

7. Remove bouquet garni. Taste, and adjust seasonings again with herbs or vegetable seasoning.

To Serve: Take casserole to table (or transfer chicken to a heated tureen). Serve a scoop of Steamed Brown Rice (see page 174) in individual shallow soup dishes with chicken, vegetables and stock. To complete the meal, serve crusty whole wheat bread or rolls, a salad, and a hot fruit compote (page 182 or 183).

Per serving: 234 calories; 24.5 gm protein; 3.3 gm fat; 13.7 gm carbohydrate; 2.3 gm fibre; 92 mg cholesterol; 2.6 mg iron; 97 mg sodium; 57 mg calcium; 272 mg phosphorus; 4387 IU Vitamin A; 0.14 mg thiamine; 0.33 mg riboflavin; 10 mg Vitamin C; 614 mg potassium; 0.26 mg zinc; 7.8 mg niacin; 124 mcg Vitamin B_6; 0 mcg Vitamin B_{12}; 12 mcg folic acid

Stuffed Roast Chicken

(Its Beauty Is Not Only Skin Deep)

Serves: 4 (¼ chicken with stuffing = 1 serving)

This is the only chicken recipe in this book in which the skin is not removed. I use a chicken with all visible fat removed and stuff the bird under the skin. The skin keeps the stuffing and the chicken moist and may be removed before serving or eating.

1 1-kg/2-lb chicken, split; wing tips, excess skin and all visible fat removed
Juice of ½ lemon
1 teaspoon herbes de Provence
1 small onion, finely chopped
1 clove garlic, or ½ teaspoon garlic powder
1 large shallot, or 2 spring onions finely chopped
2 our Stock Cubes, melted (see page 21)
450 g/1 lb courgettes, grated and squeezed dry, or 1 275g /10-oz packet chopped

spinach, defrosted and squeezed dry
100 g/4 oz skim-milk ricotta cheese
1 size 1 extra-large egg white
1 teaspoon low-sodium vegetable seasoning (see page 24)
Few grains crushed red pepper
Freshly ground nutmeg
2 tablespoons grated Sap Sago cheese, toasted (see page 16)
Hungarian paprika

Watercress and tiny tomatoes for garnish

1. Using kitchen shears and your fingers, loosen chicken skin, forming pockets to hold the stuffing.

2. Sprinkle chicken under skin with lemon juice and herbs. Marinate in refrigerator several hours or overnight.

3. *To make stuffing:* Sauté onion, garlic and shallot in stock cubes until transparent. Add courgettes and sauté 5 minutes more. Cool slightly.

4. Blend cheese in blender or food processor. Add egg white, vegetable seasoning, crushed red pepper, nutmeg and Sap Sago cheese and blend. Stir in courgette mixture and blend well.

*5. Stuff pockets formed between skin and body of chicken with courgette cheese mixture and secure with skewers.

6. Place chicken in an attractive shallow roasting dish, skin-side-up. Sprinkle with Hungarian paprika.

7. Roast in a preheated 230°C, 450°F, Gas Mark 8 oven for 10 minutes; lower oven to 190°C, 375°F, Gas Mark 5 and continue to roast for 45 to 60 minutes, or until done.

8. Cut chicken into quarters. (Remove skin if desired and sprinkle stuffing with Hungarian paprika.)

To Serve: Garnish with watercress and tomatoes, serve immediately.

Variations: Sometimes I just use small chicken breasts for stuffing, particularly if I'm serving 8 or more guests. I also vary the stuffing occasionally, sometimes using a favourite bread stuffing.

Per serving: 324 calories; 48.3 gm protein; 6.5 gm fat; 11 gm carbohydrate; 4.4 gm fibre; 113 mg cholesterol; 4.8 mg iron; 146 mg sodium; 174 mg calcium; 453 mg phosphorus; 916 IU Vitamin A; 0.19 mg thiamine; 0.53 mg riboflavin; 29 mg Vitamin C; 861 mg potassium; 0.47 mg zinc; 16.5 mg niacin; 40 mcg Vitamin B$_6$; 0.09 mcg Vitamin B$_{12}$; 7 mcg folic acid

Quick and Colourful Microwaved Chicken Orientale

Serves: 6 (100 g/4 oz cooked chicken = 1 serving)

This dish has appeal because of its relatively short preparation time and low calorie content—to say nothing of its colourful appearance.

* May be prepared several hours ahead through step 5.

100 g/4 oz canned unsweetened pineapple chunks or crushed pineapple, drained (reserve juice)

4 tablespoons drained pineapple juice

2 tablespoons mild soy sauce

2 tablespoons dry sherry

2 tablespoons brown rice vinegar

2–3 tablespoons salt-free Dijon mustard with herbs

1 teaspoon ground ginger

1 clove garlic, finely chopped

1 1.4-kg/3-lb frying chicken, skinned, defatted, wing tips removed, and cut in serving pieces, or 3 skinned, defatted, and halved chicken breasts

225 g/8 oz mushrooms, washed and sliced

1 green pepper, seeded, cut in 2.5 cm/1 inch cubes

1 red pepper, seeded, cut in 2.5 cm/1 inch cubes

1 2.5-g/7½-oz can bamboo shoots, drained

1 275-g/10-oz packet frozen broccoli florets, defrosted

100 g/4 oz spring onions, diagonally sliced

1. Combine drained pineapple, pineapple juice, soy sauce, sherry, vinegar, mustard, ginger and garlic in a large glass measuring jug or a glass bowl. Cook in microwave oven on high until mixture boils. Taste and adjust seasonings.

2. Arrange chicken in a shallow oval or rectangular glass or ceramic baking dish. (Place thick side of breast toward edge of dish.)

*3. Pour sauce over chicken, coating all sides.

4. Cover with greaseproof paper and cook in microwave on high for 10 minutes.

5. Turn chicken over. Add mushrooms and green and red pepper cubes, and cook on high 10 additional minutes. Baste chicken with sauce.

6. Add bamboo shoots and defrosted broccoli florets. Cook 3 additional minutes on high, or until chicken is cooked through.

To Serve: Sprinkle with sliced spring onions and serve with Steamed Brown Rice (page 174).

Variations: Boneless chicken breasts cut in 5-cm/2-inch strips may be substituted for whole breasts. In this case, reduce cooking time in step 4 to 5 minutes.

---

* May be prepared several hours ahead of time through step 3.

If desired, you may thicken sauce by mixing 2 tablespoons cornflour with 120 ml/4 fl oz drained pineapple juice and add to mixture in step 6.

Per serving: 206 calories; 30.3 gm protein; 2.23 gm fat; 14.87 gm carbohydrate; 2.5 gm fibre; 66 mg cholesterol; 2.1 mg iron; 287 mg sodium; 64 mg calcium; 311 mg phosphorus; 2429 IU Vitamin A; 0.25 mg thiamine; 0.34 mg riboflavin; 100 mg Vitamin C; 811 mg potassium; 0.97 mg zinc; 14.5 mg niacin; 734 mcg Vitamin B_6; 0.43 mcg Vitamin B_{12}; 14 mcg folic acid

Turkey Piccata

Serves: 6 (75 g/3 oz cooked turkey = 1 serving)

Turkey is no longer just associated with Christmas, it is a popular meat used in a variety of ways. Turkey breast slices nicely into escalopes that have a relatively short cooking time. Be careful not to over-cook them, they'll become dry and tough.

25 g/1 oz unbleached flour
100 g/4 oz our Seasoned
   Breadcrumbs (see page 25)
Freshly ground pepper
½ teaspoon Hungarian
   paprika
6 thin turkey fillets (675 g/1¼
   lb turkey breast), flattened
   (see page 108)

250 ml/8 fl oz buttermilk,
   strained of fat
6 thin lemon slices
1 tablespoon capers, rinsed
   and drained
120 ml/4 fl oz lemon juice

Watercress or parsley sprigs
   for garnish

1. Combine flour, breadcrumbs, pepper and paprika.
2. Dip turkey fillets in buttermilk, then breadcrumb mixture.
3. Arrange on nonstick baking dish and bake in a preheated 190°C, 375°F, Gas Mark 5 oven for 30 minutes.
4. Place lemon slices and capers in the lemon juice and bring to the boil.

To Serve: Remove browned turkey to a heated platter; place a lemon slice on each fillet; drizzle with lemon juice and capers. Garnish with sprigs of watercress or parsley and serve immediately. To complete the meal, serve with penne (a tubular macaroni) with Fresh Tomato Sauce with Fresh Basil (page 169) and steamed asparagus. Strawberry Yogurt Sorbet (page 195) would be a refreshing finish.

Variation: These same flattened turkey fillets can be seasoned with lemon juice and low-sodium vegetable seasoning, cooked on a nonstick griddle, and served as a turkey burger on a whole wheat bun.

Per serving: 293 calories; 39.6 gm protein; 7.5 gm fat; 15.4 gm carbohydrate; 0.4 gm fibre; 102 mg cholesterol; 2.7 mg iron; 246 mg sodium; 68 mg calcium; 346 mg phosphorus; 278 IU Vitamin A; 0.13 mg thiamine; 0.31 mg riboflavin; 14 mg Vitamin C; 540 mg potassium; 2.50 mg zinc; 9.3 mg niacin; 16 mcg Vitamin B$_6$; 0 mcg Vitamin B$_{12}$; 11 mcg folic acid

Turkey Curry

(When You're in a Hurry)

Serves: 12

2 large onions, finely chopped
2 celery stalks, thinly sliced
4 tablespoons dry white wine
1 kg/2 lb mushrooms, quartered or sliced
Juice ½ lemon
2 cloves garlic, finely chopped
2 apples, peeled, cored and diced
3 tablespoons flour

1 tablespoon curry powder, or to taste
750 ml/1¼ pints our Chicken Stock (see page 22) or Turkey Stock (see page 47), or leftover turkey gravy
1.5 kg/3 lb cooked turkey breast, diced
2 tablespoons chopped fresh parsley

1. Sauté onions and celery in white wine until transparent and tender.

2. Add mushrooms, lemon juice and garlic. Cook a few minutes, then add apples, flour and curry; stir to combine. Add stock and continue to cook, stirring constantly, until sauce coats the spoon (15 to 20 minutes).

3. Add diced turkey and parsley. Simmer until heated through. Taste, and adjust seasonings.

4. May be frozen; if so, omit apples. May also be prepared a day ahead and reheated.

To Serve: Serve curried turkey in a ring of Steamed Brown Rice (page 174), with Raita (page 213) and several of the following condiments: chopped spring onion, chopped green pepper, toasted horseradish,* plumped raisins or currants (or add directly to the curry), chutney, chopped egg whites, and sliced bananas in orange juice.

*Helpful Hint: *To make toasted horseradish,* grate raw horseradish root and place on a baking sheet in a 190°C, 375°F, Gas Mark 5 oven until golden brown. You will be pleasantly surprised at the transformation in its taste—from sharp to scrumptious. The street vendors in Vienna, Austria, use this as a topping for (you should excuse the expression) knockwurst.

Per serving: 204 calories; 25.7 gm protein; 4.7 gm fat; 13.9 gm carbohydrate; 3.2 gm fibre; 62 mg cholesterol; 2.4 mg iron; 113 mg sodium; 27 mg calcium; 284 mg phosphorus; 220 IU Vitamin A; 0.14 mg thiamine; 0.5 mg riboflavin; 12 mg Vitamin C; 691 mg potassium; 1.57 mg zinc; 8.8 mg niacin; 138 mcg Vitamin B_6; 0 mcg Vitamin B_{12}; 32 mcg folic acid

Turkey Kebabs

Serves: 12 (75 g/3 oz cooked turkey = 1 serving)

The turkey chunks for these kebabs should be marinated overnight before they are used so that they absorb the flavour of the marinade. This dish looks beautiful—without a lot of fuss and work.

1 onion, cut in 2.5-cm/1-inch cubes
1 stalk celery with leaves, chopped
1 carrot, chopped
5 cloves garlic, finely chopped
3 bay leaves, crumbled
2 teaspoons mixed thyme, marjoram, fennel, and savory
175 ml/6 fl oz dry red wine
Juice and rind of 1 lemon
175 ml/6 fl oz our Turkey Stock (see page 47) or Chicken Stock (see page 22)

1 1.5–1.75-kg/4–5-lb turkey breast, boned and cut in chunks
3 red peppers, seeded and cut in eighths
3 green peppers, seeded and cut in eighths
450 g/1 lb mushrooms, wiped clean and stalks removed

12 bamboo skewers

1. Combine all ingredients except turkey, peppers and mushrooms. Pour over turkey and marinate overnight in refrigerator.

2. Drain turkey chunks, reserving marinade, and thread onto skewers alternating with pepper pieces and mushrooms.

3. Brush kebabs with marinade and grill until crispy on all sides, about 10 minutes.

To Serve: Serve on a bed of Steamed Brown Rice (page 174) with steamed green beans and a wedge of fresh pineapple.

Per serving: 265 calories; 37.5 gm protein; 4.1 gm fat; 8.5 gm carbohydrate; 2.4 gm fibre; 100 mg cholesterol; 2.7 mg iron; 127 mg sodium; 39 mg calcium; 415 mg phosphorus; 2062 IU Vitamin A; 0.16 mg thiamine; 0.41 mg riboflavin; 89 mg Vitamin C; 878 mg potassium; 2.8 mg zinc; 16.4 mg niacin; 144 mcg Vitamin B_6; 0 mcg Vitamin B_{12}; 25 mcg folic acid

Turkey Tonnato

(Roast Turkey with Tuna Sauce)

Serves: 8 (75 g/3 oz cooked turkey = 1 serving)

Turkey tonnato is a low-cholesterol adaptation of the traditional Italian vitello tonnato (veal with tuna sauce). It may be served as a beautiful main course on a cold buffet or as an elegant appetizer. The meat must be roasted a day ahead.

1 200-g/7-oz can salt-free tuna in water, well drained	turkey breast, roasted and chilled overnight
150 ml/¼ pint nonfat yogurt	
2 tablespoons fresh lemon juice	1 bunch watercress, washed and trimmed, for serving and garnish
1 teaspoon capers, drained and rinsed	
15 g/½ oz watercress leaves, washed	1 tablespoon capers, rinsed and drained, for garnish
1 1.25–1.5-kg/2½–3½-lb	Tiny tomatoes for garnish
	Radish roses for garnish

1. *To make sauce:* Purée drained tuna in a blender or food processor.

2. Add yogurt gradually while machine is in motion. Scrape down bowl and blend thoroughly.

3. Add lemon juice, capers and watercress. Process until flecks of green appear.

4. Chill sauce until serving time. Sauce may be prepared a day ahead.

5. Just before serving time, skin chilled turkey breast and slice into 5-mm/¼-inch slices.

To Serve: Arrange overlapping turkey slices on a bed of watercress. Spoon sauce over turkey slices, sprinkle with capers, and garnish with tomatoes and radish roses. When served as a main course, a cold rice salad makes a lovely accompaniment.

Per serving: 200 calories; 37.5 gm protein; 3.7 gm fat; 1.6 gm carbohydrate; 0 gm fibre; 85 mg cholesterol; 1.5 mg iron; 96 mg sodium; 45 mg calcium; 288 mg phosphorus; 289 IU Vitamin A; 0.07 mg thiamine; 0.2 mg riboflavin; 4 mg Vitamin C; 454 mg potassium; 1.9 mg zinc; 13.5 mg niacin; 2 mcg Vitamin B_6; 0 mcg Vitamin B_{12}; 7 mcg folic acid

RED MEAT

Served Rarely

Marinated Steak

Marinated Beef and Vegetable Salad

Old-Fashioned Baked Meat Loaf

Stuffed Cabbage Loaf

Hearty Steak with Peppers

Hamburgers are an American fast-food favourite. Yet few people realize that over 50 percent of the calories in the average hamburger are derived from fat.

Limit your red meat to a 100 g/4 oz serving *no more than once a week*. Pork and lamb are to be limited also because of their high fat and cholesterol contents. Veal, comparable to beef in cholesterol because it is milk-fed, but half as high in fat because it is not old enough to be marbled, should also be eaten sparingly. Ham should also be avoided, not only because of its fat and cholesterol content, but because of its high sodium content resulting from processing. Beef, of course, is high in both cholesterol and fat.

In order to minimize your intake of fat and cholesterol when preparing red meat, use the leaner cuts of beef such as top rump steak and topside. I particularly recommend flank steak because of its lack of marbling and the ease with which you can remove its visible fat.

Marinated Steak

Serves: 6 (75 g/3 oz cooked beef = 1 serving)

2 tablespoons mild soy sauce
1 teaspoon powdered ginger
   or grated fresh ginger root
2 tablespoons frozen
   unsweetened pineapple
   juice concentrate
4 spring onions, diced
1 teaspoon garlic powder,
   or 2 cloves garlic, crushed

675 g/1½ lb top rump steak
   (all visible fat removed),
   scored lightly

Watercress or parsley sprigs
and 175 g/6 oz fresh
pineapple chunks for
garnish

1. Combine the first 5 ingredients, place in a plastic bag. Add steak and marinate 4 to 6 hours. Turn meat in marinade from time to time.
2. Remove meat from marinade and grill 5 minutes on each side, or to personal taste.
3. Cut *diagonally* into 1-cm/½-inch slices for serving.

To Serve: Place steak slices on a warm platter, garnish with watercress or chopped parsley, and sprinkle pineapple chunks over meat. Accompany with Larry's Crispy Potatoes (page 158) and Courgette Tian (page 164).

Per serving: 172 calories; 25 gm protein; 6.5 gm fat; 1.1 gm carbohydrate; 0.2 gm fibre; 70 mg cholesterol; 3.7 mg iron; 243 mg sodium; 16 mg calcium; 281 mg phosphorus; 13 IU Vitamin A; 0.1 mg thiamine; 0.35 mg riboflavin; 0 mg Vitamin C; 403 mg potassium; 0 mg zinc; 6.1 mg niacin; 0 mcg Vitamin B_6; 0 mcg Vitamin B_{12}; 0 mcg folic acid

Marinated Beef and Vegetable Salad

Serves: 12

1 560-g/20-oz packet frozen cut green beans

1 275-g/10-oz packet frozen artichoke hearts, or 1 240-g/8½ oz can quartered artichoke hearts

450–675 g/1–1½ lb top rump steak* (all visible fat removed), prepared and cooked as in Marinated Steak (see page 131) and cooled

1 215-g/7½-oz can hearts of palm, cut in 10-cm/4-inch circles

675 g/1½ lb mushrooms, stalks removed and sliced

4 spring onions, chopped

1½ tablespoons red wine vinegar

5 tablespoons our Chicken Stock (see page 22)

2 tablespoons lemon juice

4 tablespoons nonfat yogurt

2 tablespoons salt-free Dijon mustard

Freshly ground pepper

1 lettuce, rinsed and dried, for serving

2 ripe tomatoes, peeled, seeded and sliced, for garnish

3 tablespoons finely chopped fresh parsley for garnish

1. Cook beans as directed on packet. Drain and chill.
2. Cook artichoke hearts as directed on packet. Drain and chill.
3. Slice cooked steak across the grain into 5-mm/¼-inch slices.
4. Combine meat with beans, artichoke hearts, hearts of palm, mushrooms and spring onions in a salad bowl.

**5. *To make salad dressing:* Shake the next 6 ingredients in a screwtop jar until thoroughly blended.

6. Pour just enough salad dressing on salad to coat ingredients. Toss lightly and marinate 1 hour.

To Serve: Pile on a lettuce-lined platter or bowl. Arrange tomatoes around mixture and sprinkle with chopped parsley.

Variation: Leftover roast chicken may be substituted for steak. For a delicious cold pasta salad, add 100 g/4 oz of chilled cooked pasta spirals.

---

* May also be prepared from leftover steak that has been frozen.
** May be prepared through step 5 the day before.

Per serving: 118 calories; 14.9 gm protein; 3.1 gm fat; 8.8 gm carbohydrate; 2.5 gm fibre; 35 mg cholesterol; 2.5 mg iron; 46 mg sodium; 42 mg calcium; 156 mg phosphorus; 518 IU Vitamin A; 0.14 mg thiamine; 0.45 mg riboflavin; 14 mg Vitamin C; 559 mg potassium; 0.04 mg zinc; 4.7 mg niacin; 89 mcg Vitamin B_6; 0 mcg Vitamin B_{12}; 15 mcg folic acid

Old-Fashioned Baked Meat Loaf

Serves: 6 (2 slices = 1 serving)

1 carrot, cut in 4 pieces
1 onion, cut in 4 pieces
1 stalk celery, cut in 4 pieces
15 g/½ oz fresh parsley
1 large clove garlic
2 slices whole wheat or rye bread, quartered

2 egg whites
120 ml/4 fl oz nonfat milk
450 g/1 lb minced top rump steak or very lean minced beef
Freshly ground pepper

1. Place carrot, onion, celery and parsley in food processor or blender. Process until chopped.
2. While food processor is in motion, add garlic clove to vegetable mixture. Continue to process until finely chopped. Scrape down sides of bowl from time to time.
3. Add bread and process until crumbled.
4. Add egg whites and milk and process.
5. Place minced meat in a mixing bowl and add vegetable mixture. Sprinkle with ground pepper.
6. Blend gently with a fork until mixture is well blended. (Do not overmix; it will make the meat loaf tough.)
7. Shape into a loaf in a 20-cm/8-inch square glass baking dish and bake in a preheated 180°C, 350°F, Gas Mark 4 oven for 50 to 60 minutes.

To Serve: Serve with baked potatoes and tomato halves.

Per serving: 150 calories; 18.6 gm protein; 4 gm fat; 8.8 gm carbohydrate; 1.1 gm fibre; 47 mg cholesterol; 2.8 mg iron; 96 mg sodium; 54 mg calcium; 113 mg phosphorus; 1686 IU Vitamin A; 0.7 mg thiamine; 0.33 mg riboflavin; 9 mg Vitamin C; 353 mg potassium; 0.2 mg zinc; 2.6 mg niacin; 66 mcg Vitamin B_6; 0.8 mcg Vitamin B_{12}; 9 mcg folic acid

Stuffed Cabbage Loaf

Serves: 8 (2 slices = 1 serving)

For those of you who find making traditional stuffed cabbage a chore, here is an easy version that is superdelicious. It may be made ahead of time and frozen before or after baking. In choosing your cabbage, look for firm, green, crisp ones.

1 medium green cabbage, quartered and cored
1 medium onion, finely chopped
1 clove garlic, crushed
1 *thin slice* peeled ginger root, finely chopped
15 g/½ oz fresh parsley, finely chopped
1 teaspoon low-sodium vegetable seasoning (see page 24)
Freshly ground pepper
2 egg whites
3 slices whole wheat bread,

pulled into fine crumbs
150 ml/¼ pint nonfat milk
500 g/1¼ lb very lean minced beef*
165 g/5½ oz Steamed Brown Rice (see page 174)
1 450-g/16-oz can salt-free tomato sauce
1 medium onion, chopped
4 tablespoons defrosted frozen unsweetened apple juice concentrate

Chopped fresh parsley for garnish

1. Cover cabbage with boiling water and cook 10 minutes. *Drain well.*
2. Combine onion, garlic, ginger root, parsley, vegetable seasoning, pepper and egg whites in a large bowl. Mix well.
3. Soak breadcrumbs in milk until milk is absorbed. Combine with onion mixture.
4. Add minced meat and brown rice to onion mixture. Stir lightly with a fork (or hands) until blended. *Do not overmix.*
5. Combine tomato sauce with chopped onion and apple juice concentrate.
6. Lightly spray a glass 23 × 13-cm/9 × 5-inch loaf tin with nonstick spray. Fill loaf tin with alternate layers of meat mixture, cabbage leaves, and 3 tablespoons of tomato sauce mixture. Begin and end with meat.

* You may substitute minced turkey for the minced lean beef.

7. Pour remaining tomato sauce over top of meat.

8. Bake in a preheated 190°C, 375°F, Gas Mark 5 oven for about 1 hour.

To Serve: Unmould meat loaf on a heated platter, sprinkle with additional chopped parsley, and surround with steamed new potatoes and frozen petits pois, or, if you're watching calories, substitute carrots or asparagus for the potatoes. To complete the meal, serve with a crisp mixed green salad, apple sauce, and Strawberry Yogurt Sorbet (page 195) for dessert.

Per serving: 250 calories; 20 gm protein; 4.7 gm fat; 27.1 gm carbohydrate; 3.9 gm fibre; 44 mg cholesterol; 3.3 mg iron; 96 mg sodium; 96 mg calcium; 160 mg phosphorus; 1106 IU Vitamin A; 0.15 thiamine; 0.25 mg riboflavin; 44 mg Vitamin C; 476 mg potassium; 0.46 mg zinc; 3.5 mg niacin; 160 mcg Vitamin B_6; 0.09 mcg Vitamin B_{12}; 32 mcg folic acid

Hearty Steak with Peppers

Serves: 8

3 tablespoons burgundy wine
675 g/1½ lb top rump steak
    (all visible fat removed),
    cut in 2.5-cm/1-inch cubes
1 tablespoon unbleached flour
2 celery stalks with leaves,
    sliced
1 onion, sliced
2 cloves garlic, crushed
120 ml/4 fl oz our Vegetable

Stock (see page 49) or
    water
1 teaspoon low-sodium
    vegetable seasoning (see
    page 24)
Few grains crushed red pepper
1 green pepper, seeded and
    cut in 2.5-cm/1-inch cubes
1 red pepper, seeded and cut
    in 2.5-cm/1-inch cubes

1. Heat burgundy in a sauté pan; when boiling, add steak and sauté until brown.

2. Add flour to steak mixture and stir.

3. Add celery, onion, garlic and stock or water; stir and simmer 15 minutes covered.

4. Add vegetable seasoning, crushed red pepper, and green and red pepper cubes. Cover and cook 15 additional minutes, or until meat is tender.

To Serve: Serve over Steamed Brown Rice (page 174).

Per serving: 135 calories; 18.1 gm protein; 4.3 gm fat; 4.8 gm carbohydrate; 1 gm fibre; 53 mg cholesterol; 2.7 mg iron; 47 mg sodium; 24 mg calcium; 108 mg phosphorus; 709 IU Vitamin A; 0.08 mg thiamine; 0.16 mg riboflavin; 44 mg Vitamin C; 333 mg potassium; 0.08 mg zinc; 2.9 mg niacin; 62 mcg Vitamin B_6; 0 mcg Vitamin B_{12}; 6 mcg folic acid

✌ Casseroles ❧

Hungarian Stuffed Cabbage
Broad Bean Peasant Casserole
Judith's Fish Goulash
Noodle Lasagna
Sally's Vegetarian Lasagna

Turkey Noodle Casserole
Red and Green Peppers Stuffed
  with Vegetables
Baked Potatoes Provençale

Casseroles are especially desirable because we can minimize the animal protein content of the meal with the addition of vegetables, rice, pasta and the like. We use the animal protein as a seasoning in the casserole, or in some cases we eliminate it completely.

Two questions that were frequently asked in my classes were: Can I make it ahead of time? Can I freeze it? Many of the casserole dishes that follow answer these needs. On that rainy day or on one when you have much energy that needs to be directed, try a few and put them away in the freezer for those unexpected but welcome guests that frequent every happy home.

If frozen, the casserole should be removed from the freezer and placed in the refrigerator the night before, defrosted at room temperature for 4 to 6 hours (depending on the casserole), and then baked at the oven temperature and baking time in the recipe. (If you don't have time to bring it to room temperature, place in a *cold* oven and double the baking time.)

Hungarian Stuffed Cabbage

Serves 6: (2 cabbage rolls = 1 serving)

1 large green cabbage
1 small onion, grated
1 shallot, finely chopped
2 egg whites
1 clove garlic, finely chopped
1 carrot, grated
15 g/½ oz fresh parsley, chopped
90 g/3½ oz brown rice, partially cooked in 250 ml/8 fl oz our Chicken Stock (see page 22) for 25 minutes
225 g/8 oz extra lean minced beef
15 g/½ oz breadcrumbs
1 teaspoon low-sodium vegetable seasoning (see page 24)
4 tablespoons salt-free tomato juice (optional)
100 g/4 oz frozen peas
1 450-g/16-oz can tomato sauce, or can tomatoes, puréed
80 ml/3 fl oz frozen unsweetened apple or pineapple juice concentrate
½ teaspoon Hungarian paprika
Chopped fresh parsley for garnish

1. Core the cabbage and cook it in boiling water until barely tender. Drain and separate 12 large leaves and trim stalks.
2. Combine onion, shallot, egg whites, garlic, carrot and parsley until thoroughly blended.
3. Combine onion mixture with rice, minced beef, breadcrumbs, vegetable seasoning and tomato juice, using a fork to mix. Add frozen peas.
4. Place a twelfth of the mixture in each cabbage leaf and roll up, tucking in sides. Makes 12 rolls.
5. Shred remaining cabbage; sprinkle in bottom of a casserole.
6. Place cabbage rolls in casserole seam-side down, packing tightly.
7. Combine tomato sauce, or puréed tomatoes, juice concentrate and paprika.
8. Pour sauce over cabbage rolls. Cook, covered, in a preheated 160°C, 325°F, Gas Mark 3 oven for 2 hours.*
9. This recipe may be prepared a day before serving and reheated, or it may be frozen for future use. Double the recipe, use one casserole, freeze the other. *To Reheat:* Leave at room temperature for several hours and cook, covered, in 160°C,

325°F, Gas Mark 3 oven for 1 hour or until thoroughtly heated.
To Serve: Garnish with chopped parsley and serve with noodle pudding and steamed carrots.

*Helpful Hint: Place casserole on a baking sheet to collect the drips!

Per serving: 300 calories; 18.8 gm protein; 3.5 gm fat; 43.3 gm carbohydrate; 5.5 gm fibre; 36 mg cholesterol; 3.6 mg iron; 105 mg sodium; 91 mg calcium; 167 mg phosphorus; 3302 IU Vitamin A; 0.22 mg thiamine; 0.25 mg riboflavin; 65 mg Vitamin C; 552 mg potassium; 0.47 mg zinc; 3.9 mg niacin; 215 mcg Vitamin B_6; 0.01 Vitamin B_{12}; 41 mcg folic acid

Broad Bean Peasant Casserole

Serves: 8–10

3 our Stock Cubes (see page 21)
2 large onions, thinly sliced
3 cloves garlic, finely chopped
6 ripe tomatoes, peeled, seeded and chopped, or 1 800-g/28-oz can tomatoes
120 ml/4 fl oz tomato purée (if using fresh tomatoes)
Freshly ground white pepper
1 teaspoon Italian herb seasoning
2 teaspoons dried savory,

crushed, or 2 tablespoons fresh savory, chopped
1 bay leaf
1.4 kg/3 lb broad beans, shelled
1 teaspoon crushed red pepper
450 g/1 lb beef knuckle bones, fat removed
120 ml/4 fl oz our Chicken Stock (see page 22) optional

1. Melt stock cubes in a large nonstick frying pan. Add onions and garlic, and cook, covered, over low heat about 15 minutes, or until transparent and lightly browned. Stir from time to time.
2. Add chopped tomatoes, purée, pepper, herb seasoning, savory and bay leaf. Simmer a few minutes.
3. Put tomato mixture in a covered casserole. Add beans, crushed red pepper and bones.
*4. Blend mixture and cover tightly.
5. Place in a preheated 180°C, 350°F, Gas Mark 4 oven and bake 45 to 60 minutes, or until beans are tender. If the mixture seems too dry, add chicken stock.

*May be prepared the day before through step 4.

6. Remove bones before serving.

To Serve: This casserole may be served as a main dish with steamed vegetables and brown rice or as an accompaniment to a hot or cold chicken dish.

Per serving: 136 calories; 9.5 gm protein; 0.9 gm fat; 25.2 gm carbohydrate; 5.1 gm fibre; 0 mg cholesterol; 4.2 mg iron; 66 mg sodium; 83 mg calcium; 189 mg phosphorus; 3240 IU Vitamin A; 0.35 mg thiamine; 0.24 mg riboflavin; 77 mg Vitamin C; 845 mg potassium; 0.34 mg zinc; 2.6 mg niacin; 106 mcg Vitamin B$_6$; 0 mcg Vitamin B$_{12}$; 14 mcg folic acid

Fish Goulash

Serves: 4

2 tablespoons red or white wine
1 medium onion, chopped
1 clove garlic, crushed
3 ripe tomatoes, peeled, seeded, and quartered
3 small courgettes, sliced
450 g/1 lb cod, cut into 2.5-cm/1-inch cubes
300 g/11 oz Steamed Brown Rice (see page 174)
1 teaspoon low-sodium vegetable seasoning (see page 24)
Freshly ground pepper
Hungarian paprika
5 tablespoons water
3 tablespoons chopped fresh parsley

1. Heat the wine in a saucepan. Add chopped onion and garlic to the wine and sauté until transparent and soft. Add tomatoes and blend.

2. Add, in alternate layers, tomatoes, courgettes, fish and rice. Sprinkle each layer with vegetable seasoning, pepper and paprika.

3. Add water and cover firmly with lid.

4. Allow to cook over medium heat for about 25 to 30 minutes.

To Serve: Sprinkle with freshly chopped parsley and serve.

Variation: The same dish may be prepared using 2 diced potatoes instead of rice and 2 leeks and 3 carrots instead of courgettes and tomatoes.

Per serving: 375 calories; 37.8 gm protein; 7.1 gm fat; 38.1 gm carbohydrate; 7 gm fibre; 57 mg cholesterol; 3.3 mg iron; 135 mg sodium; 107 mg calcium; 457 mg phosphorus; 1808 IU Vitamin A; 0.33 mg thiamine; 0.27 mg riboflavin; 46 mg Vitamin C; 1034 mg potassium; 0.32 mg zinc; 6.5 mg niacin; 153 mcg Vitamin B$_6$; 0 mcg Vitamin B$_{12}$; 18 mcg folic acid

Noodle Lasagna

Serves: 12

450 g/1 lb whole wheat
  noodles
2 large onions, grated
2 cloves garlic, finely chopped
3 tablespoons dry white wine,
  or 3 our Stock Cubes (see
  page 21)
675 g/1½ lb extra-lean
  minced beef
800-g/28-oz can tomatoes
  with basil, crushed
1 350-g/12-oz can salt-free
  tomato paste

2 teaspoons Italian herb
  seasoning, crushed
1 bay leaf
2 450-g/16-oz cartons Weight
  Watchers cottage cheese
2 egg whites
2 275-g/10-oz packets frozen
  chopped spinach, cooked
  and well drained
3 tablespoons grated Sap Sago
  cheese, toasted (see page
  16)

1. Cook noodles in boiling water until tender (about 10 minutes). Drain well.

2. Sauté onions and garlic in wine in nonstick frying pan until transparent. Add minced meat and cook just until it turns pink.

3. Add crushed tomatoes, tomato paste, Italian seasoning and bay leaf. Simmer 15 minutes. Remove bay leaf.

4. Combine cottage cheese and egg whites in blender or food processor and mix well. Add chopped, drained spinach and blend.

5. Spray a 2.75-litre/5-pint casserole with nonstick spray.

*6. Place a layer of sauce, then noodles, then cheese, then sauce. Repeat layering and end with sauce.

7. Sprinkle with toasted Sap Sago cheese and bake in a preheated 180°C, 350°F, Gas Mark 4 oven for 45 minutes.

To Serve: To complete the meal, serve an Italian salad (mixed greens with garbanzo beans), crisp Italian bread, and Raspberry Mousse (page 194) for dessert.

Variations: If your diet allows, 3 tablespoons Parmesan cheese may be used instead of Sap Sago and, if you like, 225 g/8 oz coarsely grated mozzarella cheese may be added between layers.

---

*May be prepared the day before through step 6, or frozen at this point for future use. If frozen, defrost 8 to 10 hours or the night before in the refrigerator before heating.

Per serving: 375 calories; 38.7 gm protein; 9.1 gm fat; 36 gm carbohydrate; 1.3 gm fibre; 54 mg cholesterol; 4.7 mg iron; 328 mg sodium; 164 mg calcium; 190 mg phosphorus; 4440 IU Vitamin A; 0.33 mg thiamine; 0.52 mg riboflavin; 26 mg Vitamin C; 760 mg potassium; 0.23 mg zinc; 5.5 mg niacin; 94 mcg Vitamin B_6; 0.01 mcg Vitamin B_{12}; 10 mcg folic acid

Sally's Vegetarian Lasagna

Serves: 12

1 large onion, chopped
3 cloves garlic, finely chopped
450 g/1 lb unpeeled aubergine, diced
2 courgettes, diced
100 g/4 oz mushrooms, sliced
4 tablespoons salt-free tomato juice
1 800-g/28-oz can tomatoes
120 ml/4 fl oz dry red wine
2 carrots, grated
3 tablespoons finely chopped fresh parsley
2 teaspoons dried oregano, crushed, or 4 teaspoons fresh oregano

1 teaspoon dried basil, crushed, or 2 teaspoons fresh basil
Freshly ground pepper
9 whole wheat lasagna sheets
450 g/1 lb skim milk ricotta cheese
2 egg whites
3 tablespoons chopped fresh parsley
3 tablespoons grated Sap Sago cheese, toasted (see page 16)

1. Cook onion, garlic, aubergine, courgettes and mushrooms for 15 minutes in tomato juice.

2. Add tomatoes, wine, carrots, parsley, oregano, basil and ground pepper. Bring to the boil and simmer for 30 minutes, stirring occasionally.

3. Cook, rinse and drain lasagna according to manufacturer's directions.*

4. Process cheese in blender or food processor until creamy. Add egg whites and chopped parsley and process briefly.

5. Spray a 23 × 33-cm/9 × 13-inch baking dish with nonstick spray. Spread a layer of vegetable sauce in dish, lay 3 sheets of lasagna lengthwise over sauce, and place 4 dollops of cheese on each sheet.

**6. Proceed with a second layer of sauce, lasagna and cheese, and a third layer of the same, ending with sauce.

7. Sprinkle with Sap Sago cheese.

8. Place dish on a baking sheet to catch those bothersome drips, and bake in a preheated 180°C, 350°F, Gas Mark 4 oven for 45 minutes.

9. Let stand 10 minutes before serving so that lasagna holds its shape.

To Serve: Vegetarian Lasagna may be served with a salad and crisp whole wheat garlic toast (page 15). A wedge of seasonal melon with lime would be an excellent dessert.

Variations: If your diet allows, grated Parmesan cheese may be used instead of Sap Sago, and grated skim-milk mozzarella may be sprinkled on the dollops of ricotta cheese in each layer (use 225 g/8 oz mozzarella in all).

*Helpful Hint: Add lasagna one at a time to boiling water, so that you do not disturb boil and sheets do not stick together.

Per serving: 250 calories; 19.1 gm protein; 2.6 gm fat; 38.2 gm carbohydrate; 2.9 gm fibre; 7 mg cholesterol; 2.2 mg iron; 200 mg sodium; 62 mg calcium; 66 mg phosphorus; 2417 IU Vitamin A; 0.26 mg thiamine; 0.27 mg riboflavin; 26 mg Vitamin C; 438 mg potassium; 0.23 mg zinc; 2.6 mg niacin; 117 mcg Vitamin B_6; 0.01 mcg Vitamin B_{12}; 11 mcg folic acid

Turkey Noodle Casserole

Serves: 8

25 g/¼ cup flour
300 ml/½ pint nonfat milk
250 ml/8 fl oz nonfat
   evaporated milk
1 slice onion
½ teaspoon thyme
1 bay leaf
½ teaspoon freshly ground
   white pepper

1 teaspoon low-sodium
   vegetable seasoning (see
   page 24)
2 tablespoons dry sherry or
   sauterne
3 our Stock Cubes, melted
   (see page 21), or 3
   tablespoons our Chicken
   Stock (see page 22)

** May be prepared a day ahead through step 6, or frozen at this point for future use. If frozen, thaw 4 to 6 hours at room temperature and bake 1½ hours at 180°C, 350°F, Gas Mark 4.

100 g/4 oz mushrooms, sliced
3 spring onions, chopped
1 150-g/5-oz can water chestnuts, drained and sliced
100 g/4 oz green pepper, chopped
1 50-g/2-oz jar pimento, drained and chopped.
1 tablespoon mild soy sauce
175 g/6 oz whole wheat noodles, cooked *al dente*
1 bunch fresh broccoli, steamed and coarsely chopped
675 g/1½ lb cooked turkey, cubed
3 tablespoons our Seasoned Breadcrumbs (see page 25)
2 tablespoons grated Sap Sago cheese, toasted (see page 16)

1. *To make sauce:* Mix flour with cold milk. Blend with a wooden spoon or whisk, place over heat, and stir constantly until mixture coats spoon. Add onion, thyme, bay leaf, freshly ground pepper, vegetable seasoning and dry sherry and simmer 5 minutes more to evaporate alcohol. Remove from heat and cover until ready to use.

2. Place stock cubes in a 25-cm/10-inch nonstick frying pan. Add mushrooms and spring onions and sauté 5 minutes.

3. Add water chestnuts, green pepper, pimento and soy sauce. Mix and simmer. Cover and simmer for 2 minutes more.

4. Place cooked, drained noodles on bottom of a 33 × 23 × 5-cm/13 x 9 × 2-inch glass or earthenware casserole that has been sprayed lightly with nonstick spray.

5. Cover noodles with mushroom mixture. Spread chopped broccoli on top of mushroom mixture, reserving some florets for garnish.

*6. Add a layer of diced turkey and top with sauce (onion and bay leaf removed).

7. Sprinkle with seasoned breadcrumbs and toasted Sap Sago cheese.

8. Bake in a preheated 180°C, 350°F, Gas Mark 4 oven for 30 to 35 minutes.

To Serve: Garnish with reserved broccoli florets and serve. Complete the menu with a crispy green salad, hot rolls, and a chilled white wine. Our Festive Fruit Cake (page 183) provides a special ending for a holiday buffet.

* May be prepared the day before through step 6 or frozen at this point for future use.

Variation: If your diet allows, use Parmesan cheese instead of Sap Sago.

Per serving: 316 calories; 31.8 gm protein; 5.2 gm fat; 32.7 gm carbohydrate; 2.4 gm fibre; 64 mg cholesterol; 3 mg iron; 234 mg sodium; 190 mg calcium; 330 mg phosphorus; 1570 IU Vitamin A; 0.25 mg thiamine; 0.49 mg riboflavin; 61 mg Vitamin C; 725 mg potassium; 1.90 mg zinc; 7.1 mg niacin; 82 mcg Vitamin B_6; 0.23 mcg Vitamin B_{12}; 34 mcg folic acid

Red and Green Peppers Stuffed with Vegetables

Serves: 8 (½ stuffed green pepper and ½ stuffed red pepper = 1 serving)

4 red peppers, halved, seeded
4 green peppers, halved, seeded
450 g/1 lb potatoes, cooked and mashed with 120 ml/4 fl oz skim milk
225 g/8 oz skim-milk ricotta cheese
100 g/4 oz onion, chopped
2 cloves garlic, finely chopped
2 shallots, finely chopped
225 g/8 oz courgettes, cooked and chopped
2 large carrots, grated coarsely

1 275-g/10-oz packet chopped broccoli, cooked, or 450 g/1 lb fresh broccoli, steamed and chopped
1 275-g/10-oz packet frozen petits pois
1 teaspoon low-sodium vegetable seasoning (see page 24)
1 teaspoon freshly ground pepper
2 800-g/28-oz cans crushed tomatoes

1. Parboil the peppers for 5 minutes. Drain and cool.
2. Mix mashed potatoes, cheese, onion, garlic, shallots, courgettes, carrots, broccoli and peas.
3. Season to taste with vegetable seasoning and freshly ground pepper.
4. Use mixture to fill pepper halves. Place filled peppers in a baking dish, alternating red and green peppers.
5. Bake in a preheated 190°C, 375°F, Gas Mark 5 oven for 30 to 35 minutes. While baking, heat tomatoes.
6. Spoon tomatoes over stuffed peppers and bake another 10

minutes. May be prepared several hours ahead of time and preheated for serving.

To Serve: These delicious peppers are lovely served with Orange and Onion Salad (page 79) as an accompaniment.

Per serving: 200 calories; 12 gm protein; 3.1 gm fat; 34.9 gm carbohydrate; 7.5 gm fibre; 16 mg cholesterol; 3.3 gm iron; 134 mg sodium; 192 mg calcium; 232 mg phosphorus; 7999 IU Vitamin A; 0.38 mg thiamine; 0.3 mg riboflavin; 240 mg Vitamin C; 1047 mg potassium; 1 mg zinc; 3.4 mg niacin; 475 mcg Vitamin B_6; 0.14 mcg Vitamin B_{12}; 37 mcg folic acid

Baked Potatoes Provençale

Serves:6

2 large onions, thinly sliced
1 clove garlic, finely chopped
½ green pepper, seeded and chopped
3 tablespoons our Chicken Stock (see page 22)
2 tomatoes, peeled, seeded and chopped, or 4 canned tomatoes, drained and chopped
1 kg/2 lb potatoes, peeled and sliced 1-cm/½-inch thick
2 teaspoons thyme, crushed

1 teaspoon low-sodium vegetable seasoning (see page 24)
Freshly ground pepper
450 ml/¾ pint our Chicken Stock
1 tablespoon mild soy sauce
2 tablespoons grated Sap Sago cheese, toasted (see page 16; optional)

Chopped fresh parsley, basil or chives, for garnish

1. Sauté onions, garlic and pepper in the 3 tablespoons chicken stock until softened. Add chopped tomato.
2. Place half the onion mixture in a 23-cm/9-inch square or round flameproof baking dish sprayed with nonstick spray. Next spread on half of the potatoes. Sprinkle potatoes with crushed thyme, vegetable seasoning and freshly ground pepper.
3. Repeat layers.
4. Pour the 450 ml/¾ pint stock and the soy sauce into the dish (just enough to cover potatoes). Cover dish with foil and bake 45 minutes in a preheated 190°C, 375°F, Gas Mark 5 oven.
5. Remove foil and bake 15 minutes more, or until potatoes are tender.
6. Sprinkle with grated Sap Sago cheese and brown potatoes under grill.

To Serve: Garnish with chopped parsley, fresh basil or chives. These potatoes may be served with a variety of main dishes such as Barbecue-Style Grilled Chicken (page 113), Old-Fashioned Baked Meat Loaf (page 133), or Marinated Steak (page 131).

Variation: If your diet permits, Parmesan cheese may be substituted for Sap Sago.

Per serving: 167 calories; 5.9 gm protein; 0.4 gm fat; 36.5 gm carbohydrate; 6.5 gm fibre; 0 mg cholesterol; 2.6 mg iron; 96 mg sodium; 53 mg calcium; 121 mg phosphorus; 530 IU Vitamin A; 0.23 mg thiamine; 0.11 mg riboflavin; 58 mg Vitamin C; 859 mg potassium; 0.27 mg zinc; 2.9 mg niacin; 131 mcg Vitamin B_6; 0 mcg Vitamin B_{12}; 19 mcg folic acid

❦ Vegetables ❧

Vegetables are generally low in calories because of their high water content and low sugar content. They are a good source of carbohydrates, provide a generous supply of a wide variety of nutrients, and are a valuable source of fibre in our diets. Dried peas, beans and lentils are important sources of protein.

When you buy vegetables, your first choice should always be fresh vegetables. Steam or cook them in as little water as possible, and for as short a time as possible. If you happen to have any vegetable liquid left after cooking the vegetables, save it for use in sauces or stocks at a future time. It would be foolish to waste the food value and flavour left in these liquids.

People frequently question the difference in the vitamin and mineral content of canned and frozen vegetables. There is little. However, canned vegetables do contain more sodium because of added salt, and sometimes because of preservatives. Canned vegetables also often contain added sugar. And the high temperatures used in the canning process change their texture, flavour, and nutrient content. So if you cannot buy fresh vegetables, I recommend you use frozen.

One of the main challenges in vegetable cookery is avoiding the boredom that comes from buying the same vegetables and cooking them in the same ways day in and day out. I've discovered incredible variety among vegetables. Cabbages alone include broccoli, cauliflower, red cabbage, green cabbage, brussels sprouts, kohlrabi, Chinese cabbage, and savoy cabbage, to name a few. The following lists will give you an idea of the wonderful range of vegetables you can learn to prepare (in addition to cabbages), and the recipes in this chapter will get you started.

Leaves—round lettuce, Webb's Wonderful lettuce, iceberg lettuce, Cos lettuce, escarole, chicory, endive, sorrel, spring greens, kale, radicchio, spinach.

Roots—Salsify, radishes (red, black-white), daikons (Japanese radish), turnips, swede, beetroot, carrots, celeriac, parsnips, potatoes, yams, sweet potatoes, horseradish.

Pods and Seeds—corn, broad beans, French beans, runner beans, bean sprouts, peas, mange tout peas.

Vegetable-Fruits—Aubergines, tomatoes, Italian plum tomatoes, okra, cucumbers, red peppers, green peppers, cucumber.

Stalks—green or white asparagus, celery, Swiss chard, fennel.

Squash—Courgette, pumpkin.

Onions—red, white, spring onions, leeks, shallots, garlic.

Artichokes—globe, Jerusalem.

Mushrooms—white, brown, morels, cepes. (Use fresh when possible; however, dried mushrooms after 30 to 60 minutes' soaking are delicious.)

Basic Stir-Fried Vegetables
The Glory That Was Not "Grease"

Serves: 4

Chinese-style cooking lends itself to our methods of food preparation quite easily and happily, for several reasons. First of all, vegetables predominate; meat, fish and poultry are used in small quantities as seasonings. Dairy products like butter, cheese and milk are practically unknown to Chinese cooking. The soybean, whose protein resembles that of meat, has been converted to a frequently used cheese called tofu. Desserts rarely accompany family meals, and if served, they are frequently fresh fruit. The use of sweets is negligible, so that our fruit juice concentrate works quite well. The omnipresent rice gives us the whole grain we prefer—of course, we use brown rice instead of white.

Our method of Chinese cookery depends upon certain basic ingredients such as fresh vegetables, chicken, fish, lean steak, mild soy sauce, ginger root, garlic, spring onions, crushed red pepper and a good defatted, salt-free chicken stock (we use our own; see page 22). There are also some acceptable Chinese spices and seasonings—containing no fat, salt, MSG, or sugar—available through Chinese food stores (remember, read the labels carefully).

How does one teach an experienced chef how to cook without oil and MSG, and with only a minimal amount of mild soy sauce? Where do I begin? This was the dilemma I was confronted with when I was asked to teach a chef in Palm Springs, California. I was greeted with cordiality but scepticism—and so we began. The techniques of steaming and stir-frying are both great in our way of preparing food, so the transition was really not very difficult. I taught him how to use our Stock Cubes (page 21) instead of oil in stir-frying and to depend upon subtle spices instead of strong (sodium-laden) soy sauce, and he taught me some of the nuances I have incorporated into many of my recipes to share with you. The following recipe is a basic technique for stir-fried vegetables we perfected together.

Stir-fried vegetables are characterized by crispness, bright colour, and natural flavour. The secret, of course, is minimal cooking time. The choice of stir-frying or steaming or a combination of both techniques is determined by the way the vegetable is cut. The diagonal or julienne cut is the traditional one for Chinese-style stir-frying, but this can certainly be varied with thin slices. What is important is uniformity of cut within each recipe so that the vegetables can cook evenly and be esthetically pleasing.

450 g/1 lb mixed fresh
   vegetables (100 g/4 oz
   carrots, 100 g/4 oz
   broccoli, 100 g/4 oz

mushrooms, 100 g/4 oz
   peas, fresh or frozen)
4–5 tablespoons our Chicken
   Stock (see page 22) or

Vegetable Stock (see page 49)
1 tablespoon mild soy sauce
1 tablespoon frozen unsweetened pineapple juice concentrate (optional, to vary taste)
2 our Stock Cubes (see page 21)
1 clove garlic, finely chopped
3 thin slices ginger root, finely chopped or crushed

1. Cut vegetables as desired, slicing by hand or using a 5-mm/¼-inch slicing blade in food processor.

2. Combine stock, soy sauce and pineapple juice concentrate (if desired).

3. Heat stock cubes in a wok or a nonstick sauté pan.

4. Add garlic and ginger root and stir-fry ½ minute.

5. Add vegetables—if using a mixture, add slow-cooking ones first. Adjust heat. Stir-fry 3 minutes and steam covered 1 minute, then add remaining vegetables. Stir-fry to heat through.

6. Add stock mixture, stir gently, cover and simmer over medium heat until vegetables are done *but crisp.*

To Serve: Vegetables may be placed in a bowl or on a platter and served as an accompaniment, or they may be served over steamed brown rice and used as a delicious main dish, in which case the recipe would serve only 2 people.

Variation: Add 1 teaspoon cornflour and 2 tablespoons dry sherry in step 2. Use 1 finely chopped clove garlic and 1 spring onion cut into 1-cm/½-inch pieces instead of the ginger root.

Suggested Vegetables for Stir-Frying: Choose one or more of the following; *add toughest first.*

asparagus
aubergine
bamboo shoots (canned, rinsed and drained)
bean sprouts
broccoli
Chinese cabbage
cabbage (raw green)
carrots
cauliflower
celery
courgette
cucumbers
French beans
mange tout peas
mushrooms (fresh or dried)
onions (red or white)
peas (fresh or frozen)
pepper (red or green)
potatoes (white or sweet)
spinach
Swiss chard
turnips
water chestnuts (canned, rinsed and drained)

A Few Combinations:

1. 12 dried black mushrooms (soaked—see page 149); 100 g/4 oz sliced water chestnuts; ½ red pepper, sliced; 3 stalks Swiss chard, sliced.
2. 225 g/8 oz asparagus, cut in 2.5-mm/1-inch pieces; 1 stalk celery, cut in 2.5-mm/1-inch pieces; 225 g/8 oz bean sprouts.
3. 75 g/3 oz snow peas, whole; 225 g/8 oz carrots, thinly sliced; 100 g/4 oz broccoli, thinly sliced or julienne; and 100 g/4 oz Chinese cabbage, shredded.

Per serving: 59 calories; 4.4 gm protein; 0.3 gm fat; 13.8 gm carbohydrate; 3.3 gm fibre; 0 mg cholesterol; 1.3 mg iron; 144 mg sodium; 49 mg calcium; 98 mg phosphorus; 4009 IU Vitamin A; 0.17 mg thiamine; 0.25 mg riboflavin; 43 mg Vitamin C; 414 mg potassium; 0.19 mg zinc; 2.4 mg niacin; 126 mcg Vitamin B$_6$; 0 mcg Vitamin B$_{12}$; 24 mcg folic acid

Nanette's Microwaved Oriental Vegetables

Serves: 6

The basics of stir-frying are replaced by the magic of microwave cooking.

350 g/12 oz mange tout peas (washed and strings and ends removed), plus 2 tablespoons water
100 g/4 oz mushrooms, sliced
100 g/4 oz water chestnuts, rinsed, drained and sliced
50 g/2 oz pimento, chopped and drained

½ teaspoon garlic powder
50 g/2 oz spring onions, sliced
75 g/3 oz bean sprouts
4 tablespoons water or our Chicken Stock (see page 22)
4 teaspoons mild soy sauce

1. Place pea pods and the 2 tablespoons water in a large covered casserole.
2. Microwave on high for 2 minutes. Stir and microwave 2 additional minutes.
3. Add remaining ingredients to pea pods, mix gently, cover and microwave on high 1 to 2 minutes, or *until crisp*.
   To Serve: Serve immediately with main dish of your choice.

Per serving: 86 calories; 5.8 gm protein; 0.4 gm fat; 16.1 gm carbohydrate; 7.7 gm fibre; 0 mg cholesterol; 1.9 mg iron; 119 mg sodium; 26 mg calcium; 115 mg phosphorus; 754 IU Vitamin A; 0.28 mg thiamine; 0.22 mg riboflavin; 33 mg Vitamin C; 426 mg potassium; 0.02 mg zinc; 2.6 mg niacin; 15 mcg Vitamin B_6; 0 mcg Vitamin B_{12}; 4 mcg folic acid

Baked Beetroot

Serves: 6 (2 beetroot = 1 serving)

Most cooks never think of baking beetroot. It is an incredibly more delicious and easy method of beetroot preparation than boiling. Once you try it, you will never go back to boiling them.

1 kg/2 lb fresh beetroot (about 2 bunches *small* beetroot)	3 carrots, grated, for garnish
	3 spring onions, finely chopped, for garnish
12 lettuce leaves for serving	Fresh dill, finely chopped, for garnish
350 ml/12 fl oz nonfat yogurt for serving	

1. Scrub beetroot with a vegetable brush. Cut off all but 1 cm/½ inch of the tops and leave the tails.

2. Place in a covered casserole and bake in a preheated 230°C, 450°F, Gas Mark 8 oven for about 45 to 60 minutes, or until tender (test with the point of a paring knife).*

3. Cut off stems and slip off skins, leaving on the tails.**

4. Chill several hours in a covered container in refrigerator.

To Serve: Line a serving dish with lettuce. Place a bed of yogurt on the lettuce leaves, arrange two small beetroot on each leaf (tails up), garnish with grated carrot and chopped spring onion, and sprinkle with finely chopped dill. Lovely to serve with poached salmon (see page 98).

Per serving: 73 calories; 5.6 gm protein; 0.12 gm fat; 19.1 gm carbohydrate; 4.6 gm fibre; 0 mg cholesterol; 1.5 mg iron; 112 mg sodium; 144 mg calcium; 49 mg phosphorus; 3377 IU Vitamin A; 0.13 mg thiamine; 0.34 mg riboflavin; 15 mg Vitamin C; 488 mg potassium; 0.12 mg zinc; 1.4 mg niacin; 42 mcg Vitamin B_6; 0 mcg Vitamin B_{12}; 2.7 mcg folic acid

* Beetroot may also be wrapped individually in foil and baked at 160°C, 325°F, Gas Mark 3 for about 2½ hours. They tend to be juicier baked in foil at a lower temperature. For microwave cooking, place in a covered container with 350 ml/12 fl oz water and cook on high for about 20 minutes, or until tender.
** At this point, beetroot may be left whole, or sliced, diced or grated, depending upon the specific recipe.

Chopped Broccoli Chinese Style

Serves: 4

3 our Stock Cubes, melted
  (see page 21), or 3
  tablespoons our Chicken
  Stock (see page 22)
1 bunch spring onions, sliced
  in 1-cm/½-inch pieces
1 560-g/20-oz packet frozen

broccoli florets, thawed just
  enough to separate
250 ml/8 fl oz our Chicken
  Stock
1½ tablespoons mild soy
  sauce
1 tablespoon cornflour

1. Heat stock cubes or stock in a wok or frying pan; add onions
and cook 1 minute.

2. Add broccoli. Cover with lid and cook 1 minute; shake pan
vigorously while cooking *with cover on*.

3. In a cup or small jar, mix the 250 ml/8 fl oz stock, the soy
sauce and the cornflour vigorously to combine.

4. Add cornflour mixture to broccoli and simmer, stirring
gently until mixture thickens—it takes about 3 minutes.

To Serve: Serve family-style in a serving bowl. Delicious with
Turkey Piccata (page 126).

Variation: Cook 1 275-g/10-oz packet frozen sweetcorn kernels
with the broccoli, and add 1 50-g/2-oz jar of chopped pimento,
drained, at the end of the cooking—just before serving.

Per serving: 65 calories; 6.1 gm protein; 0.5 gm fat; 12.9 gm carbohydrate; 2.1 gm
fibre; 0 mg cholesterol; 1.2 mg iron; 150 mg sodium; 91 mg calcium; 91 mg
phosphorus; 4042 IU Vitamin A; 0.11 mg thiamine; 0.19 mg riboflavin; 105 gm
Vitamin C; 383 mg potassium; 0.05 mg zinc; 0.9 mg niacin; 0 mcg Vitamin B_2; 0
mcg Vitamin B_{12}; 2 mcg folic acid

Hilda's Braised Red Cabbage

Serves: 10

5 tablespoons our Chicken
  Stock (see page 22), or 3
  our Stock Cubes, melted
  (see page 21)

50 g/2 oz onion, finely
  chopped
1 medium red cabbage (about
  450 g/1 lb), shredded

4–6 dessert apples, peeled, cored and sliced

120 ml/4 fl oz apple cider vinegar or raspberry wine vinegar

120 ml/4 fl oz our Chicken Stock

120 ml/4 fl oz red wine

5 tablespoons frozen unsweetened apple juice concentrate

½ teaspoon freshly ground nutmeg

¼ teaspoon ground allspice

1. Heat the 5 tablespoons chicken stock in a flameproof casserole. Add onion and cook over moderate heat 5 minutes. Add cabbage, apples, vinegar and the 120 ml/4 fl oz stock. Stir.

2. Simmer 2 hours on top of cooker, or in a preheated 160°C, 325°F, Gas Mark 3 oven.

3. Add red wine, apple juice concentrate, nutmeg and allspice. Cook 30 minutes more and taste to adjust seasonings.

To Serve: Serve cabbage from casserole or in a warmed serving dish.

Variation: Add 450 g/1 lb chestnuts. Cut an X on the rounded side of each chestnut and parboil for 10 minutes. Remove outer and inner skins and chop coarsely. Add with the wine in step 3.

Per serving: 91 calories; 1.3 gm protein; 0.4 gm fat; 20.1 gm carbohydrate; 3.9 gm fibre; 0 mg cholesterol; 0.6 mg iron; 15 mg sodium; 36 mg calcium; 30 mg phosphorus; 106 IU Vitamin A; 0.05 mg thiamine; 0.05 mg riboflavin; 28 mg Vitamin C; 254 mg potassium; 0.24 mg zinc; 0.3 mg niacin; 102 mcg Vitamin B_6; 0 mcg Vitamin B_{12}; 19 mcg folic acid

Corn Cooked in Milk

Serves: 6

Corn is a good source of complex carbohydrates, and the technique of cooking it in milk seems to enhance its delicious flavour.

120 ml/4 fl oz nonfat milk

1 tablespoon nonfat powdered milk

450 g/1 lb fresh corn kernels,* cut from the cob with a sharp knife and chilled until ready to use

4 tablespoons chopped pimento or chopped red pepper

½ teaspoon freshly ground white pepper

½ teaspoon low-sodium vegetable seasoning (see page 24)

* 450 g/1 lb frozen kernel corn may be substituted for fresh corn.

1. Heat milk in a saucepan until simmering.

2. Add corn, stir, and heat to simmering. Lower heat, cover and simmer 3 minutes.

3. Drain corn with a slotted spoon. Place in a heated serving dish and stir in pimento, ground pepper and vegetable seasoning.

Helpful Hint: Save remaining cooking liquid for a cream soup.

Per serving: 101 calories; 3.5 gm protein; 1.4 gm fat; 18.1 gm carbohydrate; 3.7 gm fibre; 0 mg cholesterol; 0.7 mg iron; 4 mg sodium; 10 mg calcium; 100 mg phosphorus; 897 IU Vitamin A; 0.14 mg thiamine; 0.12 mg riboflavin; 35 mg Vitamin C; 266 mg potassium; 0.02 mg zinc; 1.5 mg niacin; 2 mcg Vitamin B_6; 0.02 mcg Vitamin B_{12}; 0 mcg folic acid

Corn, Tomato, Onion and Courgette Casserole

Serves: 6

2 × 275-g/10-oz packets frozen sweetcorn kernels, defrosted

6 small courgettes, cut in 1-cm/½-inch slices

4 ripe tomatoes, cut in 5-mm/¼-inch slices

2 mild onions, thinly sliced

2 cloves garlic, finely chopped

1 teaspoon low-sodium vegetable seasoning (see page 24)

Few grains crushed red pepper

Juice of ½ lemon

4 our Stock Cubes, melted (see page 21)

1. Place corn, courgettes, tomatoes, onions, garlic, vegetable seasoning and crushed red pepper in a covered casserole. Sprinkle with lemon juice and mix together gently.

2. Pour melted stock cubes over vegetables.

3. Cover and bake in a preheated 160°C, 325°F, Gas Mark 3 oven for 45 minutes.

To Serve: Especially nice served with our Barbecue-Style Grilled Chicken (page 113) or turkey.

Per serving: 142 calories; 6.4 gm protein; 0.9 gm fat; 32.5 gm carbohydrate; 6.4 gm fibre; 0 mg cholesterol; 2.2 mg iron; 11 mg sodium; 67 mg calcium; 156 mg phosphorus; 1665 IU Vitamin A; 0.26 mg thiamine; 0.23 mg riboflavin; 58 mg Vitamin C; 751 mg potassium; 0.34 mg zinc; 3.5 mg niacin; 149 mcg Vitamin B_6; 0 mcg Vitamin B_{12}; 19 mcg folic acid

Aubergine No-Crust Pizza

Serves: 6 (1 slice = 1 serving)

6 slices unpeeled aubergine, 1 cm/½ inch thick
175 ml/6 fl oz salt-free tomato sauce
1 teaspoon low-sodium vegetable seasoning (see page 24)
1 teaspoon oregano, crushed
Freshly ground pepper
6 slices ripe tomato, 1 cm/½ inch thick
2 tablespoons grated Sap Sago cheese, toasted (see page 16)
6 thin slices our Yogurt Cheese (see page 205) or skim milk mozzarella cheese, grated
12 thin slices green pepper
1 tablespoon chopped fresh basil

1. Squeeze aubergine slices with kitchen paper towels to remove bitter juices.
2. Dip aubergine slices in tomato sauce seasoned with vegetable seasoning, oregano and ground pepper.
3. Heat a heavy frying pan sprayed lightly with nonstick spray and sear aubergine slices until browned on each side.
4. Arrange aubergine slices in 1 layer on a nonstick baking sheet. Sprinkle with freshly ground pepper.
5. Cover each slice with a tomato slice and sprinkle with toasted Sap Sago cheese.
6. Cover each pizza with a slice of Yogurt Cheese and bake in a preheated 160°C, 325°F, Gas Mark 3 oven for 10 minutes, or until Yogurt Cheese has melted.
7. Garnish with two crossed green pepper strips and sprinkle with freshly chopped basil.

To Serve: Serve hot as either part of a main course on a vegetable plate or an accompaniment to roast chicken.

Variations: If your diet permits, grated Parmesan cheese may be substituted for the Sap Sago.

Per serving: 109 calories; 3.5 gm protein; 5.9 gm fat; 12.1 gm carbohydrate; 2.3 gm fibre; 1 mg cholesterol; 1.8 mg iron; 22 mg sodium; 80 mg calcium; 59 mg phosphorus; 1281 IU Vitamin A; 0.1 mg thiamine; 0.1 mg riboflavin; 27 mg Vitamin C; 261 mg potassium; 0.06 mg zinc; 1.3 mg niacin; 56 mcg Vitamin B_6; 0 mcg Vitamin B_{12}; 3 mcg folic acid

Larry's Crispy Potatoes

Serves: 6

When my son smells these potatoes baking in the oven, he's sure to stay home for dinner!

1 kg/2 lb potatoes, boiled in skins until tender
1 bunch spring onions, chopped
2 teaspoons Italian herb seasoning or basil, crushed
Freshly ground pepper

120 ml/4 fl oz our Chicken Stock (see page 22)
Hungarian paprika

3 tablespoons chopped fresh parsley or fresh basil for garnish

1. Peel cooked potatoes and dice in 2.5-cm/1-inch cubes.
*2. Place in a 20 × 28 × 5-cm/8 × 11 × 2-inch baking dish that has been sprayed with nonstick spray. Sprinkle with chopped spring onions, Italian seasoning and freshly ground pepper. Mix gently with a fork to distribute the ingredients.
3. Pour chicken stock over the potatoes and sprinkle generously with Hungarian paprika.
4. Bake in a preheated 200°C, 400°F, Gas Mark 6 oven on upper shelf. Stir every 15 minutes until nicely browned and crisp, about 45 minutes. Place under grill to complete browning before serving.

To Serve: Garnish with freshly chopped parsley or fresh basil. Because it is so easy to prepare, this dish lends itself nicely to outdoor entertaining for large parties. It's wonderful to serve with grilled steak or chicken.

Variation: In step 4, after stirring, spray with a mixture of 3 tablespoons mild soy sauce and 4 tablespoons water placed in a plastic spray bottle. Stir again. Spray and stir every 15 minutes. This will, of course, increase the sodium content of the recipe.

Per serving: 125 calories; 3.8 gm protein; 0.2 gm fat; 28.1 gm carbohydrate; 3.6 gm fibre; 0 mg cholesterol; 1.5 mg iron; 7 mg sodium; 35 mg calcium; 90 mg phosphorus; 553 IU Vitamin A; 0.15 mg thiamine; 0.08 mg riboflavin; 32 mg Vitamin C; 685 mg potassium; 0.49 mg zinc; 2.4 mg niacin; 266 mcg Vitamin B$_6$; 0 mcg Vitamin B$_{12}$; 13 mcg folic acid

*May be prepared through step 2 several hours ahead and refrigerated.

Spinach, Cheese and Mushroom Squares

Serves: 8 (1 10 × 7.5-cm/4 × 3-inch square = 1 serving)

3 tablespoons dry white wine
350 g/12 oz mushrooms, cleaned and sliced
4 spring onions, thinly sliced
1 teaspoon low-sodium vegetable seasoning (see page 24)
1 tablespoon Worcestershire sauce

3 275-g/10-oz packets frozen chopped spinach, defrosted and well drained
75 g/3 oz soft whole wheatcrumbs
450 ml/¾ pint Weight Watchers cottage cheese, rinsed and drained
6 egg whites

1. Bring wine to the boil in a nonstick frying pan. Add mushrooms and spring onions and sauté until just tender.
2. Add vegetable seasoning, Worcestershire sauce and drained spinach. Blend well and transfer to a mixing bowl.
3. Add breadcrumbs and drained cottage cheese. Blend.
4. Beat egg whites until stiff and fold into spinach mixture.
*5. Spray a 33 × 23 × 5-cm/13 × 9 × 2-inch glass baking dish with nonstick spray and place spinach mixture in dish.
6. Bake, uncovered, in a preheated 180°C, 350°F, Gas Mark 4 oven for 30 minutes, or until firm.
7. Let stand 10 minutes before cutting into 8 portions for serving.

Variations: May be cut into smaller squares and served as an appetizer. Frozen chopped broccoli may be substituted for the spinach.

Per serving: 153 calories; 16.2 gm protein; 1.5 gm fat; 18.6 gm carbohydrate; 2.3 gm fibre; 0 mg cholesterol; 3.5 mg iron; 312 mg sodium; 189 mg calcium; 106 mg phosphorus; 8561 IU Vitamin A; 0.2 mg thiamine; 0.6 mg riboflavin; 34 mg Vitamin C; 657 mg potassium; 0.02 mg zinc; 3 mg niacin; 56 mcg Vitamin B_6; 0.02 mcg Vitamin B_{12}; 11 mcg folic acid

* If you wish to freeze this dish for future use, prepare through step 5, cool, wrap baking dish in an airtight plastic bag or foil, and freeze. To reheat, place at room temperature for several hours and bake at 180°C, 350°F, Gas Mark 4 for 30 minutes.

Spinach Ring

Serves: 4

Spinach, and other leafy vegetables such as Swiss chard, are high in iron, Vitamin A and calcium. However, they also contain oxalic acid, which inhibits the absorption of calcium in the body, so they should be eaten in limited amounts.

1 kg/2 lb fresh spinach, or 2 275-g/10-oz packets frozen chopped spinach
50 g/2 oz Weight Watchers cottage cheese, rinsed and drained

2 spring onions
Dash freshly grated nutmeg
2 hard-boiled egg whites, chopped, for garnish
1 tablespoon chopped fresh parsley for garnish

1. Wash spinach carefully, discarding wilted leaves.* Cook in water that clings to leaves. Cover, start at moderate heat; cook 5 minutes, or until wilted, stirring once or twice.
2. Remove cover and stir until completely wilted. If there is any remaining liquid, drain it. (If using frozen spinach, cook according to package directions, drain and squeeze dry.)
3. Purée cottage cheese in blender or food processor.
4. Add spinach and spring onions to cheese and chop. Season with nutmeg.
5. Pack into a ring mould sprayed lightly with nonstick spray. Keep mould in a pan of hot water until ready to serve.
To Serve: Unmould onto a hot plate and sprinkle with chopped egg whites and parsley. For a more attractive presentation, fill the centre of the ring with steamed carrots. Spinach cooked this way will retain its green colour and fresh flavour.

Variation: Frozen chopped broccoli may be substituted for the spinach.

*Helpful Hint: When washing fresh spinach, place in generous amounts of fresh water and rinse. Then *remove spinach from water*, rinse grit from container, refill container, and repeat until remaining water is clear. If you just remove the water and not spinach from bowl, grit remains in bowl with spinach.

Per serving: 82 calories; 11 gm protein; 1 gm fat; 11 gm carbohydrate; 8.1 gm fibre; 0 mg cholesterol; 7.2 mg iron; 218 mg sodium; 230 mg calcium; 121 mg phosphorus; 18,557 IU Vitamin A; 0.23 mg thiamine; 0.54 mg riboflavin; 119 mg Vitamin C; 1119 mg potassium; 1.82 mg zinc; 1.5 mg niacin; 637 mcg Vitamin B_6; 0.02 mcg Vitamin B_{12}; 176 mcg folic acid

Vegetable Pie with a Cabbage Crust

Serves: 8–10 ($^1/_{10}$ of pie = 1 serving)

1 small green cabbage
3 spring onions, cut in 1-cm/½-inch slices
225 g/8 oz mushrooms, sliced thin
2 our Stock Cubes, melted (see page 21), or 1½ tablespoons our Chicken Stock (see page 22)
1 teaspoon Worcestershire sauce
½ teaspoon thyme
Freshly ground pepper
1½ tablespoons our Chicken Stock
1 small onion, finely chopped
1 small carrot, finely chopped

3 tablespoons chopped fresh parsley
½ teaspoon garlic powder
1 teaspoon herbes de Provence
2 275-g/10-oz packets frozen chopped spinach, thawed and well drained
225 g/8 oz skim-milk ricotta cheese
Freshly ground nutmeg
2 egg whites, lightly beaten
120 ml/4 fl oz salt-free tomato sauce, with ½ teaspoon oregano
1½ tablespoons grated Sap Sago cheese, toasted (see page 16)

1. Remove hard centre core of cabbage and parboil cabbage for 20 minutes.

2. Drain and separate cabbage leaves; try not to tear. Drain well on kitchen paper towels.

3. Sauté spring onions and mushrooms in stock cubes and Worcestershire sauce for about 5 to 10 minutes. Add thyme and freshly ground pepper.

4. Place chicken stock in a nonstick frying pan. Add onion, carrot and parsley. Sauté until transparent. Add garlic powder, herbs and drained, chopped spinach. Blend well.

5. Remove from heat, cool slightly and add ricotta cheese, freshly ground nutmeg and egg whites. Blend well.

6. Lightly spray a 25-cm/10-inch glass pie plate with nonstick spray. Arrange cooked cabbage leaves around bottom and sides of pie plate. Overlap leaves to thickness of about 5 leaves. (Leaves should extend 2.5 cm/1 inch over the edge of the plate.)

7. Spoon the drained mushroom mixture over the cabbage, spreading over bottom of plate. Then place the cheese mixture over the mushroom mixture.

8. Curl cabbage leaves over filling, leaving centre of pie uncovered.

9. Spoon tomato sauce over top of pie and sprinkle with toasted Sap Sago.

10. Bake in a preheated 150°C, 300°F, Gas Mark 2 oven for 20 to 30 minutes, or until filling is set. Remove pie from oven and drain any excess liquid. Let pie set for 2 minutes and cut into 8 to 10 wedges for serving.

To Serve: Serve with roast chicken.

Variation: If your diet permits, substitute grated Parmesan cheese for the Sap Sago.

Per serving: 115 calories; 11.5 gm protein; 3.1 gm fat; 12.7 gm carbohydrate; 4.3 gm fibre; 7 mg cholesterol; 2.6 mg iron; 176 mg sodium; 179 mg calcium; 128 mg phosphorus; 6921 IU Vitamin A; 0.15 mg thiamine; 0.38 mg riboflavin; 62 mg Vitamin C; 617 mg potassium; 0.35 mg zinc; 2 mg niacin; 176 mcg Vitamin B_6; 0.01 mcg Vitamin B_{12}; 34 mcg folic acid

Tomato Pie

Serves: 6 (⅙ of pie = 1 serving)

4 slices whole wheat bread
1 800-g/28-oz can tomatoes, drained and mashed (juice reserved)
50 g/2 oz onion, chopped
2 spring onions, chopped

2 tablespoons chopped fresh basil, or 2 teaspoons dried basil
Few grains crushed red pepper
2 egg whites
2 teaspoons oregano, toasted*

*Toast dried oregano lightly in a dry frying pan and enjoy the change of flavour.

1. Tear bread into small pieces. Pour juice from tomatoes over bread and mix.

2. Combine mashed tomatoes, onion, basil and crushed red pepper in a bowl.

3. Beat egg whites until fluffy.

4. Combine tomato and onion mixture with bread mixture.

5. Fold egg whites into tomato and bread mixture. Spoon into a 23-cm/9-inch pie dish that has been lightly sprayed with nonstick spray and bake in a preheated 190°C, 375°F, Gas Mark 5 oven for 45 minutes, or until lightly browned.

To Serve: Sprinkle with toasted oregano before serving.

Per serving: 82 calories; 4.4 gm protein; 0.8 gm fat; 15.6 gm carbohydrate; 1.4 gm fibre; 0 mg cholesterol; 1.7 mg iron; 235 mg sodium; 42 mg calcium; 38 mg phosphorus; 1443 IU Vitamin A; 0.1 mg thiamine; 0.1 mg riboflavin; 26 mg Vitamin C; 370 mg potassium; 0.32 mg zinc; 1.3 mg niacin; 135 mcg Vitamin B_6; 0.01 mcg Vitamin B_{12}; 9 mcg folic acid

Sesame, Courgette and Tomatoes

Serves: 2

1 tablespoon sesame seeds
2 tablespoons our Chicken Stock (see page 22)
1 small clove garlic, very finely chopped

3 courgettes, thinly sliced
3 spring onions, chopped
6 tiny tomatoes, halved
2 tablespoons chopped fresh parsley

1. Toast sesame seeds in a dry frying pan over low heat and set aside.

2. Heat chicken stock and garlic in a wok or sauté pan.

3. When hot, add sliced courgettes and spring onions. Stir until crisp, cover, and steam 2 minutes.

4. Stir in tomatoes and chopped parsley and heat through.

To Serve: Remove to a heated platter and sprinkle with toasted sesame seeds. Serve with Grilled Halibut Steaks (page 103).

Variation: If your diet permits, use 1 teaspoon oil instead of chicken stock.

Per serving: 35 calories; 1.9 gm protein; 1.2 gm fat; 5.3 gm carbohydrate; 3.1 gm fibre; 0 mg cholesterol; 0.7 mg iron; 4 mg sodium; 36 mg calcium; 46 mg phosphorus; 708 IU Vitamin A; 0.06 mg thiamine; 0.09 mg riboflavin; 25 mg Vitamin C; 258 mg potassium; 0.05 mg zinc; 1.1 mg niacin; 18 mcg Vitamin B_6; 0 mcg Vitamin B_{12}; 3 mcg folic acid

Courgette Tian

Serves: 8

A tian is a vegetable casserole from the region of Provence in France. It is usually a mixture of vegetables or a combination of vegetables and rice that is baked in a gratin dish.

4 tablespoons our Vegetable Stock (see page 49), our Chicken Stock (see page 23), or dry vermouth

1 small onion, finely chopped

1 clove garlic, finely chopped

1 bunch spring onions, finely chopped

1 kg/2 lb courgettes, thinly sliced

1 teaspoon chopped herbes de Provence

225 g/8 oz Weight Watchers cottage cheese, rinsed and drained

15 g/½ oz fresh parsley, chopped

3 egg whites, lightly beaten

150 g/5 oz brown rice, parboiled 30 minutes and drained

3 tablespoons our Seasoned Breadcrumbs (see page 25)

2 tablespoons grated Sap Sago cheese, toasted (see page 16)

1. Heat stock in a large frying pan and add onion and garlic. Sauté until soft.

2. Add spring onions, courgettes and herbs. Cook, covered, 10 minutes over low heat, stirring occasionally. Remove from heat.

3. Combine cheese, parsley, egg whites and cooked brown rice.

4. Add courgette mixture to rice mixture and mix well.

5. Spray a gratin dish or a 25-cm/10-inch glass pie plate with nonstick spray. Place courgette and rice mixture in baking dish and sprinkle with a mixture of breadcrumbs and cheese.

6. Bake uncovered in a preheated 180°C, 350°F, Gas Mark 4 oven for 35 minutes.

To Serve: Lovely with parsleyed potatoes and Filets de Poisson aux Tomates (page 93).

Variation: If your diet allows, use grated Parmesan cheese instead of Sap Sago.

Per serving: 91 calories; 8 gm protein; 1 gm fat; 13.2 gm carbohydrate; 4.6 gm fibre; 1 mg cholesterol; 1.5 mg iron; 102 mg sodium; 108 mg calcium; 71 mg phosphorus; 1055 IU Vitamin A; 0.1 mg thiamine; 0.24 mg riboflavin; 35 mg Vitamin C; 380 mg potassium; 0.07 mg zinc; 1.7 mg niacin; 25 mcg Vitamin B_6; 0.01 mcg Vitamin B_{12}; 7 mcg folic acid

Stuffed Courgettes

Serves: 6 as main course (1 whole courgette per person) or 12 as garnish ($\frac{1}{2}$ courgette per person)

Many vegetables are appropriate in size and shape for stuffing, if they hold their shape after cooking. One of the most popular of these is courgette.

6 courgettes
1½ teaspoons low-sodium vegetable seasoning (see page 24)
1 medium onion, finely chopped
3 large cloves garlic, finely chopped
1 shallot, finely chopped
2 our Stock Cubes (see page 21)
225 g/8 oz fresh tomatoes, seeded and chopped, or 1 225-g/8-oz can tomatoes, drained and chopped (juice reserved)
1 canned green chilli, finely chopped
1 carrot, grated
90 g/3½ oz brown rice, cooked in 350 ml/12 fl oz our Chicken Stock (see page 22) or Vegetable Stock (see page 49)
1 egg white, lightly beaten
3 tablespoons chopped fresh parsley
1 tablespoon mild soy sauce
225 g/8 oz leftover cooked chicken or beef, finely chopped
120 ml/4 fl oz salt-free tomato sauce (if fresh tomatoes are used)
75 g/3 oz fine whole wheat breadcrumbs
2½ tablespoons grated Sap Sago cheese, toasted (see page 16)

1. Wash courgettes thoroughly under cold running water. Cut in half lengthwise, scoop out pulp leaving a 5-mm/¼-inch shell (a grapefruit spoon works well for this), and season with vegetable seasoning.

2. Chop pulp coarsely and set aside.

3. Sauté onion, garlic and shallot in stock cubes for 2 to 3 minutes.

4. Add courgette pulp, tomatoes, chilli and carrot. Cook slowly for 7 to 10 minutes, until most of the liquid is removed. Stir occasionally.

5. Combine with brown rice and cool.

6. Add egg white, parsley, soy sauce and chicken. Combine with a fork and taste for additional seasoning.

*7. Stuff courgette shells and place in a glass baking dish that has been lined with 120 ml/4 fl oz tomato sauce (reserved from the canned tomatoes, if used).

8. Mix breadcrumbs with toasted Sap Sago cheese and top courgettes with mixture.

9. Bake in a preheated 200°C, 400°F, Gas Mark 6 oven for about 45 minutes to 1 hour, or until golden brown.

To Serve: You may serve this as a vegetable garnish with grilled chicken or as one of the main dishes on a vegetable plate accompanied by a baked potato and parsleyed carrots.

Per Serving: 187 calories; 14.1 gm protein; 1.8 gm fat; 30.7 gm carbohydrate; 9.6 gm fibre; 21 mg cholesterol; 2.7 mg iron; 166 mg sodium; 108 mg calcium; 177 mg phosphorus; 2875 IU Vitamin A; 0.26 mg thiamine; 0.33 mg riboflavin; 74 mg Vitamin C; 876 mg potassium; 0.19 mg zinc; 5.7 mg niacin; 84 mcg Vitamin B$_6$; 0.01 mcg Vitamin B$_{12}$; 11 mcg folic acid

*May be prepared ahead through step 7.

❧ Pastas and Grains ❧

Pastas

Basic Marinara Sauce
Fresh Tomato Sauce with
  Fresh Basil
Tuna-Pasta Salad

Marilyn's Pasta Salad
Pasta Salad Jardinière
Courgettes with Pasta Shells

Grains

Barley Casserole
Steamed Brown Rice
East African Pavlava Sauce
  with Brown Rice

Cracked Wheat Pilaf
Wild Rice, Brown Rice and
  Mushrooms

There are two kinds of carbohydrates—sugars and complex carbohydrates (such as cellulose and starches). We need complex carbohydrates in our diets because they are a very efficient source of fuel. Sugar enters the bloodstream quickly; starches, however, must be broken down gradually and stored in the body to be released as needed. Good sources of complex carbohydrates are whole grains (in cereals and brown rice, flours, bread products and whole grain pasta), legumes and starchy vegetables such as corn, potatoes and peas. Today, only approximately 25 percent of the calories we consume are derived from complex carbohydrates whereas people in Third World nations have approximately 75 percent of their calories derived from complex carbohydrates. We should avoid all refined cereals, flours and cereal products— especially those with sugar or preservatives added. Processed and refined cereal products have had the bran (the outer covering of grains which is rich in cellulose or fibre, and vitamins and minerals) and sometimes the germ (which is rich in protein, fat, vitamins B and E) removed. Instead of having to add bran or wheat germ to our foods, why not eat the whole grain as nature has provided it—in proper proportions?

I remember when pasta used to mean just plain spaghetti and meat balls. Today, there is a whole new world of pasta out there, with many varieties of shape, size, and texture. Not just unbleached white flour is used; there is pasta made from whole wheat flour, corn flour, artichoke flour, buckwheat flour, soy flour, and combinations thereof. Because we now realize the importance of complex carbohydrates in our diets, people are eating more pasta and more often without fearing the calories. Pasta is like the much-maligned potato; its final caloric content is controlled by what you put on it. Hence, if we top our pastas with light sauces, less meat and more vegetables or even fish, we have a calorie-controlled delight.

I suggest using mostly whole-grain pastas, or if not, at least those made without added fat or eggs. Remember to read your package labels. You will find more variety in your local Italian delicatessen than in most neighbourhood supermarkets. Most pastas are variations of four general shapes: strands, twists, shells, and tiny pasta bits.

One of the most popular ways of serving pasta today is the cold pasta salad, which presents endless possibilities for creativity and variety. In this chapter I have given you a few hot and cold pasta suggestions I know you will enjoy. After trying some of the recipes here you can vary them by changing the pasta, dressing or vegetables and adding meat, fish or poultry. Be adventurous.

PASTAS

Basic Marinara Sauce

Serves: 6

The beauty of this classic Italian sauce is that by preparing it quickly, the fresh flavours are retained. It is not necessary to cook it all day.

1 small onion, finely chopped
1 small carrot, finely chopped
1 shallot, finely chopped
2 cloves garlic, finely chopped

3 tablespoons our Chicken Stock (see page 22), or 3 our Stock Cubes (see page 21)

1.4 kg/3 lb ripe, fresh tomatoes, peeled, seeded and coarsely chopped, or 1 800-g/28-oz can tomatoes in sauce, chopped

3 tablespoons salt-free tomato paste, to be used with fresh tomatoes only

3 tablespoons chopped fresh basil or 1½ tablespoons dried basil

2 tablespoons chopped fresh parsley

2 tablespoons grated Sap Sago cheese, toasted (see page 16; optional)

1. Sauté onion, carrot, shallot and garlic in stock for 5 minutes.
2. Add tomatoes, tomato paste, basil and parsley. Add Sap Sago cheese if desired.

To Serve: Serve over cooked spaghetti, topped with additional chopped fresh basil or parsley if desired. Complete the meal with a crisp green salad and rolls.

Variations: Add 1 tablespoon dry red wine for last 5 minutes.

For a delicious and distinctive variation, *"Spaghetti Tonnato,"* add 2 215-g/7½-oz cans of salt-reduced tuna in water (drained) to sauce in step 2 and simmer 30 minutes. Serve over spaghetti or noodles.

Per serving: 73 calories; 4.3 gm protein; 0.6 gm fat; 16.2 gm carbohydrate; 4.5 gm fibre; 0 mg cholesterol; 2.3 mg iron; 16 mg sodium; 75 mg calcium; 87 mg phosphorus; 3458 IU Vitamin A; 0.17 mg thiamine; 0.13 mg riboflavin; 62 mg Vitamin C; 745 mg potassium; 0.55 mg zinc; 2 mg niacin; 263 mcg Vitamin B_6; 0 mcg Vitamin B_{12}; 24 mcg folic acid

Fresh Tomato Sauce with Fresh Basil

Yield: 550 g/1¼ lb (50 g/2 oz = 1 serving)

This is *not* a sauce for all seasons! Prepare it *only* at the height of the tomato crop for best results.

1 small onion, finely chopped
1 large garlic clove, finely chopped
2 tablespoons dry white wine

8 large ripe tomatoes, peeled, seeded and chopped
2½ tablespoons chopped fresh basil

1 tablespoon chopped fresh
   Italian parsley
Freshly ground pepper
	Low-sodium vegetable
	   seasoning (see page 24)
	   optional

1. Sauté onion and garlic in white wine until softened.

2. Add tomatoes; bring to the boil and simmer 10 to 15 minutes, or until most of the liquid has evaporated. (*Do not overcook.*)

3. Add basil, parsley and freshly ground pepper.

4. Taste, and adjust seasonings with pepper and a little vegetable seasoning if desired.

To Serve: May be served with pasta or with grilled fish or chicken.

Variation: Just before serving, combine all ingredients and chop coarsely in food processor. Place in saucepan and heat. Pour over freshly cooked and drained pasta. In this method of preparation, the sauce retains even more of its fresh flavour.

Per serving: 41 calories; 1.9 gm protein; 0.3 gm fat; 8.5 gm carbohydrate; 2.6 gm fibre; 0 mg cholesterol; 1.4 mg iron; 6 mg sodium; 52 mg calcium; 49 mg phosphorus; 1385 IU Vitamin A; 0.09 mg thiamine; 0.06 mg riboflavin; 34 mg Vitamin C; 406 mg potassium; 0.31 mg zinc; 1.1 mg niacin; 150 mcg Vitamin B$_6$; 0 mcg Vitamin B$_{12}$; 14 mcg folic acid

Tuna-Pasta Salad

Serves: 4 as main dish (25 g/1 oz pasta = 1 serving), 8 as an appetizer

250 ml/8 fl oz nonfat yogurt
2 tablespoons brown rice
   vinegar
1 teaspoon low-sodium
   vegetable seasoning (see
   page 24)
1 clove garlic, finely chopped
15 g/½ oz fresh parsley,
   chopped
100 g/4 oz fusilli (twisted
   macaroni), cooked *al dente*,
   rinsed and drained
1 215-g/7½-oz can salt-free
	tuna in water, rinsed,
	   drained and flaked
	175 g/6 oz frozen peas or
	   steamed fresh peas
	100 g/4 oz celery, sliced
	50 g/2 oz red onion, chopped
	2 tablespoons chopped fresh
	   dill, or 1 tablespoon dried
	   dill weed
	1 tomato, peeled, seeded and
	   diced, for garnish
	Fresh parsley sprigs for
	   garnish

1. In a large salad bowl, stir together yogurt, brown rice vinegar, vegetable seasoning, garlic and parsley until smooth.

2. Add remaining ingredients (except garnish) and toss with 2 forks to coat well.

3. Cover and chill several hours.

To Serve: Garnish with diced tomato and sprigs of fresh parsley. Use as main course with our Banana Bread (page 200) for dessert.

Variation: Substitute 250 ml/8 fl oz our Italian Dressing (see page 13) for the yogurt and vinegar dressing.

Per serving: 255 calories; 23.7 gm protein; 1.1 gm fat; 37.7 gm carbohydrate; 3.3 gm fibre; 31 mg cholesterol; 4.1 mg iron; 148 mg sodium; 170 mg calcium; 218 mg phosphorus; 1717 IU Vitamin A; 0.51 mg thiamine; 0.39 mg riboflavin; 38 mg Vitamin C; 596 mg potassium; 0.58 mg zinc; 10.3 mg niacin; 158 mcg Vitamin B_6; 0 mcg Vitamin B_{12}; 23 mcg folic acid

Marilyn's Pasta Salad

Serves: 6

25 g/1 oz dried mushrooms, soaked in hot water 30 minutes, then rinsed several times, squeezed dry, stemmed and slivered

1 tablespoon mild soy sauce

225 g/8 oz pasta shells, cooked *al dente*, rinsed and drained

1 teaspoon Chinese sesame oil

2 whole chicken breasts (450 g/1 lb chicken) roasted and cut in chunks, or 450g/1 lb leftover chicken or turkey

1 teaspoon low-sodium vegetable seasoning (see page 24)

175 g/6 oz defrosted frozen peas

1 215-g/7½-oz can artichoke quarters, rinsed and well drained

3 spring onions, sliced

1 red pepper, seeded and cut in slivers

250 ml/8 fl oz Vinaigrette Dressing (see page 13)

1 large ripe tomato, peeled, seeded and diced, for garnish

2 tablespoons chopped fresh basil or parsley for garnish

1. Marinate mushrooms in soy sauce for 30 minutes while preparing rest of salad.

2. In a large salad bowl, combine pasta, sesame oil, chicken,

vegetable seasoning, peas, artichokes, spring onions and red pepper.

3. Add dressing and toss with 2 forks to coat well.

4. Cover and chill 1 hour. Before serving, add marinated mushrooms and toss.

To Serve: Garnish with diced tomato and fresh basil or Italian parsley, and serve. Serve with crisp Italian bread.

Per serving: 255 calories; 20.7 gm protein; 1.9 gm fat; 41.1 gm carbohydrate; 3.3 gm fibre; 38 mg cholesterol; 3.2 mg iron; 99 mg sodium; 55 mg calcium; 267 mg phosphorus; 1356 IU Vitamin A; 0.54 mg thiamine; 0.41 mg riboflavin; 53 mg Vitamin C; 625 mg potassium; 0.06 mg zinc; 8.1 mg niacin; 86 mcg Vitamin B_6; 0 mcg Vitamin B_{12}; 8 mcg folic acid

Pasta Salad Jardinière

Serves: 4 as a main dish, 6 as an appetizer

250 ml/8 fl oz nonfat yogurt
2 tablespoons chopped spring onion
1 tablespoon lemon juice
1 teaspoon dried basil, or 1 tablespoon chopped fresh basil
Freshly ground pepper
100 g/4 oz thin spaghettini, cooked *al dente*, rinsed and drained
175 g/6 oz cucumber, chopped
100 g/4 oz green beans, cut in 2.5-cm/1-inch pieces and steamed

100 g/4 oz carrots, thinly sliced and steamed
100 g/4 oz courgettes, thinly sliced, cut in half and steamed
50 g/2 oz radishes, thinly sliced
50 g/2 oz green pepper, chopped

15 g/½ oz fresh parsley, chopped, for garnish

1. *To make salad dressing,* combine the first 5 ingredients in a large salad bowl.

2. Add pasta, cucumber, beans, carrots, courgettes, radishes and green pepper. Toss with 2 forks to coat well.

3. Cover and chill.

To Serve: Garnish with parsley and serve. As a main dish serve with sliced tomato salad, melba toast, and Helen's San Francisco Peach Surprises (page 193) for dessert.

Variation: Add 175 g/6 oz diced cooked chicken or turkey.

Per serving: 186 calories; 7.9 gm protein; 0.9 gm fat; 35.8 gm carbohydrate; 3.2 gm fibre; 0 mg cholesterol; 2 mg iron; 39 mg sodium; 111 mg calcium; 41 mg phosphorus; 3663 IU Vitamin A; 0.23 mg thiamine; 0.21 mg riboflavin; 42 mg Vitamin C; 304 mg potassium; 0.14 mg zinc; 1.9 mg niacin; 91 mcg Vitamin B_6; 0 mcg Vitamin B_{12}; 14 mcg folic acid

Courgettes with Pasta Shells

Serves: 8 (50 g/2 oz pasta = 1 serving)

120 ml/4 fl oz our Chicken Stock (see page 22) or Vegetable Stock (see page 49)
½ large onion, finely chopped
2 shallots, finely chopped
1 clove garlic, finely chopped
1 kg/2 lb small, firm courgettes, thinly sliced
2 teaspoons chopped fresh rosemary, or 1 teaspoon

dried rosemary, crushed
Freshly ground pepper
450 g/1 lb pasta shells, cooked *al dente*, rinsed, and drained
150 g/5 oz Weight Watchers cottage cheese, rinsed and drained

3 tablespoons chopped fresh Italian parsley for garnish

1. Place stock in a large nonstick frying pan. Bring to the boil. Add onion, shallots and garlic and cook until transparent, stirring constantly.

*2. Add sliced courgettes, rosemary and pepper. Stir and cook 2 to 3 minutes.

3. Add drained pasta and cottage cheese to pan and stir until pasta is well coated and heated through (2 to 3 minutes).

To Serve: Turn onto a heated platter, sprinkle with chopped parsley and *serve immediately*.

Per serving: 253 calories; 11.2 gm protein; 1 gm fat; 49.4 gm carbohydrate; 5.8 gm fibre; 0 mg cholesterol; 2.4 mg iron; 48 mg sodium; 74 mg calcium; 131 mg phosphorus; 501 IU Vitamin A; 0.57 mg thiamine; 0.37 mg riboflavin; 25 mg Vitamin C; 393 mg potassium; 0.03 mg zinc; 4.7 mg niacin; 50 mcg Vitamin B_6; 0 mcg Vitamin B_{12}; 3 mcg folic acid

*The vegetable mixture may be prepared through step 2 to be combined with freshly cooked pasta at serving time.

GRAINS

Barley Casserole

Serves: 8

Barley is a frequently neglected whole grain cereal that makes a satisfying and delicious casserole. This easy recipe is tasty with Hearty Steak with Peppers (page 135).

200 g/7 oz barley
1 litre/1¾ pints our Chicken Stock (see page 22) or our Vegetable Stock (see page 49)
1 carrot, sliced
1 small leek (white part only), sliced

1 small onion, chopped
Few grains crushed red pepper
½ teaspoon thyme, crushed
½ teaspoon low-sodium vegetable seasoning (see page 24)

Chopped fresh parsley for garnish

1. In a 2-litre/3½-pint casserole, combine all ingredients except parsley.
2. Cover and bake in a preheated 180°C, 350°F, Gas Mark 4 oven for about 2 hours. Stir barley with a fork from time to time while baking.
3. Remove lid and garnish with parsley before serving.

Variation: Add a 50-g/2-oz jar of pimento, chopped and drained, with the parsley before serving.

Per serving: 117 calories; 3.8 gm protein; 0.3 gm fat; 25.3 gm carbohydrate; 2.4 gm fibre; 0 mg cholesterol; 0.9 mg iron; 9 mg sodium; 19 mg calcium; 60 mg phosphorus; 1106 IU Vitamin A; 0.05 mg thiamine; 0.03 mg riboflavin; 3 mg Vitamin C; 113 mg potassium; 0.08 mg zinc; 0.9 mg niacin; 86 mcg Vitamin B_6; 0 mcg Vitamin B_{12}; 4 mcg folic acid

Steamed Brown Rice

Serves: 4–6 (about 65 g/2½ oz = 1 serving)

Another outstanding and many times overlooked whole grain cereal is brown rice. It has far more food value than white rice and

a better flavour (a nutlike quality), though because of its bran, it must be cooked longer.

1 cup* brown rice, washed   Vegetable Stock (see page
2¼ cups* water, our Chicken   49)
    Stock (see page 22), or our

1. Place cold water or stock in saucepan and bring to the boil.**
2. Add washed rice to boiling liquid slowly and return to boil. Reduce to simmer.
3. Cover and cook 40 to 45 minutes, until all liquid has been absorbed. Fluff rice with a fork before serving.

To Serve: Brown rice may be served with Stir-Fried Vegetables (see page 149) as a main course or steamed and combined with cooked courgettes, peas, mushrooms or asparagus as an accompaniment.

Variations: Add 1 tablespoon soy sauce, 1 teaspoon basil, 2 tablespoons chopped fresh parsley and 4 finely chopped spring onions with the rice.

You may also add crushed red pepper, 1 teaspoon toasted, dehydrated onion and 1 teaspoon soy sauce to cooking liquid.

The Armenians moisten their cooked rice with yoghurt before serving. It's low-calorie and delicious!

Per serving: 116 calories; 2.7 gm protein; 0.7 gm fat; 28.1 gm carbohydrate; 2.6 gm fibre; 0 mg cholesterol; 0.6 mg iron; 3 mg sodium; 12 mg calcium; 80 mg phosphorus; 0 IU Vitamin A: 0.12 mg thiamine; 0.02 mg riboflavin; 0 mg Vitamin C; 78 mg potassium; 0 mg zinc; 1.7 mg niacin; 0 mcg Vitamin B_6; 0 mcg Vitamin B_{12}; 0 mcg folic acid

East African Pavlava Sauce with Brown Rice

Serves: 8

My thanks to the students of the College of the Redwoods, Eureka, California, their teacher, Rose Stebbins and Geoffrey

* Use a 250-ml/8-fl oz cup.
** Rice may be added to boiling liquid in an ovenproof casserole, covered and baked at 180°C, 350°F, Gas Mark 4 for 45 minutes to 1 hour instead of being boiled on top of the cooker.

Bain, who discovered this recipe during his stay in the Peace Corps in an African village. The recipe is adapted to ingredients available in the West.

3 bunches (1.4–1.8 kg/3–4 lb) spring greens, washed and drained thoroughly
675 g/1½ lb boned, skinned, and defatted chicken breasts, diced
2 teaspoons low-sodium vegetable seasoning (see page 24)
1 litre/1 ¾ pints our Chicken Stock (see page 22)

4 medium onions, finely chopped
4 hot African dried peppers (they look like dried red chilli peppers), chopped, or 1 7.5-cm/3-inch chilli pepper, chopped
1 150-g/5-oz can unsalted tomato paste
550 g/1¼ lb Steamed Brown Rice (see page 174)

1. Cut washed greens into very small pieces.
2. Season diced chicken with vegetable seasoning.
3. Add 120 ml/4 fl oz of the chicken stock to a sauté pan and bring to the boil. Add seasoned chicken pieces and sauté.
4. Remove sautéed chicken from pan and add chopped greens, onions, the remaining chicken stock, the peppers and the tomato paste. Blend well.
5. Bring mixture to the boil, reduce to a simmer, cover and cook for 15 to 20 minutes.
6. Add sautéed chicken pieces and simmer 10 to 15 minutes more.

To Serve: Serve sauce over the steamed brown rice.

Per serving: 347 calories; 32.4 gm protein; 3.5 gm fat; 50.8 gm carbohydrate; 5.6 gm fibre; 49 mg cholesterol; 4.1 mg iron; 164 mg sodium; 457 mg calcium; 383 mg phosphorus; 13,672 IU Vitamin A; 0.64 mg thiamine; 0.78 mg riboflavin; 199 mg Vitamin C; 1198 mg potassium; 1.05 mg zinc; 14.7 niacin; 532 mcg Vitamin B_6; 0.32 mcg Vitamin B_{12}; 21 mcg folic acid

Cracked Wheat Pilaf

Serves: 8

A delicious alternative to brown rice is cracked wheat or bulgur. Cracked wheat is rich in potassium, phosphorus and niacin. It has a nutlike flavour and somewhat chewy texture.

3 our Stock Cubes (see page 21), or 4 tablespoons our Chicken Stock (see page 22)
5 tablespoons chopped celery with leaves
2 shallots, chopped
1 medium onion, chopped
100 g/ 4 oz mushrooms, sliced
½ green pepper, seeded and chopped
1 teaspoon low-sodium vegetable seasoning (see page 24)
250 g/9 oz cracked wheat
Few grains crushed red pepper
1 litre/1¾ pints our Chicken Stock
1 50-g/2-oz jar chopped pimento, drained

3 tablespoons chopped fresh parsley for garnish

1. Melt stock cubes in a saucepan; when boiling, add celery, shallots and onion. Sauté until transparent, stirring constantly.

2. Add mushrooms, green pepper and vegetable seasoning. Sauté 2 minutes.

3. Place cracked wheat in a shallow pan under grill and toast until golden. *Watch carefully and stir.*

4. Add browned cracked wheat to sautéed vegetables and stir over low heat a few minutes.

5. Add crushed red pepper and the 1 litre/1¾ pints chicken stock. Bring to the boil and lower heat to simmer.

6. Cover and simmer cracked wheat mixture 15 minutes. Stir in pimento.

To Serve: Place in a serving dish and sprinkle with chopped parsley. This may be served instead of the more commonly used brown rice or potatoes with Stir-Fried Vegetables (page 149) or with Orange-Glazed Chicken (page 106).

Per serving: 81 calories; 3.7 gm protein; 0.4 gm fat; 16.8 gm carbohydrate; 1.3 gm fibre; 0 mg cholesterol; 1.1 mg iron; 16 mg sodium; 23 mg calcium; 83 mg phosphorus; 399 IU Vitamin A; 0.1 mg thiamine; 0.08 mg riboflavin; 20 mg Vitamin C; 189 mg potassium; 0.06 mg zinc; 1.1 mg niacin; 52 mcg Vitamin B_6; 0 mcg Vitamin B_{12}; 8 mcg folic acid

Wild Rice, Brown Rice and Mushrooms

Serves: 12

Wild rice is not a grain, but the elegant seed of a grass. Like pasta, it tastes best when cooked *al dente*—around 45 minutes. Wild rice is expensive, so frequently we combine it with brown rice (which also cooks for 45 minutes) to cut down on the cost as well as provide an interesting combination of flavours.

1 litre/1¾ pints our Chicken Stock (see page 22) or our Vegetable Stock (see page 49)
1 teaspoon dried shallots or onion
Few grains crushed red pepper
½ teaspoon thyme, crushed
1 bay leaf
200 g/7 oz brown rice
200 g/7 oz wild rice
2 our Stock Cubes (see page 21)
1 tablespoon dry white wine
1 small onion, finely chopped
225 g/8 oz mushrooms, wiped clean and sliced
2 spring onions, chopped
1 tablespoon lemon juice
1 tablespoon mild soy sauce
1 tablespoon salt-free Dijon mustard
1 100-g/4-oz jar chopped pimento, drained

1. Place stock, shallots, pepper, thyme and bay leaf in a 2.75-litre/5-pint pan. Bring stock to the boil; add brown rice and wild rice. Bring to the boil again, reduce heat, cover and simmer 45 minutes.

*2. Remove any excess liquid.

3. While rice is cooking, melt stock cubes with wine in a nonstick frying pan. When simmering, add onion and sauté 5 minutes, or until transparent.

4. Add mushrooms, spring onions and lemon juice. Sauté a few minutes. Add soy sauce and mustard; blend with mushrooms using a fork.

5. Blend mushroom mixture with precooked rice and pimentos.

6. Place in an ovenproof casserole sprayed with nonstick spray, cover with foil, and heat in a preheated 160°C, 325°F, Gas Mark 3 oven for 20 to 30 minutes, or until quite hot and ready to serve.

To Serve: This casserole combines nicely with roast turkey or Marinated Steak (page 131).

Variation: When cold, this cooked rice mixture combines nicely with vegetables and leftover diced chicken for an unusual luncheon main dish.

Helpful Hint: If rice seems dry, add a little stock to moisten after 20 minutes.

Per serving: 115 calories; 4.4 gm protein; 0.5 gm fat; 23.2 gm carbohydrate; 1.8 gm fibre; 0 mg cholesterol; 1.2 mg iron; 50 mg sodium; 14 mg calcium; 96 mg phosphorus; 298 IU Vitamin A; 0.12 mg thiamine; 0.18 mg riboflavin; 12 mg Vitamin C; 178 mg potassium; 0.03 mg zinc; 2.2 mg niacin; 35 mcg Vitamin B_6; 0 mcg Vitamin B_{12}; 7 mcg folic acid

* Can be prepared ahead or the day before through step 2 and chilled until needed. Bring precooked rice to room temperature before using.

❧Sweets and Treats❧

Desserts

Last-Minute Fruit Mélange
Baked Fruit Compote
Pantry Fruit Compote
Festive Fruit Cake
Heavenly Fresh Fruit Pie
Floating Islands with
  Strawberry or Raspberry
  Sauce
Grapefruit Baked Alaska
Your Perfect Pear
Sweet Potato Meringues

Rosy Rhubarb Sauce
Strawberries with Strawberry
  Sauce
Yogurt Dessert Mould
Poached Peaches Supreme
Helen's San Francisco Peach
  Surprises
Raspberry Mousse
Strawberry-Yogurt Sorbet
Lila's Frozen Dessert
Citron Soufflé

Quick Breads

Banana Bread
Carrot Cake Muffins
Corn Bread, Corn Sticks, or
  Corn Muffins
Geneva's Extra-Special

Muffins
Old-Fashioned Whole Wheat
  Fruit Bars

Sugar-rich foods are generally highly concentrated foods—high in calories that are empty. They are also usually readily available for rapid consumption (sweets, cookies, cakes, and the like).

In an interview with *Total Health* Magazine, I was asked where people seem to "cheat" in their diets the most. Desserts and sweets are the foods where self-discipline is most lacking. Rich desserts are excessive in calories from sugars and fat—both of which should be avoided.

Desserts are meant to be a special finish to a meal. Rich desserts, however, raise our blood sugar level quickly and then let us down quickly—frequently accounting for that de-energized feeling at the end of an otherwise lovely meal. Why not choose whole fresh fruits for dessert—and for snacks? They contain some sugar, but

their relatively high roughage content slows down the absorption of sugar in the body. They are also high in vitamins and minerals. Wonderful, ripe fruits in season, attractively served, have a luscious but light flavour all their own, and a splash of kirsch or brandy adds that something extra for a very special dessert.

However, occasionally we still have a yen for a piece of cake or a mousse. I have found that the use of unsweetened fruit juice concentrates is helpful in developing a "sweet" taste in various desserts while not adding sugar. Our Festive Fruit Cake, Raspberry Mousse, sorbets and dried fruit compotes present the diner with something special that he can enjoy "without guilt".

DESSERTS

Last-Minute Fruit Mélange

Serves: 15

I find it an enormous convenience to have packages of frozen unsweetened fruit on hand in my freezer—fresh fruits can be used in this mélange when in season.

275 g/10 oz fresh strawberries, washed, then hulled

1 tablespoon frozen unsweetened apple juice concentrate

4 tablespoons nonfat yogurt

1 teaspoon pure vanilla essence

1 560-g/20-oz packet frozen unsweetened peach slices*

1 560-g/20-oz packet frozen unsweetened blueberries*

1 560-g/20-oz packet frozen unsweetened black cherries*

2 bananas, peeled and sliced (optional)

Fresh mint sprigs for garnish

1. *To make strawberry-yogurt dressing:* Place strawberries, apple juice, yogurt and vanilla in blender or food processor. Process until puréed. Place in covered container in refrigerator until serving time.

* 350 g/12 oz fresh sliced peaches, 350 g/12 oz fresh blackstoned cherries and 350 g/12 oz fresh blueberries may be substituted for the frozen fruit.

2. About 30 minutes before serving, place frozen peaches, blueberries and cherries in an attractive glass serving bowl.

3. When ready to serve, add dressing to fruit and mix gently. Sliced bananas may be added at this time if you desire.

To Serve: Garnish with springs of fresh mint and serve in glass coupes or small Chinese white lotus bowls.

Per serving: 86 calories; 1.1 gm protein; 0.5 gm fat; 21.1 gm carbohydrate; 1.3 gm fibre; 0 mg cholesterol; 1 mg iron; 4 mg sodium; 20 mg calcium; 22 mg phosphorus; 672 IU Vitamin A; 0.04 mg thiamine; 0.09 mg riboflavin; 31 mg Vitamin C; 181 mg potassium; 0 mg zinc; 0.7 mg niacin; 18 mcg Vitamin B$_6$; 0 mcg Vitamin B$_{12}$; 3 mcg folic acid

Baked Fruit Compote

Serves: 12

Most times, we think of fruit served cold. However, this hot fruit compote is a welcome change, particularly in the months when many fresh fruits are not in season.

450-g/16-oz can unsweetened fruit salad, drained (save juice)
1 450-g/16-oz packet mixed dried fruit, no sulphur dioxide added

1 450-g/16-oz packet stoned prunes
½ lemon
3 bananas, sliced
2 tablespoons brandy
2 tablespoons dry sherry

1. Pour drained fruit salad juice over dried fruit and prunes, adding enough water to cover fruit, and soak overnight.

2. Add juice of lemon and lemon itself and cook 30 minutes. Remove lemon.

*3. Add canned fruit salad, sliced bananas, brandy and sherry to cooked fruit and place in a 2.25-litre/4-pint covered casserole.

4. Bake in a preheated 180°C, 350°F, Gas Mark 4 oven for 30 minutes.

To Serve: Serve hot in individual fruit compotes.

Per serving: 208 calories; 1.9 gm protein; 0.5 gm fat; 52.9 gm carbohydrate; 3.6 gm fibre; 0 mg cholesterol; 2.5 mg iron; 7 mg sodium; 35 mg calcium; 58 mg phosphorus; 2019 IU Vitamin A; 0.05 mg thiamine; 0.11 mg riboflavin; 9 mg Vitamin C; 573 mg potassium; 0.06 mg zinc; 1.6 mg niacin; 201 mcg Vitamin B$_6$; 0 mcg Vitamin B$_{12}$; 4 mcg folic acid

* May be prepared a day ahead through step 3.

Pantry Fruit Compote

Serves: 16

All those canned fruits on hand in your pantry can be prepared into a pleasant last-minute dessert.

450-g/16-oz can stoned red
  sour cherries
1 560-g/20-oz can
  unsweetened pineapple
  chunks
1 450-g/16-oz can sliced
  peaches in natural juice
2 tablespoons frozen

unsweetened apple juice
  concentrate
1 450-g/16-oz can
  unsweetened apple sauce,
  or stewed apples
Cinnamon
Freshly ground nutmeg

1. Drain cherries, pineapple and peaches.
2. When well drained, place a layer of each fruit in a casserole.
3. Add apple juice concentrate to apple sauce and pour a thin layer over the top. Sprinkle with cinnamon and freshly ground nutmeg.
4. Bake in a preheated 180°C, 350°F, Gas Mark 4 oven around 20 to 30 minutes, or until hot.
To Serve: Serve in sherbet glasses while still warm.

Per serving: 55 calories; 0.7 gm protein; 0.2 gm fat; 14.1 gm carbohydrate; 0.9 gm fibre; 0 mg cholesterol; 0.5 mg iron; 2 mg sodium; 13 mg calcium; 14 mg phosphorus; 500 IU Vitamin A; 0.05 mg thiamine; 0.04 mg riboflavin; 6 mg Vitamin C; 163 mg potassium; 0.03 mg zinc; 0.4 mg niacin; 26 mcg Vitamin B_6; 0 mcg Vitamin B_{12}; 1 mcg folic acid

Festive Fruit Cake

Serves: 24 (1 slice = 1 serving)

This luscious holiday fruit cake makes an impressive presentation. For once you can have your cake and eat it.

350 g/12 oz dried fruit,
  coarsely chopped
4 tablespoons apricot brandy
1 teaspoon grated lemon rind

5 egg whites
3 ripe bananas, mashed
120 ml/4 fl oz dry sherry
250 ml/8 fl oz frozen

unsweetened apple juice or
pear and grape juice
350 ml/12 fl oz mixed frozen
unsweetened apple juice,
orange juice and pineapple
juice
1 tablespoon vanilla essence
175 g/6 oz whole wheat flour
175 g/6 oz unbleached flour
25 g/1 oz soya flour

2 teaspoons bicarbonate of
soda
½ teaspoon low-sodium
baking powder
2 teaspoons ground cinnamon
1 teaspoon mixed nutmeg,
cloves and allspice
175 g/6 oz courgettes, grated
350 g/12 oz raisins

1. Simmer the dried fruit with the apricot brandy until liquid is absorbed. Stir in lemon rind and cool. Let marinate overnight.

2. Beat egg whites until fluffy; add mashed banana, sherry, all juice concentrates and vanilla. Beat until stiff.

3. Sift dry ingredients and stir into egg white mixture.

4. Stir in courgettes, raisins and marinated fruit mixture until just blended.

5. Spoon into 2 nonstick 23 × 13 × 10-cm/9 × 5 × 4-inch loaf tins sprayed with nonstick spray.

6. Bake in a preheated 160°C, 325°F, Gas Mark 3 oven for 1 hour 10 minutes until a skewer comes out clean.

7. Cool on a rack for approximately 1 hour. Wrap in cling film and then foil. Store overnight before serving. This may be stored 2 weeks in refrigerator before using or 3 months in freezer.

Variation: For an added dimension of flavour, sprinkle 2 tablespoons of apricot brandy over the cake!

Per serving: 190 calories; 3.8 gm protein, 0.5 gm fat; 43.2 gm carbohydrate; 2.7 gm fibre; 0 mg cholesterol; 1.8 mg iron; 33 mg sodium; 58 mg calcium; 78 mg phosphorus; 856 IU Vitamin A; 0.09 mg thiamine; 0.1 mg riboflavin; 8 mg Vitamin C; 402 mg potassium; 0.09 mg zinc; 1.1 mg niacin; 112 mcg Vitamin B_6; 0.01 mcg Vitamin B_{12}; 4 mcg folic acid

Heavenly Fresh Fruit Pie

Serves: 8–10 (1 slice = 1 serving)

This gorgeous dessert is so easy to make that you'll spend more time reassuring guests of its low calorie content than preparing it.

4 size 1 extra-large egg whites,
at room temperature
¼ teaspoon cream of tartar
1½ teaspoons pure vanilla
essence
2 large ripe bananas, mashed
(skin practically black—it

will be easier to mash and
taste sweeter)
550 g/1¼ lb ripe
strawberries, washed, then
sliced
2 tablespoons kirsch or
framboise liqueur

1. Using an electric mixer or whisk, beat the egg whites until foamy, then add cream of tartar.

2. Beat at high speed. When soft peaks form, add vanilla and puréed banana gradually. Continue beating until whites are shiny and form stiff peaks that do not slide in bowl.

3. Spray a 25-cm/10-inch glass pie plate with nonstick spray. Place spoonfuls of stiffly beaten egg white mixture in pie plate and form a case with back of spoon.

4. Bake in a *very slow oven* preheated to 110°C, 225°F, Gas Mark ¼ for 1½ hours. Turn off heat, leave oven door partially ajar, and let case dry in oven several hours. (This meringue will not be as crisp as the one made with sugar, so don't compare tastes or texture.)

5. *While case is baking, make fruit filling.* Sprinkle sliced berries with liqueur of your choice and let marinate several hours to develop flavour.

6. *To assemble pie,* fill case with fruit just before serving.

Variation: Peaches may be substituted for strawberries, in which case, use 450 g/1 lb sliced peaches, 1 teaspoon almond essence, and 2 tablespoons of apricot liqueur.

Per serving: 57 calories: 3.1 gm protein; 0.4 gm fat; 10.4 gm carbohydrate; 1.8 gm fibre; 0 mg cholesterol; 0.7 mg iron; 36 mg sodium; 45 mg calcium; 42 mg phosphorus; 68 IU Vitamin A; 0.04 mg thiamine; 0.14 mg riboflavin; 37 mg Vitamin C; 219 mg potassium; 0.13 mg zinc; 0.5 mg niacin; 130 mcg Vitamin B_6; 0.11 mcg Vitamin B_{12}; 7 mcg folic acid

Floating Islands with Strawberry or Raspberry Sauce

Serves: 8 (1 meringue = 1 serving)

1 litre/1¾ pints nonfat milk
½ vanilla pod, split
3 egg whites, at room
  temperature
Few grains cream of tartar
1 teaspoon pure vanilla
  essence
275 g/10 oz fresh strawberries
  or raspberries,* washed,
  then hulled
Juice of ½ lemon, or to taste
1 tablespoon kirsch or
  framboise liqueur
Frozen unsweetened apple
  juice concentrate to taste,
  depending upon sweetness
  of fruit
Fresh mint leaves for garnish

1. In a 25-cm/10-inch frying pan, bring milk to the boil with split vanilla pod. Lower heat to maintain a *gentle simmer*. Remove skin from milk.

2. Combine egg whites and cream of tartar in a metal or glass bowl and beat until stiff. Add vanilla.

3. With 2 oval soup spoons, form meringues into 8 ovals. Drop one by one into simmering milk.

4. Poach meringues 4 minutes on each side. Turn once with a slotted spoon.

5. Drain on kitchen paper towel; chill, covered with cling film. (Will keep in refrigerator several days.)

6. *To make strawberry or raspberry sauce:* Purée berries in blender or food processor, reserving several whole berries for garnish. (You may strain sauce if desired.) Add lemon juice and kirsch or framboise. Taste, and adjust seasonings. If necessary, add apple juice concentrate to sweeten.

7. Chill sauce in a covered container in refrigerator until time to serve. Sauce may be refrigerated up to 1 week or frozen for future use.

To Serve: Choose lovely glass dessert dishes. Place an eighth of the sauce on each plate and gently float an island of meringue on sauce. Garnish with fresh strawberries or raspberries and mint leaves. If desired, grated orange rind may be sprinkled over meringue before serving.

* You may use frozen strawberries or raspberries instead of fresh.

Helpful Hint: Leftover cooked milk may be used in baking or in preparing hot cereals.

Per serving: 70 calories; 6 gm protein; 0.3 gm fat; 10.6 gm carbohydrate; 0.8 gm fibre; 0 mg cholesterol; 0.4 mg iron; 82 mg sodium; 158 mg calcium; 126 mg phosphorus; 23 IU Vitamin A; 0.06 mg thiamine; 0.28 mg riboflavin; 25 mg Vitamin C; 261 mg potassium; 0.49 mg zinc; 0.4 mg niacin; 74 mcg Vitamin B_6; 0.5 mcg Vitamin B_{12}; 5 mcg folic acid

Grapefruit Baked Alaska

Serves: 6 (½ grapefruit = 1 serving)

Beneath a snowy topping, hot from the oven, lies a grapefruit, and as a surprise in the centre a spoonful of raspberry sorbet!

3 grapefruits (preferably seedless)
3 tablespoons frozen unsweetened apple juice concentrate
3 egg whites, at room temperature
Pinch cream of tartar

4 tablespoons frozen unsweetened apple juice concentrate
1 teaspoon pure vanilla essence
½ recipe our Strawberry-Yogurt Sorbet (see page 195)

1. Cut each grapefruit in half and remove core. (Cut out more than usual.)

2. Section grapefruit and sprinkle each half with 2 teaspoons apple juice concentrate; chill thoroughly.

3. Beat egg whites until frothy; add cream of tartar, beat until soft peaks form. Gradually add the 4 tablespoons apple juice concentrate and vanilla, beating until stiff and shiny.

4. When ready to serve, put 1 heaped tablespoon sorbet in centre cavity of each grapefruit half.

5. Cover grapefruit completely with meringue.

6. Place on a baking sheet and brown meringue in a preheated 240°C, 475°F, Gas Mark 9 oven. Watch closely so that meringue does not burn.

7. Serve at once.

Per serving: 100 calories; 3.3 gm protein; 0.2 gm fat; 22.3 gm carbohydrate; 0.7 gm fibre; 0 mg cholesterol; 0.7 mg iron; 36 mg sodium; 44 mg calcium; 33 mg phosphorus; 144 IU Vitamin A; 0.06 mg thiamine; 0.06 mg riboflavin; 43 mg Vitamin C; 215 mg potassium; 0.04 mg zinc; 0.5 mg niacin; 37 mcg Vitamin B_6; 0.05 mcg Vitamin B_{12}; 3 mcg folic acid

Your Perfect Pear

Serves: 4 (1 pear = 1 serving)

4 ripe dessert pears
4 tablespoons fresh orange
juice or apple juice

½ teaspoon cinnamon
½ teaspoon freshly ground
nutmeg

1. Core each pear starting at the bottom, and leave stem intact.
2. Peel 4 1-cm/½-inch strips down the sides of each pear.
3. Place pears in a glass baking dish and sprinkle with orange juice or apple juice, cinnamon and nutmeg.
4. Cover baking dish and bake on high in microwave oven* for 13 minutes, or until barely fork-tender. *Do not overcook.*

To Serve: Serve warm in glass fruit coupes or white lotus cups. Pour some warm juice over each pear. For a special touch, add a green camellia or lemon leaf as a garnish.

Variation: Stuff 1 teaspoon seeded raisins, prunes, apricots or dates into the space of the removed core of each pear before baking. If you choose, you may mix the dried fruit with 1 teaspoon dry sherry or muscatel before stuffing the pear.

Per serving: 70 calories; 0.8 gm protein; 0.5 gm fat; 17.3 gm carbohydrate; 2.5 gm fibre; 0 mg cholesterol; 0.4 mg iron; 2 mg sodium; 13 mg calcium; 14 mg phosphorus; 52 IU Vitamin A; 0.04 mg thiamine; 0.04 mg riboflavin; 11 mg Vitamin C; 161 mg potassium; 0.01 mg zinc; 0.2 mg niacin; 21 mcg Vitamin B$_6$; 0 mcg Vitamin B$_{12}$; 2 mcg folic acid

Sweet Potato Meringues

Serves: 8 (1 potato mound = 1 serving)

Satisfying enough to be a dessert, this may also be served as an accompaniment to chicken.

75 g/3 oz seeded raisins
120 ml/4 fl oz fresh orange
juice

1 tablespoon dry sherry
6 medium sweet potatoes or
yams, scrubbed and cooked

* You may use a conventional oven, baking for 30 to 40 minutes at 180°C, 350°F, Gas Mark 4, but the results will not be nearly as delicious!

in skin until tender
Grated rind of 1 orange and 1
lemon
¼ teaspoon allspice
¼ teaspoon freshly grated
nutmeg

3 egg whites, at room
temperature
Few grains cream of tartar
1 *very ripe* banana, mashed
until syrupy

1. Plump raisins in orange juice and sherry for 10 to 15 minutes. Reserve liquid.

2. Peel cooked sweet potatoes, cut each potato into 6 pieces, and purée in blender or food processor.

3. Add orange juice and sherry from plumped raisins to potato mixture and blend until smooth.

4. Add grated orange and lemon rind, allspice and nutmeg, and blend.

5. Mix in plumped raisins.

*6. Shape seasoned sweet potato mixture into 8 mounds on a baking sheet. (I like to use an ice cream scoop.)

7. Place egg whites in a metal or glass bowl. Add cream of tartar and beat until soft peaks form. Add mashed banana and continue beating until stiff. (Test to see if whites slide around bowl; if you want to be brave, turn bowl upside down—they'll stay in the bowl.)

8. Cover each potato mound with beaten egg whites, sealing potato to pan.

9. Bake at 230°C, 450°F, Gas Mark 8 in top of oven until lightly browned, about 5 minutes. Remember to watch carefully—they burn quickly.

To Serve: Serve hot.

Per serving: 162 calories; 3.5 gm protein; 0.5 gm fat; 36.5 gm carbohydrate; 3.3 gm fibre; 0 mg cholesterol; 1.1 mg iron; 31 mg sodium; 44 mg calcium; 62 mg phosphorus; 8609 IU Vitamin A; 0.13 mg thiamine, 0.11 mg riboflavin; 31 mg Vitamin C; 385 mg potassium; 0.02 mg zinc; 0.8 mg niacin; 64 mcg Vitamin B$_6$; 0.01 mcg Vitamin B$_{12}$; 2 mcg folic acid

* May be prepared through step 6 several hours in advance and refrigerated. Remove from refrigerator 1 hour before adding meringue.

Rosy Rhubarb Sauce

Serves: 8

Rhubarb is tart, but here we have managed to overcome this tart
flavour *without adding sugar.*

560-g/20-oz packet frozen
   unsweetened cut rhubarb
5 tablespoons fresh orange
   juice
5 tablespoons unsweetened
   cranberry and grape juice
   nectar, or similar
3 tablespoons frozen

unsweetened apple juice
   concentrate*
150 g/5 oz fresh strawberries,
   washed, then hulled, sliced,
   and marinated in 1
   tablespoon kirsch
   (optional)

1. Place frozen rhubarb in a saucepan.
2. Add orange juice and cranberry and grape nectar to rhubarb.
Cover and simmer 30 minutes or until cooked, stirring occasionally.**
3. Add apple juice concentrate, stir, and add sliced strawberries
if desired.
4. Chill several hours or overnight before serving.

To Serve: Serve as an accompaniment to poultry, or as a simple
dessert.

Per serving: 31 calories; 0.6 gm protein; 0.1 gm fat; 7.4 gm carbohydrate; 1.9 gm
fibre; 0 mg cholesterol; 0.6 mg iron; 2 mg sodium; 70 mg calcium; 15 mg
phosphorus; 92 IU Vitamin A; 0.03 mg thiamine; 0.05 mg riboflavin; 12 mg
Vitamin C; 200 mg potassium; 0 mg zinc; 0.3 mg niacin; 4 mcg Vitamin B_6; 0 mcg
Vitamin B_{12}; 0 mcg folic acid

* 3 tablespoons unsweetened frozen pear and grape juice concentrate may be
substituted for the apple juice concentrate.
** May also be cooked on high in a microwave oven for 15 minutes or until
cooked.

Strawberries with Strawberry Sauce

Serves: 6

An easy dessert that tastes wonderful and looks lovely.

1 kg/2 lb strawberries, washed, then hulled **Strawberry Sauce (see page**	**186) Fresh mint sprigs or stemmed strawberries for garnish**

Place whole berries in a glass serving bowl, pour strawberry sauce over berries, and refrigerate several hours to develop flavour.

To Serve: Serve in glass brandy snifters or champagne glasses garnished with springs of fresh mint or stemmed strawberries.

Variation: Instead of strawberries as the basic fruit, use cubed cantaloupe melon or pineapple and prepare in the same manner.

Per serving: 71 calories; 1.1 gm protein; 0.7 gm fat; 16.6 gm carbohydrate; 3.3 gm fibre; 0 mg cholesterol; 1.5 mg iron; 3 mg sodium; 31 mg calcium; 31 mg phosphorus; 89 IU Vitamin A; 0.04 mg thiamine; 0.1 mg riboflavin; 88 mg Vitamin C; 246 mg potassium; 0 mg zinc; 0.9 mg niacin; 82 mcg Vitamin B_6: 0 mcg Vitamin B_{12}; 13 mcg folic acid.

Yogurt Dessert Mould

Serves: 6 (1 slice = 1 serving)

7 g/¼ oz powdered gelatine	**2.5-cm/1-inch pieces**
250 ml/8 fl oz fresh grapefruit juice, heated to boiling	**75 g/3 oz seeded purple grapes, halved**
250 ml/8 fl oz nonfat yogurt	**Curly endive or radicchio or lettuce for serving**
3 whole grapefruit, peeled, segmented and cut into 2.5-cm/1-inch pieces	**2 kiwi fruit, peeled and sliced, for garnish**
2 navel oranges, peeled, segmented and cut into	**4 small sprays whole purple grapes for garnish**

1. Dissolve gelatine in heated grapefruit juice.
2. Add yogurt to gelatine mixture. Stir with a whisk until smooth.

3. Chill until thick as unbeaten egg whites.

4. Reserve 6 grapefruit segments and 4 orange segments for garnish. Fold drained, cut grapefruit, orange and grapes into chilled yogurt mixture.

5. Rinse a 1-litre/1¾-pint mould with cold water and add fruit gelatine mixture.

6. Cover with cling film and chill until firm or overnight.

To Unmould and Serve: Unmould onto a platter lined with one of the suggested greens. Run a metal spatula around the edge of the mould to loosen, then invert mould over platter and shake gently. Garnish with orange and grapefruit segments, sliced kiwi, and grape sprays. This would also be delicious served as a fruit salad.

Per serving: 114 calories; 6.7 gm protein; 0.3 gm fat; 23.3 carbohydrate; 0.8 gm fibre; 0 mg cholesterol; 0.7 mg iron; 27 mg sodium; 87 mg calcium; 31 mg phosphorus; 274 IU Vitamin A; 0.11 mg thiamine; 0.13 mg riboflavin; 68 mg Vitamin C; 387 mg potassium; 0.05 mg zinc; 0.8 mg niacin; 51 mcg Vitamin B_6; 0 mcg Vitamin B_{12}; 4 mcg folic acid

Poached Peaches Supreme

Serves: 8 (½ large peach, 1 tablespoon yogurt sauce, 2 tablespoons strawberry sauce = 1 serving)

450 ml/¾ pint water
250 ml/8 fl oz chablis
1 175-ml/6-fl oz can frozen unsweetened apple juice concentrate
Grated rind of 2 lemons
1 vanilla pod, split lengthwise

4 ripe but firm large peaches or nectarines
250 ml/8 fl oz nonfat yogurt (optional)
Strawberry Sauce (see page 186)

1. In a saucepan, combine water, wine, apple juice concentrate, lemon rind and vanilla pod. Bring to the boil and simmer 20 minutes.

2. Drop peaches into simmering liquid and poach gently about 10 minutes, or until barely tender.

3. Let peaches cool in poaching liquid.

4. When cool, remove peaches and slip off skins. Halve peaches, remove stones and slice.

5. At serving time, blend yogurt with 120 ml/4 fl oz of the strawberry sauce if desired.

To Serve: Divide sliced peaches into chilled coupes, brandy snifters or large wine glasses. Place 1 tablespoon yogurt mixture over peaches and top with 1 tablespoon strawberry sauce. If you like, a stemmed strawberry or mint leaves may be used as a garnish.

Variation: *To make poached pears,* use the same poaching liquid and add 4 ripe pears, peeled and halved, and cored. Poach 7 to 8 minutes and cool in liquid. Serve pears from a large glass bowl in cooled poaching liquid. A sauce is not necessary.

Helpful Hint: Poaching liquid may be placed in an airtight container and refrigerated for several weeks for future use.

Per serving: 112 calories; 1.9 gm protein; 0.2 gm fat; 20.8 gm carbohydrate; 2 gm fibre; 0 mg cholesterol; 0.8 mg iron; 21 mg sodium; 58 mg calcium; 21 mg phosphorus; 756 IU Vitamin A; 0.04 mg thiamine, 0.12 mg riboflavin; 29 mg Vitamin C; 198 mg potassium; 0.1 mg zinc; 1 mg niacin; 46 mcg Vitamin B_6; 0 mcg Vitamin B_{12}; 5 mcg folic acid

Helen's San Francisco Peach Surprises

Serves: 6 (½ peach = 1 serving)

450-g/16-oz can peach halves in fruit juice or water
2 tablespoons frozen unsweetened orange juice concentrate
½ teaspoon almond essence
½ teaspoon grated lemon rind
Freshly ground nutmeg
Pinch cream of tartar
2 egg whites, at room temperature
2 tablespoons frozen unsweetened apple juice concentrate
1 teaspoon pure vanilla essence
275 g/10 oz raspberries or strawberries, washed, then hulled
1 tablespoon frozen unsweetened apple juice concentrate
4 tablespoons nonfat yogurt
1 teaspoon pure vanilla essence

1. Drain peaches and place cup-side-up in a shallow glass or enamel baking dish.
2. Stir together orange juice concentrate, almond essence and

grated lemon rind. Spoon into peach halves and top with freshly ground nutmeg.

3. Add cream of tartar to egg whites. Beat until soft peaks form. Add the 2 tablespoons apple juice concentrate while continually beating until stiff peaks form and egg whites are stiff but not dry. Add the first teaspoon vanilla and mix.

4. Swirl meringues over each peach half and bake in a preheated 200°C, 400°F, Gas Mark 6 oven for 8 to 10 minutes, or until meringues are lightly browned.

5. Prepare fruit sauce while peaches are baking. Place raspberries, the 1 tablespoon apple juice concentrate, the yogurt, and the second teaspoon vanilla in blender or food processor and purée.

To Serve: Serve peaches immediately in individual dessert dishes, passing fruit sauce in a separate bowl so that guests can serve themselves.

Per serving: 72 calories; 2.4 gm protein; 0.4 gm fat; 16 gm carbohydrate; 1.4 gm fibre; 0 mg cholesterol; 0.8 mg iron; 24 mg sodium; 30 mg calcium; 25 mg phosphorus; 428 IU Vitamin A; 0.04 mg thiamine; 0.11 mg riboflavin; 40 mg Vitamin C; 234 mg potassium; 0.08 mg zinc; 0.9 mg niacin; 42 mcg Vitamin B_6; 0.01 mcg Vitamin B_{12}; 6 mcg folic acid.

Raspberry Mousse

Serves: 8

For extraordinary eye appeal, as well as delectable taste, try this raspberry mousse.

1 100-g/4-oz can chilled nonfat evaporated milk, or 350 ml/12 fl oz nonfat yogurt
6 egg whites, at room temperature
1 tablespoon lemon juice
Pinch cream of tartar
15 g/½ oz powdered gelatine
120 ml/4 fl oz fresh orange juice

1 teaspoon raspberry or pure vanilla essence
1 tablespoon kirsch
450 g/1 lb freeze-dried unsweetened raspberries, thawed and puréed with 3 strips orange rind
225 g/8 oz sugar-free raspberry preserves* or puréed ripe bananas

* Fruit Preserves à la Suisse (page 204) may be used.

1. Whip chilled evaporated milk or stir yogurt in a chilled bowl (see page 19) and refrigerate.

2. Whip egg whites until soft peaks form. Add lemon juice and cream of tartar; whip until stiff.**

3. Dissolve gelatine in orange juice over low heat. Add to beaten egg whites.

4. Fold in extract and kirsch. Blend well. Gently stir in berries and preserves.

5. Add whipped milk or stirred yogurt. Blend gently.

6. Pour mousse into a 1-litre/1¾-pint soufflé dish and chill thoroughly for 4 hours in refrigerator. Serve the day it is prepared for best flavour.

To Serve: Serve directly from soufflé dish. You may top with fresh fruit or a fresh fruit sauce (made by puréeing fruit in blender or food processor with lemon rind and apple juice concentrate if necessary). Budget allowing, long-stemmed strawberries add a special touch.

Per serving: 104 calories; 7.2 gm protein; 0.4 gm fat; 19 gm carbohydrate; 5 gm fibre; 0 mg cholesterol; 0.8 mg iron; 63 mg sodium; 80 mg calcium; 27 mg phosphorus; 260 IU Vitamin A; 0.07 mg thiamine; 0.24 mg riboflavin; 26 mg Vitamin C; 268 mg potassium; 0.06 mg zinc; 1.2 mg niacin; 185 mcg Vitamin B_6; 0.02 mcg Vitamin B_{12}; 6 mcg folic acid

Strawberry Yogurt Sorbet

Serves: 8

Serve this to cleanse your palate between courses, or as a refreshing dessert.

450 g/1 lb frozen
   unsweetened strawberries
2½ tablespoons frozen
   unsweetened apple juice

concentrate
150 ml/¼ pint nonfat yogurt
4 tablespoons instant nonfat
   dry milk

1. Place half the frozen berries in blender or food processor and purée.

** If using puréed banana instead of raspberry preserves, beat into egg whites at this point.

2. Add remaining fruit and frozen apple juice concentrate. Purée.

3. Add yogurt and dry milk. Process until sorbet is formed.

4. Pour into a 28 × 18-cm/11 × 7-inch metal or glass baking dish. Freeze until nearly frozen solid.

5. Return mixture to blender or food processor. Process until broken into small pieces; then process until creamy.

6. Place mixture into individual pot au crème dishes or hollowed lemon or orange shells, or in one large container, cover with cling film, and return to freezer.

To Serve: Remove from freezer about 15 minutes before serving.

Variation: This sorbet works well in Grapefruit Baked Alaska (page 187).

Per serving: 53 calories; 2.5 gm protein; 0.2 gm fat; 11.2 gm carbohydrate; 1.5 gm fibre; 1 mg cholesterol; 0.9 mg iron; 24 mg sodium; 75 mg calcium; 42 mg phosphorus; 182 IU Vitamin A; 0.05 mg thiamine; 0.17 mg riboflavin; 17 mg Vitamin C; 167 mg potassium; 0.11 mg zinc; 0.8 mg niacin; 9 mcg Vitamin B_6; 0.08 mcg Vitamin B_{12}; 0 mcg folic acid

Lila's Frozen Dessert

Serves: 8

2 175-g/6-oz cans frozen unsweetened orange-pineapple juice concentrate

1 90-g/3½-oz packet nonfat dry milk

850 ml/1⅓ pints cold water

1 tablespoon pure vanilla essence

Orange slices or pineapple wedges for garnish

1. Place all ingredients (except garnish) in blender, food processor or mixer bowl. Blend well.

2. Pour mixture into a flat plastic freezer container and freeze until *nearly* frozen solid.

3. Put mixture back in blender, food processor or mixer and process or beat until broken in small pieces, then increase speed and beat until creamy. (It takes about 3 to 5 minutes.)

4. Put mixture in pot au crème dishes or sherbet dishes—or in one large container—and refreeze for future use.

To Serve: Remove from freezer about 5 to 10 minutes before serving and garnish with orange slices or pineapple wedges.

Per serving: 85 calories; 1.9 gm protein; 0.1 gm fat; 19.6 gm carbohydrate; 0.1 gm fibre; 1 mg cholesterol; 0.3 mg iron; 18 mg sodium; 56 mg calcium; 49 mg phosphorus; 166 IU Vitamin A; 0.13 mg thiamine; 0.06 mg riboflavin; 44 mg Vitamin C; 300 mg potassium; 0.14 mg zinc; 0.5 mg niacin; 12 mcg Vitamin B_6; 0.1 mcg Vitamin B_{12}; 1 mcg folic acid

Citron Soufflé

Serves: 8–10

7 g/¼ oz plus 1 teaspoon powdered gelatine
2 tablespoons fresh orange juice
Grated rind of 4 lemons
120 ml/4 fl oz lemon juice
175 g/6 oz frozen unsweetened apple juice

concentrate
8 egg whites, at room temperature
⅛ teaspoon cream of tartar
250 ml/8 fl oz nonfat evaporated milk, chilled several hours in freezer

1. Dissolve gelatine in cold orange juice. Liquefy gelatine over low heat; transfer to a mixing bowl.
2. Add lemon rind, lemon juice and apple juice concentrate to the dissolved gelatine. Place bowl with gelatine mixture in refrigerator until mixture thickens.
3. Beat egg whites until foamy, add cream of tartar, and beat until stiff.
4. Whip chilled nonfat evaporated milk in a *chilled* bowl until peaks form (see page 19).
5. Add thickened gelatine mixture to whipped milk.
6. *Fold* stiffly beaten egg whites into milk and gelatine mixture and place in a 2-litre/3½-pint soufflé dish.
7. Chill 3 to 4 hours or overnight before serving, or freeze for future use.

To Serve: Garnish with thin lemon slices and fresh mint leaves.

Variations: *Make a lemon chiffon pie* by adding mixture to a baked 25-cm/10-inch pastry case and topping with sprinkled Grape-nuts.

To make an orange soufflé, substitute grated rind of 4 oranges and 120 ml/4 fl oz frozen unsweetened orange juice concentrate

for the lemon rind and 120ml/4 fl oz lemon juice.

Soufflé may also be divided into lemon or orange shells and frozen for future use.

Per serving: 69 calories; 5.7 gm protein; 0.1 gm fat; 11.2 gm carbohydrate; 0 gm fibre, 0 mg cholesterol; 0.1 mg iron; 69 mg sodium; 77 mg calcium; 54 mg phosphorus; 106 IU Vitamin A; 0.02 mg thiamine; 0.15 mg riboflavin; 10 mg Vitamin C; 153 mg potassium; 0.2 mg zinc; 0.1 mg niacin; 22 mcg Vitamin B_6; 0.09 mcg Vitamin B_{12}; 3 mcg folic acid

QUICK BREADS

Why pay more money for using a prepared mix with less nutritious food value, when you can easily prepare your own quick bread that is neither complicated nor time-consuming? Quick breads use a quick-acting leavening—baking powder or bicarbonate of soda and sour milk—instead of slow-acting yeast. The nutritious approach to preparing quick breads is to minimize their fat, sugar and sodium content, and still make them delicious. We have done this by eliminating added fat or oil; substituting fresh or dried fruits and unsweetened fruit juice concentrates for sugar; eliminating salt; substituting low-sodium baking powder for regular baking powder; and, of course, using no preservatives. Whenever possible, we have also used whole wheat flour instead of white flour.

Quick breads are easy to prepare and freeze well. Here are a few helpful hints that will make expert bakers out of beginners:

1. Always preheat your oven 10°C, 25°F, 1 Gas Mark higher than the recipe calls for—then lower it to the suggested temperature when baked goods are placed in the oven. (For example, if the recipe calls for 180°C, 350°F, Gas Mark 4, preheat oven to 190°C, 375°F, Gas Mark 5, and lower to 180°C, 350°F, Gas Mark 4 when you put the tin in the oven.)
2. Read recipe thoroughly, assemble ingredients, and have tin ready before you begin preparation.
3. Measure dry ingredients into a bowl first; then measure liquid ingredients into a separate bowl.
4. Add dry ingredients to wet. Stir only until flour disappears—

over-mixing results in mixture not rising as much as it should.

5. Put in preheated oven *as soon as mixture is placed in tin.*

If you follow these suggestions, you will be delighted with your results!

Banana Bread

Yield: 22 slices (1 slice = 1 serving)

250 g/9 oz whole wheat pastry flour
25 g/1 oz soya flour
1 tablespoon low-sodium baking powder
¼ teaspoon bicarbonate of soda
25 g/1 oz bran
3 very ripe bananas, mashed and well blended
4 tablespoons frozen unsweetened apple juice
concentrate
150 ml/¼ pint buttermilk, strained to remove fat globules
2 teaspoons pure vanilla essence
75 g/3 oz seeded raisins, plumped in 4 tablespoons hot fresh orange juice for 15 minutes
3 egg whites, stiffly beaten

1. Preheat oven to 190°C, 375°F, Gas Mark 5.
2. Spray a nonstick 23 × 13 × 7.5-cm/9 × 5 × 3-inch loaf tin lightly with nonstick spray.
3. Combine whole wheat flour, soya flour, baking powder, baking soda and bran in a mixing bowl.
4. In a separate bowl, combine mashed bananas, apple juice concentrate, buttermilk, vanilla and raisins with orange juice.
5. Add dry ingredients to wet ingredients and stir quickly until flour disappears. *(Do not overmix.)*
6. Mix in beaten egg whites. Immediately fill loaf tin, place in oven, lower temperature to 180°C, 350°F, Gas Mark 4, and bake for 1 hour, or until golden brown. Test for doneness by inserting metal skewer. When it comes out clean, bread is finished baking. (Bread will also shrink slightly from sides of tin when done.)
7. Place loaf tin on wire rack for about 5 minutes. Remove bread from tin and complete the cooling on a rack.

Variation: Add 20 g/¾ oz poppy seeds to dry ingredients for an interesting additional flavour.

Per serving: 81 calories; 2.6 gm protein; 0.3 gm fat; 18 gm carbohydrate; 0.8 gm fibre; 0 mg cholesterol; 0.6 mg iron; 21 mg sodium; 44 mg calcium; 85 mg phosphorus; 38 IU Vitamin A; 0.04 mg thiamine; 0.05 mg riboflavin; 3 mg Vitamin C; 213 mg potassium; 0.2 mg zinc; 0.5 mg niacin; 108 mcg Vitamin B_6; 0 mcg Vitamin B_{12}; 6 mcg folic acid

Corn Bread or Corn Muffins

Yield: 12 muffins or 1 20x20 cm/8x8 inch tin cut into 12 squares
(1 muffin = 1 serving)

215 g/7½ oz yellow cornmeal
50 g/2 oz unbleached flour
1 tablespoon low-sodium
  baking powder
½ teaspoon bicarbonate of
  soda
300 ml/½ pint buttermilk,
strained to remove fat
globules
1½ tablespoons frozen
  unsweetened apple juice
  concentrate
2 egg whites

1. Preheat oven to 220°C, 425°F, Gas Mark 7. Spray a 20-cm/8-inch square tin or 12 patty tins with nonstick spray.

2. Measure cornmeal, flour, baking powder and bicarbonate of soda into a bowl and mix with a fork.

3. In a large bowl, mix buttermilk and apple juice concentrate together.

4. Beat egg whites until stiff.

5. Add cornmeal mixture to buttermilk and apple juice mixture. Blend quickly with a fork. Add beaten egg whites, blend quickly with a fork again.

6. Immediately place mixture into baking tin. Bake in 200°C, 400°F, Gas Mark 6 oven for 20–25 minutes, or until firm and lightly browned. Cool slightly on wire rack.

To Serve: This quick bread should be served warm. It is a delicious accompaniment to soup:

Variation: If your diet permits, you may add 1 tablespoon safflower oil to the buttermilk.

Per serving: 92 calories; 3.6 gm protein; 0.3 gm fat; 18.2 gm carbohydrate; 1.1 gm fibre; 1 mg cholesterol; 0.6 mg iron; 41 mg sodium; 84 mg calcium; 117 mg phosphorus; 51 IU Vitamin A; 0.11 mg thiamine; 0.12 mg riboflavin; 0 mg Vitamin C; 177 mg potassium; 0.16 mg zinc; 0.8 mg niacin; 6 mcg Vitamin B$_6$; 0.01 mcg Vitamin B$_{12}$; 2 mcg folic acid

Geneva's Extra-Special Muffins

Yield: 12 muffins (1 muffin = 1 serving)

100 g/4 oz whole wheat flour
50 g/2 oz unbleached flour
½ teaspoon bicarbonate of soda
2 teaspoons low-sodium baking powder
25 g/1 oz unprocessed bran
25 g/1 oz unsweetened whole wheat flakes
250 ml/8 fl oz buttermilk, strained to remove fat globules, or sour milk (1 tablespoon vinegar in 250 ml/8 fl oz cold milk)
2 ripe bananas, mashed
1 teaspoon pure vanilla essence
2 tablespoons frozen unsweetened orange juice or apple juice concentrate
3 egg whites, stiffly beaten
175 g/6 oz raisins,* plumped in 250 ml/8 fl oz hot water for 15 minutes, then drained

1. Preheat oven to 220°C, 425°F, Gas Mark 7. Sift whole wheat flour, unbleached flour, bicarbonate of soda and baking powder together.
2. Add bran and whole wheat flakes and stir with a fork.
3. Combine buttermilk, banana, vanilla and orange juice concentrate.
4. Add liquid to dry ingredients, stir *until flour disappears*. (The mixture will look lumpy.)
5. Fold stiffly beaten egg whites into mixture.
6. Add raisins; stir gently.
7. Fill nonstick bun or patty tins half to two-thirds full.
8. Bake in a 200°C, 400°F, Gas Mark 6 oven 15 to 20 minutes, or until lightly browned. Cool slightly on wire rack before serving.

* 100 g/4 oz frozen unsweetened blueberries may be substituted for the raisins or 75 g/3 oz chopped toasted hazelnuts may be added with the raisins.

Helpful Hint: If muffins are done a little ahead of the rest of the meal, loosen them and tip in patty tin to keep warm. Second-day muffins may taste better split and toasted before serving.

Per serving: 126 calories; 5.6 gm protein; 0.8 gm fat; 33.3 gm carbohydrate; 2.4 gm fibre; 0 mg cholesterol; 2.5 mg iron; 56 mg sodium; 75 mg calcium; 240 mg phosphorus; 129 IU Vitamin A; 0.15 mg thiamine; 0.16 mg riboflavin; 2 mg Vitamin C; 387 mg potassium; 1.54 mg zinc; 3 mg niacin; 249 mcg Vitamin B_6; 0.01 mcg Vitamin B_{12}; 37 mcg folic acid

Old-Fashioned Whole Wheat Fruit Bars

Yield: 30 4 × 5-cm/1½ × 2-inch bars (1 bar = 1 serving)

If you're looking for a healthy snack or dessert to put in a lunch box, you'll be pleased with this fruit bar. Dried fruits are high in natural sugar, however, so limit your consumption.

225 g/8 oz chopped dates
225 g/8 oz dried apricots
2½ tablespoons frozen
  unsweetened apple juice
  concentrate
2½ tablespoons frozen
  unsweetened
  pineapple-orange juice
  concentrate
450 ml/¾ pint water
1½ teaspoons almond essence

175 g/6 oz whole wheat flour
165 g/5½ oz rolled oats
1 teaspoon low-sodium
  baking powder
2½ tablespoons toasted
  sesame seeds
1 175-g/6-oz can frozen
  unsweetened orange juice
  concentrate
2 very ripe bananas, mashed
  until syrupy

1. Preheat oven to 220°C, 425°F, Gas Mark 7. Mix together in a saucepan the dates, apricots, frozen apple juice concentrate, pineapple-orange juice concentrate and water. Cover and simmer about 20 minutes, or until tender, stirring occasionally so fruit does not stick.
2. Remove from heat, stir until thick, add almond essence, and blend.
3. In a bowl, mix together flour, rolled oats, baking powder and sesame seeds.
4. Mix orange juice concentrate and syrupy banana together. Slowly add to flour mixture, mixing with a fork until well blended.

5. Lightly spray an oblong 33 × 23 × 5-cm/13 × 9 × 2-inch tin with nonstick spray. Press half of oat mixture into pan. Flatten with hands to cover bottom of pan.

6. Spread with fruit filling and crumble remaining oat mixture over top, patting lightly.

7. Bake in a 200°C, 400°F, Gas Mark 6 oven for 30 minutes, or until lightly browned. Cut into 30 bars while still warm. Cool bars in tin on a wire rack.

Per serving: 99 calories; 2.3 gm protein; 0.9 gm fat; 22.1 gm carbohydrate; 1.2 gm fibre; 0 mg cholesterol; 1.1 mg iron; 3 mg sodium; 23 mg calcium; 68 mg phosphorus; 884 IU Vitamin A; 0.09 mg thiamine; 0.04 mg riboflavin; 12 mg Vitamin C; 240 mg potassium; 0.29 mg zinc; 0.9 mg niacin; 76 mcg Vitamin B_6; 0 mcg Vitamin B_{12}; 7 mcg folic acid

❧ Potpourri ❧

Fruit Preserves à la Suisse
Yogurt Cheese
Frittata
No-Yolks Huevos Rancheros
Our Tostadas
Tuna Benedictine
Hummus
Tickled-Pink Pickled Beetroot
Chestnuts Roasted on an

Open Fire
Raita
Cultured Cucumber Sauce
Two Sauces from Cuisine
  Minceur
A Low-Calorie Whipped
  Topping
Instant Banana Milkshake

Webster defines a potpourri as a miscellaneous collection, brought together without a bond or connection. Well, here they are—all my leftover recipes, whose only bond or connection is my desire for you to enjoy them!

Fruit Preserves à la Suisse

1 tablespoon = 1 serving

1 560-g/20-oz packet frozen
  berries, or 450 g/1 lb fresh
  berries in season
2 tablespoons lemon juice

2 tablespoons fresh orange
  juice or water
15 g/½ oz powdered pectin

1. Combine fruit, lemon juice, orange juice and pectin.
2. Stir over high heat. Bring to the boil.
3. Boil 2 minutes, or until shiny.
4. Store in sterile jars in refrigerator or freeze in containers for future use.

Per serving: 5 calories; 0.1 gm protein; 0.1 gm fat; 1.2 gm carbohydrate; 0.3 gm fibre; 0 mg cholesterol; 0.1 mg iron; 0 mg sodium; 3 mg calcium; 3 mg phosphorus; 9 IU Vitamin A; 0 mg thiamine; 0.01 mg riboflavin; 8 mg Vitamin C; 24 mg potassium; 0 mg zinc; 0.1 mg niacin; 7 mcg Vitamin B_6; 0 mcg Vitamin B_{12}; 1 mcg folic acid

Yogurt Cheese

Yield: about 300 ml/½ pint (1 serving = 1⅓ tablespoons)

450 ml/¾ pint nonfat yogurt

1. Line a triple-mesh strainer with 3 thicknesses of muslin. Pour yogurt into lined strainer.
2. Place strainer over a bowl and refrigerate overnight. The curd that remains in the strainer the next day will be the yogurt cheese.
To Use: May be used in place of cottage cheese in salads and as a sandwich spread or piped onto halved artichoke hearts or other vegetables for hors d'oeuvres or buffet (use pastry nozzle for prettier effect). *Please note:* Yogurt Cheese cannot be frozen.

Variation: Yogurt Cheese may be seasoned with 3 tablespoons fresh dill, an assortment of fresh herbs, chives, pimento or chilli peppers. Mix seasonings into the yogurt before placing it in strainer.

The cheese can also be molded by puncturing holes in an empty milk carton, then adding yogurt and letting it drain over a bowl overnight. When you remove the remaining curd by cutting away the carton, you will have a square of cheese that slices nicely for sandwiches.

Per serving: 16 calories; 1.6 gm protein; 0.05 gm fat; 2.2 gm carbohydrate; 0 gm fibre; 0.4 mg cholesterol; 0.02 mg iron; 22 mg sodium; 57 mg calcium; 45 mg phosphorus; 2 IU Vitamin A; 0.01 mg thiamine; 0.07 mg riboflavin; 0.24 mg Vitamin C; 74 mg potassium; 0.28 mg zinc; 0.04 mg niacin; 15 mcg Vitamin B_6; 0.18 mcg Vitamin B_{12}; 3.5 mcg folic acid

Frittata

Yield: 1 serving

A frittata is an Italian omelette. Ours uses egg whites only, thus lowering the cholesterol content. It will be well received at breakfast, brunch or lunch.

1 tablespoon chopped onion
1 clove garlic, finely chopped
2 tablespoons salt-free tomato
   juice
1 tablespoon chopped
   courgette
2 mushrooms, sliced
1 tablespoon chopped green
   pepper
1 tablespoon chopped
   pimento

Freshly ground pepper
Dash Tabasco sauce
½ teaspoon thyme, crushed
2 size 1/large egg whites
1 teaspoon cornflour

¼ tomato,* chopped, for
   topping
1 spring onion*, chopped, or
   1 teaspoon chopped fresh
   basil, for topping

1. In a nonstick pan, sauté onion and garlic in tomato juice for 5 minutes, or until transparent.

2. Add courgette, mushrooms, green pepper, pimento, ground pepper, Tabasco and thyme. Blend and cook, covered, for about 2 to 3 minutes.

3. Beat egg whites and cornflour together just until fluffy. Add to sautéed vegetable mixture.

4. Cook, covered, over medium heat until bottom is lightly browned.

5. Lift edge to see if ready. Loosen frittata, invert, and brown lightly on other side.

To Serve: Place on a warm plate and top with chopped tomato and spring onion or basil.

Variation: Any 4 of the following vegetables may be added, chopped: bean sprouts, tomato, asparagus, cooked potatoes, chilli pepper, artichoke hearts.

Per serving: 92 calories; 10.5 gm protein; 0.4 gm fat; 12.4 gm carbohydrate; 2.5 gm fibre; 0 mg cholesterol; 2.7 mg iron; 128 mg sodium; 51 mg calcium; 73 mg phosphorous; 1128 IU Vitamin A; 0.09 mg thiamine; 0.036 mg riboflavin; 44 mg Vitamin C; 479 mg potassium; 0.14 mg zinc; 1.7 mg niacin; 90 mcg Vitamin B_6; 0.08 mcg Vitamin B_{12}; 13 mcg folic acid

* 2 tablespoons canned green chilli sauce may be substituted for tomato and spring onion.

No-Yolks Huevos Rancheros

(Ranch Eggs)

Serves: 4 (2 tortillas and 2 egg whites = 1 serving)

Mexicans have a strong influence on the cooking of those living in Southern California. This simple, economical, Mexican-style dish makes an excellent Sunday breakfast.

150 g/5 oz onion, chopped
1 large green pepper, seeded and chopped
2 cloves garlic, very finely chopped
2 800-g/28-oz cans tomatoes, drained and chopped (reserve juice)
½ teaspoon low-sodium vegetable seasoning (see page 24)
1 200-g/7-oz can green chillies, chopped
1½ tablespoons chopped fresh coriander
Freshly ground pepper
8 egg whites
8 corn tortillas
1 teaspoon low-sodium vegetable seasoning

1. In a large nonstick frying pan, sauté onion, green pepper and garlic in 4 tablespoons juice drained from tomatoes. Cook, stirring occasionally, until onions are transparent (about 5 minutes).

2. Add tomatoes, the ½ teaspoon vegetable seasoning and the chillies, coriander and pepper. Simmer sauce 30 minutes.

3. Make 8 indentations in the sauce with a spoon and drop 1 egg white into each indentation. Cover and cook eggs 3 minutes, or until set, basting with sauce from time to time.

4. Season tortillas with the 1 teaspoon vegetable seasoning and bake in a preheated 200°C, 400°F, Gas Mark 6 oven for about 3 to 5 minutes while the eggs are cooking.

To Serve: Place 2 tortillas on each warm serving plate. Arrange 1 egg white on each tortilla, spoon sauce over and around, and serve immediately. For hearty eaters, you may want to add some Steamed Brown Rice (see page 174).

Per serving: 254 calories; 18.7 gm protein; 3.4 gm fat; 71.8 gm carbohydrate; 3.4 gm fibre; 0 mg cholesterol; 5.5 mg iron; 440 mg sodium; 81 mg calcium; 230 mg phosphorus; 3813 IU Vitamin A; 1.92 mg thiamine; 0.41 mg riboflavin; 106 mg Vitamin C; 1161 mg potassium; 1.87 mg zinc; 3.5 mg niacin; 483 mcg Vitamin B_6; 0.07 mcg Vitamin B_{12}; 32 mcg folic acid

Our Tostadas

Serves: 6 (1 tortilla = 1 serving)

You prepare the various ingredients and let the family assemble their own lunch or supper.

450 g/1 lb mushrooms, sliced
1 bunch spring onions, sliced
4 our Stock Cubes, melted (see page 21), or 3 tablespoons our Chicken Stock (see page 22), or our Vegetable Stock (see page 49)
6 corn tortillas
Garlic powder
Onion powder
Low-sodium vegetable
seasoning (see page 24)
1 425-g/15-oz can chilli beans, without meat, puréed in blender or food processor
1 punnet alfalfa sprouts, or 1 Cos lettuce, shredded
2½ tablespoons our Sour Cream (see page 23)
3 ripe tomatoes, chopped
3 tablespoons canned green chilli sauce

1. Sauté mushrooms and spring onions in stock cubes or stock for 5 minutes, or until soft.

2. Place tortillas on a nonstick baking sheet and sprinkle with garlic powder, onion powder and vegetable seasoning. Bake in a preheated 180°C, 350°F, Gas Mark 4 oven for 5 minutes, or until crisp.

To Assemble: Place baked tortillas on individual serving dishes and spread with a layer of puréed beans. Next, spread with a layer of mushroom mixture. Then add a few alfalfa sprouts. Top with a dollop of sour cream, sprinkle with chopped tomatoes, finish with a spoonful of chilli sauce, and serve.

Variation: *To make chicken tostadas,* substitute 350 g/12 oz leftover diced or shredded roast chicken for mushroom mixture, or add chicken to the mushroom mixture.

Per serving: 100 calories; 7.2 gm protein; 1.6 gm fat; 30.8 gm carbohydrate; 3.2 gm fibre; 1 mg cholesterol; 2 mg iron; 50 mg sodium; 25 mg calcium; 163 mg phosphorus; 670 IU Vitamin A; 0.93 mg thiamine; 0.41 mg riboflavin; 20 mg Vitamin C; 505 mg potassium; 0.63 mg zinc; 3.8 mg niacin; 178 mcg Vitamin B_6; 0 mcg Vitamin B_{12}; 27 mcg folic acid

Tuna Benedictine

Serves: 8 (½ muffin and ½ cup topping = 1 serving)

3 tablespoons unbleached
   flour
750 ml/1¼ pints nonfat milk
1 bay leaf
½ teaspoon low-sodium
   vegetable seasoning (see
   page 24)
1 tablespoon grated onion
1½ teaspoons dry mustard

Few drops Tabasco sauce
1 200-g/7-oz can salt-free
   tuna in water, well drained
4 hard-boiled egg whites,
   sliced
4 whole wheat muffins, split
   and toasted
Chopped fresh parsley for
   garnish

1. Blend flour and milk in a cup or glass jar.
2. Place in a saucepan with bay leaf, vegetable seasoning, grated onion, mustard and Tabasco.
3. Stir constantly with a wooden spoon over moderate heat until sauce is thickened and smooth.
4. Add tuna and egg slices and heat thoroughly.

To Serve: Top each muffin half with tuna and egg mixture and sprinkle with chopped parsley. If you like, serve with grilled tomato halves and steamed broccoli spears.

Variation: Substitute 8 egg whites poached in nonfat milk for hard-boiled egg whites. Place 1 poached egg white on each muffin half and top with tuna mixture.

Per serving: 148 calories; 15.6 gm protein; 1.47 gm fat; 218 gm carbohydrate; 0.33 gm fibre; 16 mg cholesterol; 0.9 mg iron; 185 mg sodium; 124 mg calcium; 143 mg phosphorus; 220 IU Vitamin A; 0.08 mg thiamine; 0.22 mg riboflavin; 1 mg Vitamin C; 247 mg potassium; 0.40 mg zinc; 3.5 mg niacin; 41 mcg Vitamin B_6; 0.36 mcg Vitamin B_{12}; 8 mcg folic acid

Hummus

1 tablespoon = 1 serving

This is a veritable staple in Middle Eastern cooking. (Americans usually serve it as an appetizer.)

2 cloves garlic
2 tablespoons toasted sesame

seeds
2½ tablespoons lemon juice

Pinch cayenne pepper (below)
4 tablespoons our Chicken 1 425-g/15-oz can garbanzo
Stock (see page 22) or juice beans, drained
from garbanzo beans

1. Place garlic, sesame seeds, lemon juice, cayenne and stock or juice in blender or food processor. Purée.
2. Add drained garbanzo beans and continue to purée until creamy and smooth.
3. Taste and adjust seasonings.
4. Place in an airtight refrigerator container and chill, until ready to serve.

To Serve; Bring to room temperature. To serve as an appetizer, place in a bowl and surround with plain or toasted pita bread, or serve with our Caponata (see page 33). Hummus can also be served as an addition to a pita bread sandwich for lunch.

Variation: If your diet allows, 1 teaspoon olive oil may be added after step 3; blend well.

Per serving: 25 calories; 1.5 gm protein; 0.6 gm fat; 3.9 gm carbohydrate; 0.9 gm fibre; 0 mg cholesterol; 0.5 mg iron; 2 mg sodium; 15 mg calcium; 23 mg phosphorus; 3 IU Vitamin A; 0.02 mg thiamine; 0.01 mg riboflavin; 1 mg Vitamin C; 53 mg potassium; 0 mg zinc; 0.1 mg niacin; 1 mcg Vitamin B_6; 0 mcg Vitamin B_{12}; 0 mcg folic acid

Tickled-Pink Pickled Beetroot

Serves 4

1 kg/2 lb fresh beetroot 2.5-cm/1-inch piece fresh
325 ml/11 fl oz cider vinegar ginger root, peeled and cut
120 ml/4 fl oz frozen in half
unsweetened apple juice 2 bay leaves
concentrate ½ teaspoon thyme
2 tablespoons pickling spice 1 large white or red onion,
1 bay leaf thinly sliced

1. Cook beetroot in boiling water to cover for 30 to 40 minutes, or until tender.
2. Drain cooking liquid and save; cool, peel and slice beetroot.
3. Combine beetroot juice, vinegar, apple juice concentrate,

pickling spice, bay leaf and ginger root in a saucepan. Bring to the boil and simmer 10 minutes.

4. Strain hot mixture and pour over sliced beetroot. Add bay leaves, thyme and onion.

5. Place in a tightly covered container and refrigerate for 24 hours before serving.

To Serve: Drained pickled beetroot may be served as an individual salad on a lettuce leaf, garnished with grated, hard-boiled egg white. Pickled beetroot is also delicious served as a condiment with poached fish or grilled chicken.

Per serving: 39 calories; 1 gm protein; 0.1 gm fat; 9.7 gm carbohydrate; 1.8 gm fibre; 0 mg cholesterol; 0.7 mg iron; 32 mg sodium; 14 mg calcium; 22 mg phosphorus; 26 IU Vitamin A; 0.02 mg thiamine; 0.03 mg riboflavin; 6 mg Vitamin C; 204 mg potassium; 0.03 mg zinc; 0.2 mg niacin; 11 mcg Vitamin B_6; 0 mcg Vitamin B_{12}; 2 mcg folic acid

Chestnuts Roasted on an Open Fire

(Or in Your Oven)

Yield: Approx 225 g/8 oz roasted chestnuts from 450 g/1 lb raw (2 chestnuts = 1 serving)

Each chestnut contains about 16 calories—it's the only nut that you can crack without feeling some guilt.

Roasting: (for chestnuts to eat as a snack)

1. Pick over chestnuts and discard any that are soft or wormy.

2. Cut an × on rounded side of each chestnut. Place cut-side-up on a nonstick baking sheet.

3. Place in a preheated 220°C, 425°F, Gas Mark 7 oven and roast for 1 hour, or until done. Sprinkle with a few tablespoons of water every 15 or 20 minutes during cooking. The chestnuts will burst open when ready.

To Serve: Remove outer shells and inner skins before eating.

Parboiling: (for chestnuts to use in cooking)

1. Pick over chestnuts and discard any that are soft or wormy.

2. Cut an × on rounded side of each chestnut and add to boiling water.

3. Bring to the boil again and simmer about 10 minutes.

To Use: Remove outer shells and inner skins before using. May be frozen for future use.

Per serving: 32 calories; 0.5 gm protein; 0.2 gm fat; 6.9 gm carbohydrate; 1.1 gm fibre; 0 mg cholesterol; 0.3 mg iron; 1 mg sodium; 4 mg calcium; 15 mg phosphorus; 0 IU Vitamin A; 0.04 mg thiamine; 0.04 riboflavin; 0 mg Vitamin C; 75 mg potassium; 0 mg zinc; 0.1 mg niacin; 0 mcg Vitamin B_6; 0 mcg Vitamin B_{12}; 0 mcg folic acid

Raita
A Condiment for Curries

1 tablespoon = 1 serving

250 ml/8 fl oz nonfat yogurt
2 ripe bananas, thinly sliced
1 ripe peach, peeled and diced
2 teaspoons lime juice
1 tablespoon finely chopped
   fresh coriander
1 teaspoon grated peeled fresh

ginger root
1–1½ teaspoons cumin
   powder, lightly toasted in
   oven or dry frying pan
½ teaspoon low-sodium
   vegetable seasoning (see
   page 24) optional

1. Combine yogurt, bananas, peach, lime juice, coriander, ginger root, toasted cumin and vegetable seasoning in a bowl.

2. Blend well and store in a covered container in refrigerator for several hours before serving.

To Serve: Use as one of the condiments with Turkey Curry (page 127) or any favourite curry, or with Tandoori Chicken (page 112).

Per serving: 22 calories; 0.9 gm protein; 0.1 gm fat; 5.1 gm carbohydrate; 0.6 gm fibre; 0 mg cholesterol; 0.3 mg iron; 9 mg sodium; 25 mg calcium; 6 mg phosphorus; 147 IU Vitamin A; 0.02 mg thiamine; 0.05 mg riboflavin; 2 mg Vitamin C; 77 mg potassium; 0.04 mg zinc; 0.3 mg niacin; 77 mcg Vitamin B_6; 0 mcg Vitamin B_{12}; 2 mcg folic acid

Cultured Cucumber Sauce

1 tablespoon = 1 serving

450 g/1 lb cucumbers peeled
½ onion, finely chopped
1 large clove garlic, finely
   chopped

350 ml/12 fl oz nonfat yogurt
1 teaspoon onion powder
Freshly ground pepper
Few drops Tabasco sauce

1. Shred cucumber in food processor.
2. Add chopped onion and garlic to cucumber and very finely chop.
3. Squeeze and drain well.
4. Combine yogurt, onion powder, ground pepper and Tabasco. Blend well.
5. Fold in cucumber mixture.
6. Chill 4 to 6 hours in the refrigerator.
To Serve: Use as a sauce for fish or as a dip.

Per serving: 8 calories; 0.6 gm protein; 0 gm fat; 1.4 gm carbohydrate; 0.2 gm fibre; 0 mg cholesterol; 0 mg iron; 8 mg sodium; 18 mg calcium; 4 mg phosphorus; 26 IU Vitamin A; 0.02 mg thiamine; 0.04 mg riboflavin; 2 mg Vitamin C; 28 mg potassium; 0 mg zinc; 0.2 mg niacin; 2 mcg Vitamin B_6; 0 mcg Vitamin B_{12}; 0.5 mcg folic acid

Two Sauces from Cuisine Minceur

Serves 6

Two low-calorie sauces to be used with vegetables or grilled or poached fish or poultry.

Piquant Sauce from Cuisine Minceur

½ onion, sliced
2 stalks celery, sliced
3 carrots, sliced
5 tablespoons water or our Chicken Stock (see page 22) or our Vegetable Stock (see page 49)
3 tomatoes, chopped

20 g/¾ oz fresh sorrel leaves
1 clove garlic, crushed
1 bay leaf
½ teaspoon dried thyme, or 1½ teaspoons chopped fresh thyme
Freshly ground nutmeg
Few grains crushed red pepper

1. Cook onion, celery, carrots and water or stock in a small saucepan for 15 minutes.
2. Add tomatoes, sorrel, garlic, bay leaf, thyme, nutmeg and crushed red pepper. Simmer 15 minutes, adding water if necessary.
3. Purée and strain.

Per serving: 40 calories; 1.5 gm protein; 0.4 gm fat; 8.8 gm carbohydrate; 2.8 gm fibre; 0 mg cholesterol; 1.2 mg iron; 32 mg sodium; 37 mg calcium; 41 mg

phosphorus; 4877 IU Vitamin A; 0.07 mg thiamine; 0.06 mg riboflavin; 21 mg Vitamin C; 355 mg potassium; 0.32 mg zinc; 0.8 mg niacin; 143 mcg Vitamin B$_6$; 0 mcg Vitamin B$_{12}$; 12 mcg folic acid

Mushroom Sauce from Cuisine Minceur

½ onion, chopped
2 carrots, chopped
2 stalks celery, chopped
4 mushrooms, chopped
2 tablespoons chopped fresh

parsley
1 bay leaf
½ teaspoon herbes de Provence
250 ml/8 fl oz nonfat yogurt

1. Place first 7 ingredients in a saucepan. Add water just to cover.
2. Cook 20 to 30 minutes, stirring occasionally.
3. Purée and strain. Add yogurt and combine.

Per serving: 37 calories; 2.5 gm protein; 0.2 gm fat; 7.2 gm carbohydrate; 1.5 gm fibre; 0 mg cholesterol; 0.9 mg iron; 47 mg sodium; 89 mg calcium; 27 mg phosphorus; 3205 IU Vitamin A; 0.05 mg thiamine; 0.15 mg riboflavin; 10 mg Vitamin C; 195 mg potassium; 0.13 mg zinc; 0.9 mg niacin; 67 mcg Vitamin B$_6$; 0 mcg Vitamin B$_{12}$; 8 mcg folic acid

A Low-Calorie Whipped Topping

1 tablespoon = 1 serving

25 g/1 oz instant nonfat dry milk
4 tablespoons ice water or iced unsweetened orange or pineapple juice

1 teaspoon lemon juice
2 tablespoons frozen unsweetened apple juice concentrate

1. Chill beaters and a narrow, deep bowl.
2. Beat instant milk with ice water on highest speed for 3 minutes, or until soft peaks form.
3. Add lemon juice and beat until stiff.
4. Add apple juice concentrate and blend.
To Serve: Serve at once.

Per serving: 6 calories; 4 gm protein; 0 gm fat; 1.1 gm carbohydrate; 0 gm fibre; 0 mg cholesterol; 0 mg iron; 6 mg sodium; 14 mg calcium; 11 mg phosphorus; 0 IU Vitamin A; 0 mg thiamine; 0.02 mg riboflavin; 0 mg Vitamin C; 25 mg potassium; 0.05 mg zinc; 0 mg niacin; 5 mcg Vitamin B_6; 0.04 mcg Vitamin B_{12}; 1 mcg folic acid

Instant Banana Milkshake

Serves: 2

250 ml/8 fl oz chilled nonfat milk
1½ tablespoons nonfat powdered milk*
1 tablespoon frozen

unsweetened apple juice concentrate*
½ ripe banana, sliced
½ teaspoon pure vanilla essence

1. Combine milk, powdered milk and fruit concentrate in a chilled glass measuring jug. Beat until milk starts to form peaks.
2. Add banana slices and vanilla and continue beating until thick and creamy.

To Serve: This delicious, nourishing snack should be served immediately in chilled glasses. (Since there is no fat in the milk, if not served immediately it will fall back; the only thing holding it up is the air you have beaten into it.)

Variations: Either 75 g/3 oz sliced strawberries, 75 g/3 oz drained unsweetened crushed pineapple, or 75 g/3 oz sliced fresh or frozen peaches may be substituted for the banana. My favourite is peaches with ½ teaspoon almond essence.

Per serving: 110 calories; 7.3 gm protein; 0.4 gm fat; 20.1 gm carbohydrate; 0.8 gm fibre; 4 mg cholesterol; 0.4 mg iron; 106 mg sodium; 249 mg calcium; 206 mg phosphorus; 309 IU Vitamin A; 0.09 mg thiamine; 0.31 mg riboflavin; 5 mg Vitamin C; 487 mg potassium; 0.87 mg zinc; 0.4 mg niacin; 238 mcg Vitamin B_6; 0.77 mcg Vitamin B_{12}; 13 mcg folic acid

* If you eliminate these ingredients, the calories in each serving will be reduced by almost 50 percent.

⊰§ Index ⧽•